# THE PASSIONATE LIFE

*Harper & Row, Publishers, San Francisco*
Cambridge, Hagerstown, New York, Philadelphia
London, Mexico City, São Paulo, Sydney

*1817*

# The Passionate Life

## STAGES OF LOVING

### Sam Keen

**Library of Congress Cataloging in Publication Data**

Keen, Sam.

THE PASSIONATE LIFE.

Bibliography: p.
Includes index.
1. Sex. 2. Love. I. Title.
HQ21.K256   1983      306.7        82-48932
ISBN 0-06-250469-X
ISBN 0-06-250468-1 (pbk.)

84  85  86  87  88   10  9  8  7  6  5  4  3  2

# Contents

If people were told: what makes carnal desire imperious in you is not its pure carnal element. It is the fact that you put into it the essential part of yourself—the need for Unity, the need for God—they wouldn't believe it. To them it seems obvious that this quality of imperious need belongs to the carnal desire as such. In the same way it seems obvious to the miser that the quality of desirability belongs to gold as such, and not its exchange value.

SIMONE WEIL,
*First and Last Notebooks*

The body is the spirit *incognito.*

SANDOR McNAB

# 1.
# The Erotic Crisis: Love, Sex, and the Human Spirit

## THE APOCALYPTIC ORGASM

The last time we made love was sad, violent, filled with the awfulness of endings. For two years we had met on empty evenings and odd weekends in hidden places. Not because ours was "an affair." Neither one of us was married at the time. But we belonged to different worlds. She was twenty-seven, a romantic free spirit, a psychedelic voyager. Her mind and body were given instantly to the passing moment. She asked no promises. Took no hostages against the future. I was forty-one, burdened with seriousness, and trailing the chains of broken promises and a good marriage gone wrong. I suppose she "loved" me more than I loved her, or at least it was her way to have fewer reservations. Her heart neither hesitated nor deliberated. She would have married me if I had asked. I didn't.

Whenever we tried to venture into each other's world, cacaphony resulted, as if two radios were simultaneously playing a Bach chorale and the Rolling Stones. So we finally agreed to meet in exile, on the island of the flesh. When the heat was upon us we came together, made love, had a meal together, and went our separate ways. We pretended the void between us was neutral space. Our agreement was mutual, rational, and satisfying to us both. More than that. Since we limited our relationship so severely, the brief contact between our flesh was supercharged. Usually we met, exchanged nonsequiturs while we fondled each other, and careened into bed unable to wait. Sex was always very good; a swollen stream coursing through a narrow canyon, sweeping everything before it, washing away the accumulated debris of winter, finally trickling out into the desert sand, spent. We were thankful to each other for the cleansing.

Yet the more we rode the edge of mounting excitement, surfed the waves of sensation, the more a mood of sullen, unspoken violence grew between us. Something in us did not respect our contract. Our agreement to sever sense from spirit violated our longing for the unconditional. The ghost of the bonds we would not acknowledge returned to haunt us, until we came to hate each other for all that was missing. As the novocaine of our shared pleasure wore off, we were each left with our individual ache. Each orgasm reminded us of abandoned and abandoning arms, days not linked to days by shared memories, too many meals eaten with strangers, broken promises, the missing center.

On the last night, the pools of pleasure and pain we had managed to keep separate overflowed and the waters mingled. We made love again and again, hoping against the knowledge of our betrayal that we could salve the wounds we had helped inflict on each together. In the late darkness, the illusion shattered. As we came together, our arms stretched wide, the words exploded in my ear: "It is finished." The end had come. It was time for us to take our separate journeys, to discover how eros might be married to something abiding, whole, holy.

### THE DEATH OF LOVE

> The degree and kind of a man's sexuality reaches up into the topmost summit of his spirit (Nietzsche).[1]

The twentieth century began with Nietzsche's lament that God had died. *Time* magazine finally got around to running the obituary in 1967. As the century ends, the pantheon of idols with which we sought to replace the absent God is disintegrating. Reason has failed to bring sanity into the affairs of men, women, or nations. Knowledge and fact have overwhelmed us and, in direct proportion, Wisdom has disappeared. Power has increased, and with it the propensity toward nuclear suicide, or cosmocide. Communication networks span the globe, but they have not increased compassion. Lately, the youngest and most resilient of the substitute gods is in failing health. Love, in its three epiphanies—romance, marriage, sex—is a dying God. The romantic myth and the hope of living happily ever after are continually shattered by experience. And sex, which we embraced to make up for our disappointment with love, is failing under the burden of our expectations. Already the news of our erotic dis-ease has reached the media and we've seen the headline, "Sex Is Dead."

Why?

There is no more revealing place to begin our search to understand our erotic crisis than with the words themselves.

It is common sophistry to proclaim that our problem lies with the vagueness of the word "love." The Greeks supposedly had an easier time because they could distinguish between *agape* (a godly kind of altruistic, self-giving love, such as Mother Teresa's ministry to the wounded and dying of Calcutta), *eros* (a hungry, desirous longing to possess the other), and *philia* (brotherly love, or friendship). We often hear the lament that English is a poverty-stricken language; it forces the single word "love" to cover a multitude of sins and virtues, everything from lust to compassion. We "love" our wives, our children, our cars, our dogs. "Love" is the answer to all problems that can't be solved by science. "God is love." "What the world needs now is love sweet love." Psychiatrists warn us that we must "love or perish." No doubt, the Gospel of John and Elmer Gantry are right in theory. Love is the alpha and omega, the morning and the evening star. But the very universality of the appeal to love seems to invalidate it.

In fact, the English language is as inventive, subtle, and adequate to the problem of *talking about* love as any other. *Roget's Thesaurus* suggests several hundred moods of love, including affection, friendship, charity, protectiveness, possessiveness, kindness, tenderness, beneficence, attraction, compatibility, sympathy, fellow-feeling, understanding, fondness, inclination, devotion, fancy, caprice, sentimentality, loyalty, enchantment, fascination, yearning, eroticism, respect, admiration, passion, infatuation, enthusiasm, seduction. Our language allows us, in the name of love, to span the distance between soft promises and hard commitments, between lust and adoration; to philander or take a vow; to like or be obsessed with another.

The problem of love lies in our hearts, not in our tongues; in our intentions, not in our vocabularies. We misunderstand love because we have chosen to worship power; we fail in compassion because we have become obsessed with control; we silence the reasons of the heart because we have chosen to follow a path of heartless knowledge, no matter where it takes us; we do not adore because we insist that every thing and every person be of use; we do not wonder because we reduce the real to the measurable; we do not care because we have come to believe that it profits a man or woman well above the prime rate to trade the soul for a piece of the action.

In capsule form, the history of the decline and fall of love can be traced in the changed meaning of the word "erotic." Both Webster and common usage define "erotic" as meaning "of, devoted to, or tending to arouse sexual love or desire." In definitions of related words, the aspect of sexual passion or desire is always central. Yet when we look at the root word *eros*, we discover that it means simply "to love or desire ardently." There is no suggestion in the original meaning that the desire is specifically sexual.

Plato's myth of the androgyne gives the original meaning of eros. In the beginning, according to Plato, there were three kinds of human beings: man-man, woman-woman, and man-woman. Each unit was joined back to back, had four arms, four legs, and a single head with faces front and back. These hybrid creatures could either walk upright or run cartwheel fashion, but they could never face each other. When Zeus decided to divide and conquer these powerful beings, he split each unit down the middle so that a single person would henceforth be incomplete and would have to search for his or her other half. Thus we are now motivated by eros, by a profound longing to be reunited with our missing complement. Sexual love is only one of the many modes in which eros seeks to reunite us with what is missing.

Greek philosophers considered eros the prime mover, the motivating principle in all things human and nonhuman. It was the impulse that made all things yearn and strive for fulfillment. The acorn was erotically moved by its destiny to become an oak, just as human beings were motivated by eros to become reasonable and to form a political order as just and harmonious as that of nature. Eros was inseparable from the potentiality or promise (the potency or power) that slept in the substance of all things.

Thus, in the original vision that gave birth to the word, erotic potency was not confined to sexual power but included the moving force that propelled every life-form from a state of mere potentiality to actuality. When we limit "erotic" to its sexual meaning, we betray our alienation from the rest of nature. We confess that we are not motivated by anything like the mysterious force that moves birds to migrate or dandelions to spring. Furthermore, we imply that the fulfillment or potential toward which we strive is sexual—the romantic-genital connection between two persons. Throughout this book, eros is used in its original sense, in an effort to breathe perspective back into our thinking about love and sexuality.

The analysis that follows rests upon the conviction that love, sexuality, and power can only be healed by returning to the original meaning of eros: by seeing the pleasures of the flesh within the context of a vision of the human promise, as it unfolds over the course of a lifetime within the ambience of the community and the cosmos. Our erotic dis-ease will not be solved by sex manuals, sensitivity groups, sensate focus, techniques to stimulate the nerve endings, or the discovery of a perfect lover. Our erotic potential is fulfilled only when we become cosmopolitan lovers, only when *potentia* (power) and *eros* (desire) reunite our bodies to the *polis* (the body politic) and the *cosmos* (the natural environment).

ROMANCE, MARRIAGE, AND THE CAPITALIST DREAM

To understand why we have reduced eros to its sexual meaning and elevated it in our pantheon of hopes beyond its power to grant us happiness, we must see how romance, marriage, and sex came to be foremost among the values to which we give lip service.

We Americans have come to invest our hopes for private fulfill-ment in love. We expect love sweet love to heal us from the injuries and disappointments we suffer in our public lives within corporations, factories, and bureaucracies. Freud said, and we mostly agree, that a mature person should be able to love and to work. We believe in these twin virtues. But in fact, our lives are organized around work, and love is supposed to make work worthwhile. Until recently, Americans could be characterized, without too much exaggeration, as industrious, aggressive, de-voted to competition, and hopelessly romantic.

Our longing for romance pops up everywhere. The following advertisements in the "Relationships" column of a weekly news-paper express this belief in the romantic myth.[2]

### IS ROMANCE DEAD?

I still believe that exciting, romantic relationships can happen when two happy, vibrant people decide to come together. I am an attractive, 31, W/M lawyer enjoying candlelight dinners, fireside evenings, hik-ing, music and animals. I seek an attractive lady who is happy with the life she has constructed for herself and would like to share her happi-ness with one who can appreciate it. Write . . .

59 year old W/M looking for that fabulous flight on gossamer wings to the moon with a woman who is also practical enough to help take care of the baggage on the way back. A practical romantic if that's conceivable. Write . . .

A new beginning. 26 year old W/F after being involved with a partner who never really cared about my needs searches for a loving, exciting, W/M to share such pleasures as balloon rides, rafting, sailing, sunsets, laughter, beaches, explore total sensuality and most of all the big O. Life is so short. Box . . .

I Curt am now willing to receive my ideal female partner. God, my ideal female partner, and I all know what I am thinking of. That or some-thing better now manifests. Photo appreciated. Write Curt, Box . . .

That special someone. Loving, sensitive, happy, business executive, 35, handsome, 5'10", seeks dynamic young woman who is in her twenties, loves life and is ready to share her dreams with that special man. You are physically and spiritually beautiful and are ready to begin a committed relationship that is full of love and understanding.

Wanted W/M with Herpes. Large reward—me. W/F 29, 5'2", petite, desirable personality. Searching for friendship evolving into a long lasting relationship.

Heavy legs. LA lawyer, 48, 5'11", 170, seeks W/F 25–45 over 5'6", very heavy ankles and calves, slender waist and above. Terry, Box . . .

Romance is the jewel in the crown of capitalism. Scratch an engineer, a worker, a fashion designer, and you will find a slumbering romantic. We grow up expecting that some magic day it will happen. We will fall in love with that special someone who will simultaneously fall in love with us. Then we two (after obstacles have been overcome) will join together and never be lonely. We will be all things to each other: lovers, companions, helpmates, spouses, friends, protectors, nurturers: a self-sufficient couple, with little need for others. The love-nest, well-feathered with suburban comforts, may be filled for a time with fledglings, but the romance between husband and wife will continue through thick and thin until death do us part.

Of course, the dream is a cliché. Realism and divorce statistics tell us that very few lovers live happily ever after. Romance fades. Nevertheless, the dream is tenacious. *True Romance* maintains its loyal readers year after year. Hollywood cranks out the archetypal romance, playing variations on the theme of *Love Story* to packed audiences in both rich and lean times. Old fools and young continue to fall in love again and again, hoping against the testimony of past experience that the next one will be the "right" one. Even though we acknowledge the failure in fact of romance, we continue to take pride in striving after the ideal. We are quite certain that our habit of allowing people to "fall in love," to choose their mates on the basis of private passions, is superior to a pragmatic approach to coupling.

We can't abandon our ideal of romance because it is linked to a whole system of values, at the center of which stands our belief in the individual. Each of us, in theory, has the right to forge our personal destiny, and this includes the right to choose our mate. In short, the love story functions as a myth (or what Kant called a "regulative idea") within western culture. It is a motivating fiction that focuses the energy and aspiration of the psyche, and it is an integral part of the ideology of capitalism. The promise that our lives will be crowned by romance is inseparable from the cultural decision to invest most of our eros—energy, time, and care —in work, the accumulation of money, and power. Romance is the grail that should reward our restlessness, the sacred fulfillment that is supposed to compensate us for profaning the world. It is an imagined oasis of passion in a culture that has reduced its horizon of values to the pragmatic. We expect to "fall" in love because we know we have fallen from grace. That one special person is supposed to fill the vacuum of loneliness that results from the loss of community, replace the magic that vanished from nature when Christ (with the help of the bulldozer) "killed the great god Pan," as D. H. Lawrence put it. 'Love,' as someone said, is the only green thing left in a world of concrete and steel.

We are not, of course, the first people to fall in love. Only the first to idealize and democratize romance, to make it an unofficial but very real requirement for a fulfilled adult life, to link it to sex, and to expect it to be the continuing basis for marriage.

As Robert Brain says in the excellent study *Friends and Lovers,* "the combination of spiritual love, frustrated sex, and marriage is a uniquely Western contribution to the evolution of human relationships."[3]

A brief history of romance will lend perspective.

We may safely assume that, in Stone Age tribes, some Romeo developed an inordinate passion for a neolithic Juliet. Among present-day "primitives," romance is scarcely ever the norm governing relationships; but it does occur. The Samoans, Margaret Mead describes, permit premarital and extramarital romances and emphasize the cultivation of erotic skills, but strongly disapprove of affairs that disrupt social stability. As a rule the less inhibited a culture is about sensuality and premarital and extramarital sex, the less romance will be charged with feelings of exclusiveness, jealousy, possession, and the less it will be seen as the binding force and *raison d' être* for marriage. In most tribes, marriage is far too serious a social institution to be left to the whims of individual passions. Those who get caught in romantic madness and disrupt the tribe are pitied and censured rather than held up as models for heroic passion.

Powerful sexual and romantic emotions have always existed; but the way we value, think about, encourage, discourage, or censure those emotions has changed throughout history. As recent accounts of the antiromantic mood of Red China have shown us, one society's vice is another's virtue.

Socrates fell in love with beautiful boys, Sappho with girls, Heloise and Abelard with each other. Romance appeared from time to time in the early years of western culture, but it was hardly encouraged. The Greeks worshiped reason *(logos),* loved the order of the polis above the disorderly passions of the individual, and so kept romance to a minimum. In fact, the Dionysian orgy in which the Greek spirit permitted excess was the opposite of romance. In the orgy, ecstatic passion was released by a connection with an *anonymous* other. Partners in the frenzy set aside the masks of personality and met as pure expressions of exuberant sexual energy. The orgy strips away the precise uniqueness of the person that is the basis of romance.

Nor did romance thrive in the atmosphere of Christian theology. Much of the sexual ethic of western Christendom was tainted by the Gnostic-Manichean dualism that regarded matter as degraded, nature as the creation of a demonic god (demiurge), women as inferiors, and sex as lust to be repressed or expressed only within marriage. Had Augustine not felt so guilty for loving his mistress, the Middle Ages might have recognized that sexual feelings were one of the delightful gifts of the Creator. As it was, Christianity fell into an anti-erotic posture: glorifying virginity, degrading woman, linking sex to guilt, discouraging romance, denying the flesh, casting suspicion upon sensuality. In theological terminology, this was expressed in the doctrine of the superiority of agape (which Christians defined as God-given and selfless) over eros (which they thought of as impure and lustful).

Our modern western notion of romantic love burned bright for a moment in the passions of Heloise. Ten years after their forcible separation, she wrote to Abelard:

> When little more than a girl I took the hard vows of a nun, not from piety but at your command. . . . I can expect no reward from God, as I have done nothing from love of Him. . . . God knows, at your command I would have followed or preceded you to fiery places. For my heart is not with me, but with thee.[4]

But it was the troubadours of the French Middle Ages whose songs of adulterous love for aristocratic ladies idealized romantic love. The chivalrous troubadour adored a distant, high-born woman, usually someone else's wife, to whom he wrote poetry but whom he rarely enjoyed in a sexual manner.

With the industrial revolution, the prerogatives of royalty were claimed by the growing middle class. Every home a castle; every man a king; every woman queen for a day. Everyman claimed the aristocratic right to a grand ennobling passion, to leisure for love and dalliance. In Victorian times, sex (like capital), was supposed to be chastely saved until it could be profitably invested in marriage. Capitalism demanded an ethic of postponed gratification. Eros and money were to be accumulated, not spent immediately. Thus the romantic ideal was divorced from the notion of illicit love and longing and the new concept of the romantic marriage was born. Henceforth love, sex, and romance were supposed to live happily ever after within the sanctity of marriage. We were promised that if we worked hard and waited, we would win both love, prosperity and happiness. Libido, ego, and superego (the ancient enemies) would settle down harmoniously together in a mortgaged suburban house and dwell in secure passion.

## THE SEXUAL REVOLUTION: AT THE CONVERGENCE OF TWO MYTHS

Sometime in the 1960s, the romantic myth began to lose ground and our sexual mores began to change. Premarital sex became an accepted practice. Unmarried couples lived together openly and without censure. Erotic minorities came out of the closet. Women took the pill and demanded the traditional male right to recreational sex—"the zipless fuck," as Erica Jong was later to christen it. Abortion became easy. The age of "repression" was over.

The change in our sexual attitudes and behaviors that goes under the name of the sexual revolution was actually created by a convergence of two *opposite* myths: the counterculture's myth of the return to innocence, and the dominant culture's myth of consumption.

In the beginning, the sexual revolution was a part of the blossoming of the counterculture. It went along with drugs, rock music, communes, protests against the war in Vietnam, and the "back to nature" movement. The age of Aquarius was born in an apocalyptic atmosphere created by the Damoclean sword of the arms race, by the escalating ecological threat, and by the loss of trust in our dominant institutions—government, churches, corporations. Everywhere the young looked they saw hypocrisy. With society collapsing around them, and no secure future in view, it made sense to postpone bringing children into the world, to disconnect sex and procreation, and take whatever pleasure the moment offered. Eat, smoke dope, and ball, for tomorrow we die. The youth, like Thoreau a century before, were disillusioned with "civilization" and went in quest of something "natural," something innocent. With the help of drugs, they explored the wilderness that existed in the mind just under the veneer of personality. Thousands flocked back to the land and created a rural renaissance that is still alive in Tennessee and the valleys of Oregon and Washington. And they reached out to sex, to see if they could discover a natural body, innocent sensations unpolluted by the capitalistic Victorian romantic notions of sin. With body paints and casual sex they sought to celebrate the body in an effort to protest the necrophilia, the violence, of a technological society that sacrificed everything tender to abstractions. Love-ins and free love were a reaction against everything in the American establishment that had culminated in a war for which every night Walter Cronkite reported the latest "body count" of Viet Cong killed. The counterculture's myth sought a return to innocence, to a wisdom beneath the sophistications of mind. "Lose your mind and come to your senses," Fritz Perls counseled. In sex, as in "natural foods," they sought some new immediacy, some contact with what was primal, fresh, spontaneous, pure. Their impulse was to begin again, to create a culture in harmony with nature. The flesh was their New/found/land, their New Israel, in which they hoped to worship and live free.

Alas, innocence is as fragile as it is beautiful, and experience shatters it for all but the perennially childish. The youth culture didn't count on time, aging, and the inevitable transformations of eros. No matter how pure the heart or innocent the intent, the notion of pleasure without consequence, intimacy without commitment, sensation without deliberation, is an illusion. The structure of time and the human condition is such that what is done today mortgages the future. There is karma, or consequence, an inevitable connection between today and tomorrow, between vagina and womb, semen (seed) and husbanding, anatomy and destiny, the genitals and the person. The Counterculture's love produced as much herpes and gonorrhea and as many fatherless children as the old brand of sexual irresponsibility. Only the rhetoric was different.

The dominant culture in America quickly seized upon the aspects of the sexual revolution that it could co-opt and turn to its own ends of perpetuating the status quo. Among members of the establishment, instant sex became a reactionary rather than a revolutionary activity. In the sixties, we moved from being a production to a consumption economy. Our factories turned out an excess of goods. Therefore, to keep the economy growing, it became necessary to reverse the old ethic of saving money and postponing gratification (which had the function of allowing the accumulation of capital and passion) and teach people to consume, to seek instant gratification of their desires. Advertising moved into high gear to create an endless series of needs to be satisfied. We became convinced that we would finally be happy if we bought that second car, the new TV, the latest gadget to simplify life. The new ethic was "spend, consume, allow no desire to go unsatisfied. Do it Now! Fly now, pay later." The credit card became the ticket to paradise. Establishing credit, which meant having a regular job and proving that you could handle the stress of constant debt, living beyond today's means, became the new rite of passage into adulthood. The new citizen did not worry about the mortgaged future, the national debt, the ecological, social, spiritual conse-quences of expending the world's resources to create an economy in which the gross national product was supposed to expand every year. The future would take care of itself.

Not surprisingly, the credit card society adopted instant sex. Chastity, long engagements, postponed gratification, and the dis-cipline of saving to ensure the future were replaced by sex, instant intimacy, and whatever felt good to two or more consenting adults. Spending (the Victorian word for orgasm), became the better part of wisdom in an inflationary economy. Everything is expanding, there are no limits to growth. Only the repressed and the fearful inhibit themselves.

Inevitably, the innocence of the sexual revolution was made to serve the purposes of the dominant cultural myth. The key word "natural" became the new tool of the advertisers, the instrument for manipulating our desires to purchase more and perpetuate a lifestyle wholly dependent upon experts, corporations, and the production and consumption of commodities. Producers labeled their tired old processed foods "natural." Shampoos and tooth-paste concocted from the chemical warehouses of Secaucus, New Jersey, were laced with a bit of honey, yogurt, or placenta, and sold as "super-natural." With all this, natural sex became a new hot selling item. *Playboy* and *Cosmopolitan* and true believers in liberated sex quickly packaged advice on guilt-free sex, the etiquette of affairs at the office, techniques for instant and constant ecstasy, and multiple orgasms for the masses. The use of sex in advertise-ment became standard. Sexy women and virile men suggested that our erotic fantasies would be fulfilled if we used the right deodor-ant, smoked the right cigarette, and drove the right sports car. The sort of man who read *Playboy* was always adored by two women because he dressed in the correct styles, served wine at the right temperature, and had no sexual hang-ups. We hardly noticed that Madison Avenue constantly had its hand on the genitals of the nation. It linked an endless series of products to the new myth of sexual salvation. As sex replaced romance as the form in which the promise of eros was to be fulfilled, it became the new lure that would sell the goods and perpetuate the myth of the old culture of industrial capitalism.

In itself, of course, the process of promoting, advertising, and trying to convince people to consume the goods and values of industrial culture is not sinister, but inevitable. In one way or another, every culture "advertises" its world view, promotes its myth. Within the Vatican, there was early established an office of "propaganda" to promote the true dogma. In the Middle Ages, the statues and portraits of the saints served to recommend and make attractive a Christian view of reality. A picture of St. Francis with halo was a pin-up advertising a particular notion of virtue. It was propaganda aimed at selling the idea that agape was superior to eros, that spirituality was preferable to materialism, that renunciation of sexual desire was the path to the greatest happiness. Stained glass windows and cathedrals were the media carrying the advertisements for the Gothic myth, the vision of reality as "a great chain of being," a hierarchy in which the supernatural was higher than the natural, revelation superior to reason, the church of greater authority than the state, man naturally dominant over woman, and the life of the spirit (prayer, sacraments, obedience to the church, confession) of greater dignity than secular employment.

The corporate society uses Madison Avenue as its office of propaganda and television as its medium to create icons of eros. The saints of the secular vision—the famous, the beautiful, the powerful, the sexy—promote its view of the good life. Faithful consumers are certain that the longing of the heart will finally be satisfied if they perform the correct devotions—buy the product that has officially been designated this year's "in" style. The implicit promise of the "latest model" is "Consume and be satisfied"—or, in the old language, "Take, eat, this is my body." This corpus, this corporation, serves you the elixir of immortality, or its secular equivalent, the marks of status.

In the middle of the sexual revolution, we hardly noticed that sex, along with the rest of life, was becoming mechanized, stripped of wonder, and interpreted in categories borrowed from machines. With innocent intentions but chilling results, the western mind informed love and sex with its myth.

First, love and sex, like value and fact or mind and matter, were separated. Love became a private, subjective emotion, a way of feeling about another person. Its cognitive status was denied; it was not considered a way of *knowing.* Modern philosophies of science rejected as sentimental nonsense Augustine's conclusion that we can only know what we love. Sex was reduced to a biological phenomenon that scientists could quantify and study objectively in the laboratory. The intensity and number of orgasms were measured, and the stages of arousal were reduced to standard patterns. Scientists, with a little help from sexual surrogates, repaired sexual "malfunction" (a mechanistic term) by teaching techniques of sensate focus, muscular control, and the fundamentals of communication. Reduced to an amoral, biological phenomenon, stripped of guilt and mystery, the fundamentals of sex could easily be mastered. After Kinsey and Masters and Johnson, a new profession of "sex therapists" came into being. Without benefit of any deep meditation on the nature of eros (few, for instance, read Denis de Rougement's *Love in The Western World,* Norman O. Brown's *Love's Body,* or Herbert Marcuse's *Eros and Civilization*), they began to teach the ABC's of sexual communication, innocently smuggling the western myth into their techniques. (Currently, the best sex therapists are critical of such naive scientism and are searching for ways to reconnect sexuality and spirituality.)

Love was either denied or elevated to an occult realm so far above mundane experience as to be unreachable. The technophiles said it was just a fancy word for lust, a poetic way of speaking about a biological fact. Many an adolescent girl is seduced by the argument: "Come on, honey, don't be so uptight. Sex is natural, like eating a meal or drinking a glass of water when you're thirsty." Romantics admitted that sex was just sex, but continued to hope that the "real thing," namely love, would mysteriously surprise them. Often "love" was completely desexualized, spiritualized, and defined as a pure type of godly affection that saints exhibit, but that normal people rarely experience in their daily lives, and which certainly has no relevance to *the real* world of business and politics. Either way, it was considered so vague, impractical, or mystical that few, except Erich Fromm, thought the art of loving could be taught. In no university, church, or school was there a course in the curriculum called "How to Become a Loving Person." By luck, by grace, or not at all, one fell into it, or it happened. White magic.

Meanwhile, sex, like the other facts of life, was taught in school. For the most part, the textbooks sterilized sex by the use of neutral scientific language. No joy, no juice, no celebration, no suggestion of the weeping and gratitude that may accompany the sexual-mystical ecstasy. Any brief survey of the how-to books about sex leads one to suspect that the sexual advice industry was taken over by graduates of the Massachusetts Institute of Technology. Making love required knowledge of the proper techniques and positions. Anatomy charts detailed the plumbing. Genital engineers explained the angle, thrust, lubrication, frequency, varieties of stimulation, and nature of nerve endings, which, if mastered would produce orgasms—multiple, if not simultaneous.

Inadvertently, the sex books also taught the gospel of youth that is a part of the technological myth: To be is to be productive, to be worthwhile is to work. The joy of sex was for beautiful people, playboys and playgirls. Eros belonged to the willow-waisted and smooth cheeked, the Barbie and Ken dolls, the model bodies who graced the advertisements in the pages of *Glamour, Cosmopolitan, Penthouse,* and, yes, *Ms.* It came as a shock when Simone de Beauvoir challenged the myth, telling us that desire still warmed the flesh of the old, that Marlene Dietrich wasn't the only sexy grandmother, and that "dirty old men" were only men who had not forgotten.

How successful has the selling of sex and the new technology of arousal been? The avalanche of books about sex is itself strong evidence that the perspective and advice given in sex manuals doesn't work; it is an index of frustration, disappointment, anxiety, and false hope. Our obsessive efforts to find *the* core of life's meaning and satisfaction in sexual experience is a potlatch feast dedicated to a dying god.

We need only examine the logic of experience to see the structural contradiction involved in the myth of sexual fulfillment. On the one hand, the sexual revolution focused upon the individual's right to pure sensation. At the same time that it liberated sex from guilt, it encouraged us to divorce it from love and commitment. The necessary connection between love and marriage was proclaimed to be as obsolete as the horse and carriage. You *can* have one without the other. The sensate focus, the proclamation of the right of individuals to share sexual sensations with whomever they pleased, carried with it the idea that liberated sex could be divorced from continuity of caring, from consequences, from children, from community. Stripped of its context, sex became a happening between genitals that were only incidentally connected to persons who had a history and hopes for the future. Sensation was divorced from feeling and expectation. Thus liberated, sex became a game, a sport. "Sport-fucking" became the new metaphor, the well-trained sexual athlete the new model.

On the other hand, the promise implicit in the sexual revolution was that we would be washed clean of guilt by the big O. With a little help from Wilhelm Reich, the complete orgasm was proclaimed the elixir of happiness, the badge of freedom and authenticity. Sex was not only supposed to provide pleasure, it was supposed to give *meaning* to our lives.

Obviously, the one hand did not know what the other proffered. An experience emptied of emotional and moral content became the candidate for providing fulfillment, a sure recipe for schizophrenia. We entered the double bind: The more sex failed to live up to its widely advertised claims, the more frantically we redoubled our efforts to get it right. We became obsessive about being "natural," heated about appearing cool. Why, we wondered,

doesn't this thing we have stripped of awe and made trivial provide us with a center? Liberated sex drove us almost as crazy as
the old puritanical kind. They were flip sides of the same coin. One
portrayed sex as the devil, the other as God; one promised happiness if we abstained, the other if we indulged. Both lied.

Finally, sex began to appear more and more frequently in the
presence of violence. Disconnected sex and psychotic violence
were marks of the 1970s. The sexual revolution went hand in
hand, or fist in teeth, with the public's escalating romance with
violence. The expectation that uninhibited sex would lessen aggression proved false. Why? Because *to reduce communion between persons to contact between bodies, anonymous sex organs, and nerve endings is
already an act of violence.* The touch that heals always feels and
cherishes the other as a unique person. It includes the implicit
promise of friendship, care, and respect. It is no wonder that we
have come to fill our media and imaginations with pictures of
blood-smeared flesh. On TV and in the movies, we ritualistically
watch stabbings, rapes, mutilations, fights, the sadistic punishment of the flesh. Newspapers inundate us daily with all the news
that is unfit to print. Sadism sells because it is an unconscious cry
of despair that might be translated: "If I am nothing more than a
machine made of flesh, a body divorced from spirit, then destroy
the flesh, smash the machine." In irrational violence, the exiled
spirit cries to be recognized, eros shouts its final demand for the
full promise of being human to be cherished. The actions of the
alienated individual tell us that we must discover a new sense of
the sacredness of all life, a new glimpse of the whole and holy self,
or we will commit suicide. The diminished identity we are allowed
within the horizons of the western myth is no longer sufficient to
sustain our will to love. History has brought us to a point of clarity
and choice: love or die.

Wanderers in the wasteland, disillusioned with old gods, morals, ideologies, weary from the civil warfare between mind and
body, man and woman, nation and nation, we must become pil-
grims, seekers of a new vision, cartographers of a new form of
consciousness.

EROS, MYTH, AND METAPHYSICS

Our erotic crisis is merely one symptom of the underlying dis-ease through which western culture is now passing. The western-economic-secular-technological myth is beginning to disintegrate; and, as it ceases to in-form us, its view of the erotic is no longer satisfying.

Yeats has diagnosed the problem we face:

Mere anarchy is loosed upon the world,
The blood-dimmed tide is loosed, and everywhere
The ceremony of innocence is drowned;
The best lack all conviction, while the worst
Are full of passionate intensity.

The passions that now animate our world have become demonic and we lack a vision of health. We have plenty of portraits of twisted anti-heroes, men and women obsessed with power and sex. The modern novel has outstripped psychology in providing a casebook of the varieties of pathology. But we lack a vision or a science of hygeology. What forms of passion might make us whole? To what passions may we surrender with the assurance that we will expand rather than diminish the promise of our lives? Where may we look to catch a glimpse of the kind of passionate life that would heal both the psyche and the body politic?

If we are to recover a healthy passion, we must give up the simplistic notion that our erotic dissatisfaction is the result of a lack of sufficient information about proper sexual techniques or communication skills that can be cured in a weekend at Esalen or a few sessions of sex therapy. If we insist upon treating the symptom, there is no cure for the dis-ease. It is nothing less than our foundational myth with its models of the human psyche we must consider. The problem is not in our genitals, but in our minds, in our philosophy of life.

The foundational myth of any culture, whether Bushman, Marxist, or modern American, is like a cookie cutter pressed down on the raw dough of experience. It shapes every significant action by providing the metaphors, images, and models that in-form our experience. The mythical system determines whether birth will be understood as a medical phenomenon to be presided over by doctors, or as the incarnation of a soul to be sanctified by a priest; whether death is the end of self or the graduation into immortal life; whether illness is the result of germs or a punishment for offending the gods or breaking a taboo. It also decides when, where, why, and with whom we have sex, and whether love is a byproduct of lust or a sacrament that provides our best clue to the meaning of life.

To dispel our disenchantment with love and sex, we have to discover how the western myth has in-formed and mal-formed our bodies and our erotic practices. This requires that we make the nearly impossible attempt to demythologize our consciousness, to understand the eyes with which we look at the world. Once we have done this, we may begin to explore the elements of the passionate life that will allow us once again to celebrate the full range of love as eros, philia, libido, agape, charity, compassion, sweet lust, adoration, comfort, care. As we set out on the journey beyond our cognitive homeland, we know only that we must move away from a myth that has lost its capacity to provide us with a believable and satisfying map of human life and hence can no longer heal us.

A major component of the western myth is the belief that myth is a primitive and mistaken way of thinking about the world that has been replaced by science. Commonly, the word "myth" is now used to mean an illusion or a lie, as when we speak of the rumors and myths of the engines that were supposed to run on water instead of gasoline. Enlightened moderns are accustomed to looking at the queer beliefs of the Mayas or the Tassaday and seeing them as mythical. But we look on our own belief systems as rational and rooted in the realities of politics and economics. As Joseph Campbell says: "Myth is other people's religion."

We will make no headway so long as we hold to this simplistic view of myth. We will examine the notion of myth in detail when we look at the adult. For the moment, we may describe a living myth as a set of glasses through which a people sees the world. Or, to be more exact, *myth is the system of basic metaphors, images, and stories that in-forms the perceptions, memories, and aspirations of a people; provides the rationale for its institutions, rituals, and power structure; and gives a map of the purpose and stages of life.*

A living myth remains largely unconscious for the majority. It is *the* reality, not the symbol. For instance, I once asked a Hopi who had studied anthropology in a large university from what period the Hopi legends of creation of the world could be dated. He looked at me oddly and answered: "From creation, of course." As an educated man he knew about myth, but as a Hopi he still lived mythically.

Some people in every culture, however, see through or beyond the myth. In primitive cultures these were the shamans, the healers, the divine madmen and madwomen, and those with a natural bent for philosophical reflection.

Those whose amphibious minds move both within and beyond the myth may be thought of as outlaws or metaphysicians. Myth and metaphysics are related to each other in the same way that religion is related to theology. The mythical mind is unreflective. It lives unquestioningly within a horizon of the culture's images, stories, rituals, and symbols, just as the religious person rests content within the liturgy and creedal structure of the church or cult. The metaphysical mind reflects upon the myth and tries to make it conscious. It plays with the stories and images and lifts the basic presuppositions about life into the light of consciousness. In this sense, metaphysics is the thinking person's religion. In the place of stories about heroes and villains, it has a theory about good and evil. But both myth and metaphysics rest upon a commitment to a way of seeing and acting, and are not merely speculative toys of academic minds.

Whether our tastes and temperaments run more toward the mythical or the metaphysical style, we cannot avoid the necessity of taking the risk of belief. Since human beings are fragments of a whole that can never be fully known, we must necessarily make a leap of faith. We are, by virtue of our ignorance, mythical or metaphysical animals. Every vision of the meaning of life, whether primitive or scientific, ancient or modern, sacred or secular, is mythical or metaphysical.

It has been fashionable in the twentieth century not only to debunk myth (or leave it to either Jungian therapists, historians of religion, or English professors who make a study of James Joyce), but to pretend that reasonable and educated people could avoid the embarrassment of religion and the risk of metaphysics by sticking close to demonstrable facts and testable hypotheses. However, in the course of reducing our beliefs and hopes to certainties and proofs, we impoverished and deluded ourselves. The modern anti-myth reduced human life to a story without a point, a tale told by an idiot, a process without a purpose, a journey without a goal, an affair without a climax (Godot never comes), an accidental collision of mindless atoms. What little wisdom we have salvaged from our overload of fact seems to point us toward despair and nihilism. Since there is no intrinsic point to life, we had better make up a meaning by which to live, fabricate a purpose. Our little ideologies have produced our great desecrations: concentration camps, gulags, recurring rounds of genocide dedicated to some nationalistic idol. In the process, we have hardly noticed that economics, technology, and politics have become the new myth and metaphysic. We haven't avoided myth and metaphysics, only created demeaning ones.

Metaphysics and myth-making are a game of making a whole out of parts, a way of teasing the fragments of life into a vision of completeness. To play the game, we take some important aspect of human experience and let the imagination run wild. Let's suppose the world is like a big animal, or a plant, or a city, or an artifact, or a business, or a battle, or an accident, or a dream, or a machine, or a rat race, or a love relationship. Everybody plays the game, consciously or unconsciously. There is no way not to play it. Since we never see the whole except through the distorted spectacles of some limited analogy, every perspective is tinged with foolishness. Logical positivists and theosophists alike must decide, before the evidence is in, how they will interpret and live in this mysterious, indecipherable world. And every observer is prejudiced, a part of the world being observed, a pleader of special causes. No philosophical astronaut is able to travel outside the cosmos to judge for certain whether the world is made of dumb atoms or is held in the fragrant arms of Aphrodite. This is our each and only world: Every person must wager a single life on power, or knowledge, or love, or work, or conquest, or comfort, or adventure, or on some god of clan.

## THE WESTERN MYTH AND THE EROTIC VISION: A PREVIEW

The erotic obsession with the machine dictates the logic of the western myth. Here are its rules and articles of faith:

1. Reality is quantifiable, measurable, infinitely divisible into more basic and more real units.
2. Anything that can be measured can be controlled. All problems are solvable.
3. Questions that cannot be answered should not be asked.
4. Knowledge and power are the twin pillars of human identity.
5. Anything we can will we can accomplish.
6. Time is chronological, measurable, quantitative (like money), and can be saved or wasted.
7. Events are sequential; all causes are in the past; the present is the effect of all past causes; the future will be the effect of all present causes.
8. Reality is material, law-abiding, understandable.
9. Mind is the name of the most highly organized material.
10. Knowledge consists of organized facts.
11. Human conduct should be governed by mind.
12. Emotion is irrational; sensation, intuition, and feeling are primitive, immature forms of thought.
13. The most reasonable, powerful, and controlling individuals are of most value and should govern a society.

14. Nature is that imperfectly formed chaos that is to be in-formed by human goals (i.e., it exists to provide raw materials).

15. Females are less aggressive, less rational, less valuable than males and, like nature, are to be controlled and excluded from positions of responsibility.

16. Child-rearing, homemaking, and the nurturing arts are less important than productive work.

17. Wealth is created by fabricating natural, raw materials into finished products; the production of goods is the basis of value.

18. Money is the measure of value.

19. Human life is organized around the laws of the market.

20. Economics has replaced religion as the ultimate concern.

21. The chief motivation (eros) of human beings is to accumulate and consume.

22. Desire is infinitely manipulable.

23. Advertising and propaganda are the chief erotic sciences of the modern age.

In the western myth, it is finally competition or war that makes the world go round. As Heraclitus said, war is the father of all things. At heart, reality is conflictual: Jahweh battles the Goddess; man seeks to conquer nature, woman, and his own unruly emotions. The sword and the machine are the instruments of conquest. Within the horizon of this myth, love is understood as the artificial restraining of our natural impulses toward unbridled aggression. It is an emotion invented by culture to keep us from killing each other in order that the tribe might survive. The social contract is an arrangement between competitors, each seeking to maximize self-interest, to limit carnage by civility. The relationship between man and woman is a truce in the warfare between the sexes. Nowadays, having sex or making love, like other forms of fabrication, requires the advice of technological experts, doctors, psychiatrists, and moralists.

By contrast, the erotic myth holds that love is not primarily something we *make* or *do,* but something we *are.* We do not define it so much as it defines us. Before it is ever manifest as an activity or behavior, love is that impulse, motivation, or energy that links us to the whole web of life. Eros is the bond in the ecological communion within which we live. It is not primarily an emotion, a decision, or the result of an act of will. It is the mutuality linking cell to cell, animal to environment, without which we would not be. The predestined attraction of the penis for the vagina, which we celebrate as sexuality, is nothing more than a specific instance of a universal principle. The dance of desire, the attraction and repulsion of particles, goes on within the heart of every atom and aphid. Thus the study of love is not primarily a sociological, psychological, or biological matter. It belongs to ontology—the study of being. In the erotic vision, love is, in the words of Paul Tillich, "the ontological drive toward the reunion of the separated." Love is the prime mover within Being-becoming-itself. It is the energy of linkage. As such, love is the presupposition rather than the conclusion of our search. The erotic vision is based on the assumption that we can only understand our condition by beginning with love as the central clue upon which to found a metaphysics. We argue not *to* love but *from* love. Gabriel Marcel articulates the basis of an erotic metaphysic:

> Love, in so far as distinct from desire or as opposed to desire, love treated as the subordination of the self to a superior reality, a reality at my deepest level more truly me than I am myself—love as the breaking of the tension between the self and the other, appears to me to be what one might call the essential ontological datum.[5]

Philosophy, Marcel says, must begin not with the artificially isolated ego, the Cartesian thinking or doubting self, but with the self that exists within an intersubjective communion, a self already linked to other beings. Within the tradition of erotic metaphysics, which goes back to Augustine and Plato, love is assumed to be prior to knowledge. We love in order to understand. Since it is love that under-stands us, the task of an erotic metaphysic is not to demonstrate the existence of love but to articulate the ground of our being as human beings, to give words, images, a voice to our silent knowledge, to decipher the erotic impulse that is encoded within our DNA and within the intentionality of life itself.

The tradition of erotic metaphysics is perennial. When men and women first began to think abstractly, it occurred to them that the experience of love, sexuality, fertility provided the best clue to understanding the nature of things. Vulva and breast were the earliest symbols of the erotic vision in neolithic times, when God was a woman called Mother Earth. Plato and Aristotle both saw eros as the prime mover of stars, acorns, and the affairs of men. Christian theologians later defined the ultimate reality—God—as love. In Chinese thought, the interplay of yin and yang, the feminine and masculine energies, was said to be responsible for all changes. The whole system of kundalini yoga found in Tantrism pictured the erotic energy of the universe rising like a snake up the human spine, infusing the seven centers of the body (see Appendix A). Hegel brought the erotic tradition to its most complete articulation in the nineteenth century by defining reality as spirit, and spirit as "love disporting with itself." Herbert Marcuse saw, beyond the alienation of western culture, the possibility of a utopia in which machines would serve the cause of eros rather than thanatos (death). Norman O. Brown has given the erotic vision its most imaginative contemporary form in *Love's Body*, in which he shows that imagination, language, and poetry infuse human flesh with the substance of love. In a more practical vein, Wendell Berry gives voice to the erotic vision in his essays, showing that agriculture is a way of life that practices the continuous harmony between earth and its creatures and heals the split between the holy and the world. And no thumbnail sketch would be complete without acknowledging that the women's movement today is a strong voice of the erotic vision. Susan Griffin in *Woman and Nature* and *Pornography and Silence* shows that the divisions we have made between mind and matter, culture and nature, man and woman, sex and tenderness are the essence of the pornographic mind. We can only be healed when we reunite knowledge and eros, the intellect and the sensuous knowledge of the body.

FROM EROTIC METAPHYSICS TO EROTIC PSYCHOLOGY

This book will follow in the line of the existential philosophers from Socrates to Heidegger and Marcel who have argued that our primary access to Being, God, or Reality is through the study of our own being. We inevitably read the world-story through the lens of our own autobiography. The human psyche is the gateway to whatever we may know of the beyond. Hence we may know, or trust, that the universe is friendly, only in the measure that we may come to know ourselves as beings who are motivated by the impulse to become lovers.

One of the reasons that most studies of love are so unenlightening is because they attempt to discover a *single meaning* of love or sexuality. To understand what part love plays within the human psyche (and beyond), we need to look at the varieties of love that unfold as a person moves through an entire lifetime. A human being, as Heidegger said, is spread out over time. Love is different for the newborn child than it is for the ripe old man. Thus to trace eros as the prime mover of the psyche, to study the changing imperatives, impulses, and motives that govern each stage in the life-cycle, we need something like a time-lapse film of a complete lifetime. Our definition of self, or love, can only be given in the form of a story: The nature of human being can only be defined by recounting the history of what we are becoming; the dance of love can only be detected in the postures of desire that characterize us at various stages along life's way.

The method of this book will be to construct a life-map that traces the transformations of love throughout the course of an *ideal* lifetime. Our task is to sketch an outline of an erotic developmental psychology. Our time-lapse portrait will, rather arbitrarily, divide a lifetime into five stages: the child, the rebel, the adult, the outlaw, and the lover. By looking at the modes of intercourse, the dispositions, and the developmental impulses that govern each of these stages, we will unfold a story that suggests that the goal of becoming a lover is encoded within the human DNA, that the primal reality that in-forms us, prior to all cultural myths, is love.

(Appendix B charts a summary of these stages.)

The outline of developmental erotic psychology that follows owes more to the vision of human life found in the tantric vision of kundalini yoga, Bunyan's *Pilgrim's Progress*, Daumal's *Mt. Analogue*, the hero's journey, Kierkegaard's *Stages on Life's Way*, and *Love's Body* than to the contemporary view found in such works as Erikson's *Identity and the Life Cycle*, Sheehy's *Passages*, or Levinson's *The Seasons of a Man's Life*. My interest is *normative* not *descriptive*, philosophical rather than empirical. A glance at the bloody face of human history and at our current obsession with violence is enough to make nonsense out of the claim that human beings are *in fact* motivated by love. If we count noses, thanatos appears to be winning over eros.

A normative approach asks: What is the human potential? What is the promise of human life at its best? To use an analogy: Empirical studies of developmental stages are like a survey of the state of physical health that reveals that 63.2 percent of persons regularly suffer from colds, fatigue, and bouts of depression. A normative study is concerned with super-health. Who are those people who don't fall ill, who have sustained enthusiasm and energy, who may be sad but not depressed? How does the immune system function in optimum health? These are the questions that are central to this meditation on psychosomatic-spiritual-political-ecological health: In the optimum human lifetime, what desires and motives characterize the different stages of life? How is love transformed as we pass from being children, to rebels, to adults? Are there modes of loving that surpass the normal erotic quotient (EQ) of adults? (Insofar as the quest for knowledge is central to the western myth, we are accustomed to measure IQ; and we routinely accept the idea that there are persons with superior IQs. But we have thought little and investigated less the possibility of a supernormal EQ—erotic quotient. Perhaps we fear the demand it would place upon us to become more loving.)

In addition to being biographical, the method of this book is also autobiographical. My access to being is through the psyche: My access to the psyche is through *my* psyche. Modern theories about the stages of life, like the mystical account of the ascent of consciousness that we find in *The Tibetan Book of the Dead,* or Dante's *Inferno* and *Paradiso,* are highly personal visions. John Bunyan's *Pilgrim's Progress* and Lawrence Kohlberg's stages of moral development are both disguised forms of autobiography. Neither can be demonstrated to be universal truth. While I trust, and have taken pains to show, that the intention of becoming a lover is deeply etched within the human psyche, it is without question my own vision, my *apologia pro vita sua,* my personal effort to understand and celebrate the life I have been given. In sculpting the stages of development, I have made use of a host of witnesses from many cultures and times, all of whom have stretched the human EQ to its limit. But I also make frequent use of my own experience, because there is only one case history of the development of the psyche I have followed with intimate and daily study for half a century—my own.

I share my experience of love not as an expert but an amateur, not because I know the answers but because the question has lodged itself in me. For a decade I have wondered what we moderns must do in order to recover a passionate way of life. For years I planned to write a book on love and sex. Someday, I thought, I would be mature enough to attempt to scale Mt. Eros. But after a marriage of seventeen years, two children, a divorce, five years of "exploring my sexuality" (as they say in California), a second marriage now in bloom, and an autumn child, I am as fascinated by the vision of becoming a lover as ever, but I am still no expert. The mystery seems to deepen as I move closer to it. However, after years of aspiring to become a lover, I have a certain expertise in impediments to love, romantic and antiromantic illusions, blind alleys, and procrustean beds. As a fledgling, I have little knowledge about high flying, but I can offer some advice about how to flap your wings and fall from high places with a minimum of injury. Frequent failures may produce a residue of wisdom. I feel much like those men in India who have gone to university but failed their exams, and who introduce themselves as "Surgit Singh, B.A. (Failed)." Mapping those areas of human experience

that are antithetical to love (the perversions of possession, paranoia, fear, hate, the quest for power, self-absorption) has at least
helped me to isolate the territory within which we may discover
the meaning of love. Thus I will frequently use the first person
singular, not as the voice of authority, but to say: Here is what I
have found and seen to date on my journey. I draw a portrait of
the complete lover not as a philosophical self-portrait, but as an
effort to gain a glimpse of the hope that lures me toward becoming
myself.

WARNING: THEORIES MAY BE HAZARDOUS TO YOUR
PSYCHOLOGICAL HEALTH

Philosophers, psychologists, sociologists, and especially economists should be required to place warning labels upon their theories. Any theory is designed to be an aid to clarifying vision. When
it obscures, it should be discarded. Unfortunately, we tend to turn
theories into creeds rather than allow them to remain playthings
that help us to recognize patterns.

Fair warning. The notion of stages on life's way rests upon one
of the oldest religious-psychological metaphors—life as a journey.
A stage is part of a process of development that has an end, a goal,
a *telos*. If there are stages on life's way, then there must be a journey
to be taken—a point, a purpose, a destination toward which the
process is moving. Something must in-form the direction of the
movement. Both *Passages* and *Seasons of a Man's Life* are finally de-
pressing because they do not carry out the logic of their own
metaphor. They describe stages and movement that have no point.
Both trail off and do not deal creatively with old age because they
refuse to deal with any goal in old age, any telos, that might be
seen as a triumph of human potency rather than a decline of
vitality. If we use the idea of stages and journey we are obliged
to follow the logic of our metaphors and ask where we are going
and why. If life is a journey, the end of life may be death but it
cannot be its telos. The claim of this book is that the unfolding of
eros in-forms the human journey. We age in order to become
lovers.

There are, however, implications of the metaphor of the journey against which we must guard. A journey, like a stage, suggests linear movement, a before-and-after sequence. It tempts us to date childhood from age one to twelve, adolescence from thirteen to twenty, and so on. In a moral sense, it suggests that life is like getting nearer a goal, or climbing a mountain. There is a time when we are going to get *there,* to the end. We are going to be finished, complete, perfect. In one sense, each individual's life is linear. Between birth and death we move toward our four score and ten years as an arrow flies in one direction. Hence linear modes of thought are appropriate to describe much of the life of the psyche. But, in the depths of the unconscious, there are no straight lines, no time, no before or after. Remembrance and premonition move together. In dreams and in imagination, past, present, and future are simultaneously present. When we think of this eternal dimension of our being, the circle is more appropriate than the line. If life is a journey, then, it is not a pilgrimage but an odyssey in which one leaves and returns home again. We go out into time and return again and again to the same place. Although, as T. S. Eliot reminds us, having returned we know the still point from which we never departed better, we see home with strange eyes. The circle suggests there is no progress, especially moral progress, in human life. In the depths of the saint's psyche, the murderer and the madman still play their roles. The primal impulses to good and evil are always as near to us as the archaic dimension of our own unconscious. In this sense, there is no ascent, not even a spiral upward, no higher and lower virtues, no progress toward becoming a lover. A child may be more loving, more motivated by eros, more open than an adult. Our journey may be a matter of finding ways to return to what we once knew and have forgotten. In the platonic tradition, eros is a remembering, or recollection, of the self, an effort (as Zen also says) to discover the face we had before we were born.

Recognizing both the values and dangers of the metaphors of development and journey, I have assigned no chronological dates to the stages of child, rebel, adult, outlaw, lover. Obviously, there is a progression in consciousness and in large measure we put away childishness when we pass into adulthood sometime in our twenties. But the motives of the child continue to work in us as infantile emotions long into the second half of life. Likewise, the intuition of the lover is already animating the child and drawing the adult beyond the confines of the tribal identity.

In an effort to balance the metaphors used to articulate the erotic vision, I suggest that the "stages" of life may also be thought of as

- modes of intercourse; styles of knowing, loving, and being in the world;
- erotic postures; the yoga asanas, or positions we use in relating to the self, others, the world;
- musical themes that weave together to form a symphony; the themes that are central to each stage are anticipated in the previous stage and remain as resonant subthemes in subsequent stages;
- viewpoints or perspectives from which to interpret our experience;
- impulses, neural circuits, encoded patterns, or dispositions, each of which dominates a given stage of our psychological development;
- a spectrum of color that emerges when the pure light of eros is shone through the prism of an individual life;
- a still-life photograph excerpted from a moving picture on the process of becoming a lover.

All maps of human life are composed of metaphors. All metaphors are revelatory and inaccurate. To profit by one another's experiences, we must become adept at the art of playing with metaphor, translating images, listening for the meaning beneath the non-sense of just-so stories or myths. Consciousness is poetry. We mix our metaphors in order to avoid orthodoxy, literalism, tyranny.

I invite you into a story

a life map
a moving-picture
a developmental psychology
a symphonic progression
an exploration of the postures of love
a journey, an odyssey, an amorous pilgrimage.

# 2.
# The Child

In the beginning we find the end; in our origin our telos; in the manger our eschatology. To know where we are going we must discover where we have come from. Gabriel Marcel reminds us that "hope is a memory of the future." We become lovers not by accumulating power or knowledge but by re-membering the conspiracy (breathing together) of care, the history of passion, from which our substance was created and which inform our minds and bodies. We study the child not to find who we were, but to discover who we are and yet may become. Our original condition is always present. The past re-presents itself in the faces of those we now love and hate.

Erotic philosophers advise us to return to the interface with the world we knew before we put on the masks that became our personas. Jesus: "Except you become as a little child you will never enter the Kingdom of Heaven." Nietzsche: "The child is innocence and forgetting, a new beginning, a game, a self-propelled wheel, a first movement, a sacred 'Yes.' For the game of creation, my brothers, a sacred 'Yes' is needed."[1] Freud knew that the "polymorphous perversity," the child's capacity for promiscuous enjoyment of the entire body, slept in the unconscious of every person. It scared him. Susan Griffin tells us: "When we love a child, we love human nature before it has been reshaped by culture. This is what we mean by 'innocence' and 'naiveté'; not that the child has no sexual feeling, but that this feeling has not yet been corrupted by culture's hatred and fear of nature, and that the child's idea of self has not been reshaped to a humiliating image."[2]

By returning (metanoia), we begin again. The first principle of life of the spirit is this: Those virtues, or graces, by which we are healed—trust, hope, and love—all depend upon seasoned innocence, openness to novelty, the willingness to be refreshed. Refurbish your memories of childhood and you will find fragments of an old map that will lead you to a treasure hidden in your future. Become conscious of your pre-history, your *sine qua non,* the conditions without which you would not be.

Circling, circling, the fragments of memory join hands, the rent of time is healed.

In front of the cabin on my farm, where I sit writing these words, an ancient cottonwood shades the glen, casts shadows over the waterfall that sounds in my ears. From the highest limb hangs a single strand of rope—sixty feet or more, a ship's hauser. I am interrupted by a child who comes to the cabin. "I want to swing, please." I pull the rope up the hill, lift him onto the knot that acts as a seat, push him as high above my head as I can reach. And let go. Out he goes. Over the valley, over the stream, over the years. Into the thin air of timelessness. Into the archetype. Into memory. And by the time the pendulum reverses and he returns to my arms, J. Alvin Keen, my father, has sent me soaring in Apple Buchanan's swing. Forty years have vanished and I can't remember whether I am one of the giants who, in mythical time, climbed the impossible tree and put up the paradisiacal swing, or the father whose joy is inseparable from the child, or the child, who wants only to do it again.

## A PRIMORDIAL LOVE STORY

Where does my story, or yours, begin? When I trace the roots of my being, at what point do I distinguish between *my* self and the soil in which I was planted? When can I first say "*I* am"?

I could begin with the birth of self-consciousness. One day, when I was nine years old, I was walking down Court Street in Maryville, Tennessee. Near the bottom of the hill, fifteen feet from an apple tree, on a part of the sidewalk that was smooth enough for skating, I knew suddenly and with blinding clarity that I was different than my parents, my brothers and sisters, and my play-

### The Child's Psyche

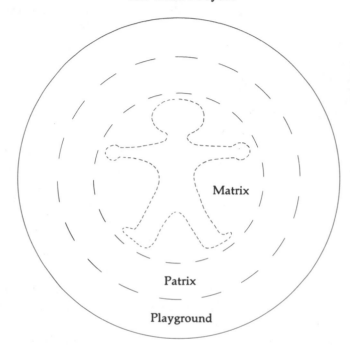

mates. Self-consciousness descended on me like a hawk. *Cogito ergo sum.* In a sense, I might date the origin of my self from this moment.

But my consciousness was swaddled in a cradle made by nature and culture long before I knew myself to be a person apart from others. I was neither father, mother, nor architect of my own being. No self-made man. I grew like a seed in humus that was composted of the residue of generations. A nexus of communion of the living and dead wove the tissue of my mind and body. My individuality was born from a web of life too intricate to unravel. Thinking back on the context that created me, I can only conclude that I must start my story with this affirmation: I was loved; therefore I am. As Martin Buber put it, "In the beginning was relationship."

The stuff and patterns of which you and I are made—atoms and blueprints coded in the DNA—have been in the making since the beginning of time. Astronomical events, Nature, God, Evolution— some immense force—shaped a place called earth, which was extraordinarily friendly to my development. My pilgrimage began eons ago, in the primordial watershed of evolution. All the information accumulated in millions of years of experiments is woven into the substance of every "innocent" child. The womb within which I was wrought was informed by all that has gone before. The sinuous knowledge of reptiles is encoded in my spinal cord. In my brainstem, the instinctual certainty of the mammal clan tutors my body in the strategies of fight and flight. Millennia of fish who gilled their way through watery worlds until they might crawl gasping onto the land contributed their research to the formation of my ears and lungs. And so the story might continue, tracing the geneology of my body until we reach the cortex, where words and images create a mirror of self-consciousness in which I may look and wonder who I am.

How are we to view this prehistory that is the prologue to each individual's story?

Two perspectives: To the objective eye of the tough-minded scientist (who resides within each psyche), the evolution of life is a hit and miss affair, a matter of "natural selection," at best an accident, the result of careless fate playing dice with unstable atoms. Or it is a tale of the triumph of selfish genes that proved fit enough to survive the battle.

To the wondering eye of the child (that remains undimmed in the oldest and wisest), it seems that some cunning god wove a cosmic tapestry in which each life is a part of a design too large for our myopic eyes to comprehend. Even seeing the flaws, the horrors of time, the indelible marks of evil, the innocent spirit gives thanks for the bittersweet cosmos that feeds and devours us.

### THE ENCOMPASSING MATRIX: THE WOMB OF LOVE

If I must pick an arbitrary beginning for my personal story, I might choose the moment of conception. One cold March evening in

Scranton, Pennsylvania, Dad and Mother surrendered to the promptings of eros, and a persistent sperm fought its way past a million hazards into the arms of a waiting ovum to consummate a love affair that turned out to be me. Twenty-three plus twenty-three chromosomes embraced, said "I do," and journeyed together into the interior of the womb. A multitude of cells formed a commune, a commonwealth, in which brain and heart and liver grew to be a single harmonious body politic—a baby boy.

In utero, there is no I and Thou, no subject or object, no self and environment. No boundaries. No in/dividuals. Only mother-and-child. Complete symbiosis. Through a million arteries of the placenta, the child receives information and nourishment from its matrix. In the amniotic fluid an island appears, a small self awash in the cosmic sea. The cords binding mother and fetus gradually create the new and separate being.

The first (and last) world is the womb. The only paradise we may regain is one we have lost. Freud tells us what every son knows but has conspired to forget (and no daughter has, perhaps, wholly forgotten): We long to return to the womb. Thus we are condemned to absurdity, for how can a man be born again? Unless, of course, we listen to the child within who re-cognizes the world as an encompassing matrix. Even in the age of science, the world is a primal encompassing presence, a living body within whom we are planted and grow. Thus we are first seminal beings, agriculturists—bearers, planters, tenders of seed. The human world is not, and never will be, a product of our hands, a fabrication.

Modern hysteria (hyster = womb) comes from the denial that we live within the womb of Being. We want to deny our helplessness and dependency. We accuse nature of being as careless as history, as warlike as nations, as mechanical and heartless as the machines we have created. She has rejected, deserted, abandoned us. We are not encompassed in a care/ful matrix. Alone, anxious, abandoned, secretly ashamed, we are forced to create a system, a controlled environment, a mechanical complex, a defended establishment to ward off her hostile intent. She is red in tooth and claw. No wonder we want to revenge ourselves on her—use, abuse, control, rape, desecrate. So long as we refuse to feel ourselves as seminal beings within the belly of time we will continue to resent and suspect nature, the feminine, and all that is succoring and unpredictable within our own psyches.

BIRTH: LOVE AS SEPARATION AND REUNION

In the fullness of time, the unity of mother and child is broken. The prodigal journey of in/dividuation begins. Contractions. Spasms. The violence and pain of separation. The trauma of birth. From this moment, the archetype of birth will forever be deeply etched into the human organism. Every crisis in which the psyche is stretched, pushed, and impelled into a larger world, invited to become spirit, will be symbolized by the trauma and triumph of birth. Without being born again, and again, there is no journey, no spirit, no love. Myth and religion teach the art of midwifery. To learn the logic of love, study the process of birth.

The passage through the narrows is dangerous. In the birth canal the child, in transit between matrix and world, is in mortal peril. The odds against its survival seem impossible. How can so small and unpracticed a traveler withstand the battering and pressure? How can it have the courage and knowledge to leave behind the easy paradise of the womb and the ambrosia freely given by the placenta to begin the lifetime work of breathing? Yet, regularly, the miracle happens. Each of us has already once passed through the valley of the shadow of death and answered the heroic call to adventure in the alien nation of time.

Birth creates distance. A space merges between I and thou. A void opens between matrix and child. The self is born from nothing—*ex nihilo.* In the empty place between mother and child, between object and subject, when the umbilical cord is cut, a new being, forever defined partially by its separation is created. Birth teaches us that we are alone. It imprints us with the fear that we may be abandoned, and the hope that we may be re-united with the ground of our being. Love and knowledge are born where we least expect them, in the manger of nothingness, in the empty and anxious space that separates us from our matrix.

Moments after birth, mother and child look at each other as intimate strangers. Each feels the separation that has occurred. Their early seamless being-together has been torn apart. Now they must learn to communicate.

## BONDING: LOVE AS BEING ONE FLESH

In the natural course of things, the rupture caused by birth is healed immediately. Mother takes the child, still connected to her through the oxygen-rich umbilical cord, to her breast. In her arms, a complex bond is woven from the touch of skin, the smell of breath, the sound of voice, the benediction of smiles, the rhythm of rocking, the resonance of the beating heart, the taste of the breast. There is immediate hormonal and sensory knowledge. This is *my* mother. The key fits the lock. Our first cognition is re-cognition.

Even *in utero,* the infant knew something of the taste, smell, and sounds of the mother. At birth, the pattern of the face is added to the familiar in-formation. A newborn is programmed for immediate face-recognition and will spend 90 percent of its waking time focused on the mother. Joseph Chilton Pearce tell us, "Establishing this face pattern gives the cornerstone on which the whole conceptual set is built after birth, the constellate around which all the rest of the infant's exploration of the mother will orient."[3] The beloved face is the first visual template, the starting point on the map—around which all knowledge will be organized. *It is the* axis mundi, *or world pole, the first mythical site that marks the center of the sacred world.* Later, the face and the arms will be replaced by new mythical beings—a lover, a spouse, a church, a tribe, a corporation. The security necessary for the child to explore the strange new world comes from basking in the presence of the smile.

(Questions: Can we truly know any reality we do not feel is smiling on us? Can love and knowledge be separated without destroying life? The abstractions upon which modern science are built proceed from a denial that man is bonded to nature. "She" has been reduced to "it." The smile has been reduced to a look of bland indifference. Are the abstractions—numbers, meter readings, hypotheses, formulas for prediction and control—that we have left after we have stripped nature of the smile and the sacred presence what we mean by knowledge? Or, is true knowledge always carnal, a re-cognition of the bonds uniting I and thou? What kind of science would arise in a culture where men loved their mothers? Their matrix?)

At the breast, we learn our first philosophy—the philosophy of familiarity, kinship, and kindness. The world is what is kin and kind to us. We belong together; isolation is death, bonding is life. Enjoyment is rooted in mutual need; I re-create the matrix that creates me; desire is mutual; the pleasure I receive is matched by the pleasure I give. Nipple and mouth form an antiphonal symphony of shared resonances. Holding and being held, receiving and giving pleasure, nourishment and love are indistinguishable. Like a plant or animal, our first knowledge is tacit. What is real is what we touch. Things make sense because we smell, see, hear, and taste. Subtle shifts in muscle tension, and in the rhythm and sound of breathing, telegraph the knowledge of distant events. When the arms that held me were supple and warm, I trusted the world. When the breast on which I lay was troubled, I knew some nameless terror threatened. The first catechism of the flesh is: Mother is anxious; therefore the world is dangerous. Or, Mother is calm; therefore the world is safe.

THE IN-FORMING PATRIX: LOVE AS CARE AND
THE WEAVING OF CHARACTER

All the while we are encompassed and succored by the mother, we are already being informed by the values, meanings, and myths of the culture that surrounds us. Language forms our minds. Rituals are woven around our naked biological beings. Water and fire baptize us into the second womb—the artificial womb of culture.

Traditionally, we have thought of nature as maternal and culture as paternal. Mother links us through the tacit, sexual, instinctual knowledge of our bodies to the eternal rhythms of nature. The fathers and elders of the tribe are the guardians of the abstract knowledge, the traditions and ceremonies that celebrate the myths and sanctify the power structure and ideology of the tribe. They create the cultural womb, which we may call the *patrix*, without which we would not be human.

The sexism and ideology implicit in this way of reading history is obvious. Our language clearly lies. There have always been women who knew and men who loved. Men form part of the matrix for the child, and women help create the patrix. Both sexes weave a conspiracy of care around the child, teach it language, traditions, and know-how.

That we are informed by a patrix means that we do not enter life as anonymous beings without names or histories. We are born heirs to an enormous trust fund from a community. From the beginning, I was entertained by and initiated into the mysteries of the Keen and McMurray clans. Sacred objects—an old pistol, a worn Bible, an arrowhead, tintype photographs of my ancestors—gave me a heroic past to imitate. Family, kin, clan, tribe were the lenses through which each of us first saw the world. Our perspective is familiar, not neutral. Your eyes grasp the world as a Smith, a Cohen, a Kozinski. Each ethnic heritage incarnates a history of care that is re-presented in the thousand stories, legends, tales that the generations have passed on until they became polished stones carried long in the pocket.

GUILT AND SHAME: LOVE'S BOUNDARIES

A child needs to dwell in a garden of innocence. It is only within the encompassing matrix and patrix that it may grow strong by learning the virtues of dependency and basic trust. Along with the care it receives from loving arms, however, a child also absorbs the values, opinions, prejudices, hatreds, and habits of the family and clan. From the beginning, it is tutored in the orthodox and righteous distinction between good and evil. The home is the first church and school. The tension and relaxation of muscles, smiles and frowns, teach us Father's and Mother's philosophy of right and wrong. A smiling countenance identifies and rewards us when we have done a good thing. A frown or an angry voice, with its implied threat of abandonment, informs us that we have done a bad thing and are treading dangerously near taboo territory.

Throughout childhood, we are conditioned to give unquestioning obedience to the family and community's dualistic system of values—ought and ought not, good and evil.

Whether we are American Methodists or Kalahari Bushmen, we are shaped by a system of oughts and taboos. The anxiety caused by the threat of abandonment or punishment keeps us within the walls of the garden. An invisible electric fence of conscience, an unconscious barrier enforced by shame and guilt, keeps us within predetermined boundaries. In childhood we remain within the circle of familiar love because, fearful of the terrors that may lurk in the unknown darkness, we are drawn by the warmth and light of the hearth. Right or wrong, good or evil, obedience or disobedience, love or abandonment, acceptance or guilt, approval or shame —these form the boundaries within which the psyche of the child finds security, trust, and courage.

We need to be clear-eyed and unsentimental about the dilemma that is built into parental love. The most perfectly bonded child, wisely nurtured by a happy mother and father, must still pay a heavy price for the gift of familiar love. The arms that hold us shape our character before we have a mind or will to choose. The author/ities imprint their official myths on our psyche before we try to tell our own story. The bonds that secure us also limit us. Love creates the prison of character.

The long period of dependency that characterizes human childhood ensures that all of us will reach adulthood being slightly, or severely, schizophrenic. We each have a character, a shell, a set of conditioned responses, preformed opinions and unexamined values, a mask or personality we wear in the presence of our parents and peers. But in the secrecy of our private self, there is also a sanctuary within which our spirit begins to develop. It is within this playground that we first taste freedom and the knowledge that our being is not finally defined by the mores of the community.

THE SYBARITIC SENSES: THE WORLD AS PLAYGROUND

A child first discovers freedom (consciousness, the ability to transcend encapsulation, spirit) in play. One legendary day, the child wanders away from the encompassing matrix and patrix to explore the wonders that lie beyond.

I watch Jessamyn, my seven-month-old daughter: She lies secure in her mother's arms. Her eyes first fix upon the face, and then dart out to gaze at a teddy bear. Her fingers, kitten-like, knead the breast and then reach out to test the textures of objects. Promiscuously, she touches and tastes everything within her reach. Without benefit of clergy, she seeks oral intercourse with fingers, spoons, pillows, the tail of the dog. Her eyes, hands, senses, mind, create a dance, a dialectic between bonding and exploring. She moves first, *with* and then *away from*. The more secure she feels the more daring her explorations. After each foray into the wilderness (today a grunting, cooing, laughing, shrieking encounter with a tangled piece of green ribbon), she returns to the known, to mother. Already she is a homesteader and a gypsy, as she will remain so long as her consciousness is alive.

Each child begins the march toward consciousness as five sense organs in search of a world. Long before the cortex affirms: "I think; therefore I am," the body sifts through mixed sensations of pleasure and pain and affirms by laughter and tears: "I sense, therefore I am." It is by playing with sensations that we put together our picture of the world. The child sits at the center of a magical theater filled with a kaleidoscope of unknown things that make indistinct impressions on the senses. Gradually, a distinct object swims into view and is distinguished from the play of light and shadow, color and form, temperature and texture. What was once something like and unlike mother's breast becomes a blanket that (unlike the breast) may be chewed upon and pulled.

Every part of the child's body is an erogenous zone, every sense an organ of intercourse. The mouth accepts the favors of the breast, the big toe, the rattle. The eyes widen to take in any movement or color. The ears delight in all but sudden or harsh sounds. The skin welcomes touch. "Tickle my body," Jessamyn demands, without words. "Do it again. More kisses." In the beginning, before they have been educated to feel shame and guilt,

children enjoy anything that feels good. They have not yet separated the body into private (erotic) and public (desensitized) parts.
Their incipient minds are formed by the explorations of their
sybaritic senses. Before the fall into culture the unadapted child,
who still exists in the depth of every psyche, is an unashamed
hedonist.

Recently, psychologists and philosophers have begun to insist
that play is, after all, rather serious business. Small chimpanzees
may seem to be monkeying around, wrestling and growling in
good fun, but they are *really* learning the grim art of fighting and
defense. Boys and girls playing guns and dolls are merely in training to assume the social roles of warriors and mothers. No doubt
there is truth in this perspective, especially for monkeys. We learn
by imitation. All the world's a stage, or at least some of it. A
sprinkle of dust in the mud pie teaches us to add cinnamon to the
apple pan dough. By playing house or doctor we learn the facts of
life. There is play that prepares us to perform our adult roles—
doctor, lawyer, merchant. Games strengthen the serious "oughts"
of a culture. Football teaches the orthodox virtues: competition is
the game; winning is the goal; cooperation is the means. But there
is also an innate and nearly indestructible spirit of play in human
personality that gives us the capacity to transcend all the molds,
morals, masks, and myths that culture would impose upon us.

In the play of the senses, the child burrows beneath the boundaries of the persona. Touching, smelling, and tasting allow us to
discover for ourselves if, and to what extent, the world makes
sense. So long as we have bodies, we may retreat into the sanctuary of experience. The senses are private oracles. When we consult
them we discover a sacred bond, deeper than the binding obligations and myths of the tribe, that unites us to life. Touch, taste,
smell, sight, hearing link us to the vibratory events that make up
our world. The child touching its own body, toys, friends, shame-
lessly enjoying the smorgasbord of sensations, discovers an asocial
self (a prototype of the outlaw).

Play, of the senses or the imagination, is the magic, the grace,
the elixir without which roles become habits, personality becomes

a facade, character becomes character-armor, culture becomes a prison.

When I celebrate freedom, I remember the wilderness that was, and always will be, just across the street beyond the reach of the watching eyes and careful "oughts." We crossed Court Street and climbed through a hole in the fence, leaving God, good manners, cleanliness, and all the polite virtues of Presbyterian children behind. The moment we were in the trees, out of sight of home, we became pagans. A short way down the path we stopped, pulled out our stolen pack of Camels from the hollow log, lit up. And coughed. All morning we worked on our fort, cutting saplings with a hatchet we borrowed from Granddad's toolbox, and wove them into walls beneath the felled forked oak. Midafternoon our domain was invaded by a party of picnickers. We became Indians and stalked the unwary, stealing two egg salad sandwiches and a cake when they were not looking. After that we dammed up the creek, went swimming, and tried to catch a crawfish. When the sun went down, we climbed back through the fence, checked to see if our breath still smelled of tobacco, put on the mask of civility, and went home for dinner.

Even as a child, I knew myself to be different from and more than the oughts, images and ideals I agreed to in order to win the love of my parents and the respect of my peers. The insatiable senses and the promiscuous imagination are never satisfied by the monogamy of the persona. Some restless, unnamable energy pushed me out of the garden of childhood, lured me into becoming a rebel.

# 3.
# Faulted Childhood and the Perversions of Eros

WE ARE ALL PERVERTS

A child is the form in which the flesh brings forth its promise. Eros in bud. Every child has an inalienable right to be bonded in welcoming arms, kindly initiated into a caring culture, allowed to play freely in the realms of the senses and imagination. As the seed is betrothed to fertile soil, sun, and rain, the child bears an organic right to nurture. This right, which is nowhere guaranteed by law and cannot be proved by abstract reason, is inscribed in our inarticulate genetic sense of the sacred. Paradoxically, our certainty of the sacredness of the promise of childhood is renewed each time we see it desecrated. The bruised and battered child calls forth in most people an instinctive moral outrage: By all that is holy, this child *ought* not to be treated in this way. Wounds bear a silent testimony to the broken promise of love.

Every community and every age can compile its own catalogue of the varieties of tragedy that twist the bodies, pervert the minds, and violate the natural rights of children. Exposure and death of unwanted infants was the earliest form of population control. Until the child labor laws were enacted to curtail the cruelty of forcing children to work twelve and fourteen hours a day in factories and mines, children were considered little adults, often harshly disciplined, forced into premature sexual activity. In China, the feet of girl children were broken, the toes bent back, to make the feet "more beautiful." Painful rites of initiation were the rule among primitive tribes. It is only recently that we have challenged the idea that children are the property of their parents.

Even in our relatively gentle century, no child enters adulthood unscarred. Millions of malnourished mothers give birth to babies already genetically stunted by protein deprivation. A majority of infants in "civilized" countries are born in hospitals where the mothers are drugged, their babies routinely taken away from them and placed in a nursery. That terror we fear most, to be unbonded and abandoned, is the first product of most modern births. Many children are born to hostile or anxious mothers and are unwanted from the day of their birth. A majority of middle-class children suffer from the vacuum of the missing father who is too busy with "important" things to enfold them in his arms, too serious to play. Warfare regularly brings injury, chaos, the loss of a parent. Even those children who are raised in privileged and normal conditions by parents who are attentive to their needs are faulted by some deficiency or excess. Some are held so tightly in over-solicitous arms they find it difficult to escape crippling dependencies; the arms become prisons. Children of ambitious parents are frequently crippled by shame, by perpetual failure to live up to impossible standards and perfectionistic ideals. Still others, raised by parents who are devoid of hope, opportunity, or passionate ideals, suffer from a vacuum of desire and motivation. Their highest goal is to get by.

Mythology tells us every childhood was faulted. In some measure we are all perverts, neurotics, sinners, imperfect specimens. The promise of childhood is not fulfilled in any of us. The myth of the Fall portrays us all as exiles from the full human potential. Our eros, our motives, our desires, our drives have been twisted. Paradise has been lost. History is the story of our efforts to repair the damage, to discover our way back to a home we have never yet inhabited, to recover a unity we have intuited only in the fragments.

Most people, liberals and moral majority alike, react negatively to the suggestion that we are all perverts. But to say we are perverse is no misanthropic judgment, no cause for despair. To the contrary, the acceptance of our imperfection is the basis of humility. We are all gnarled. "Perverse" means literally "turned the wrong way." We make many wrong turns, proceed on our journey in an indirect, often tortuous way. No one of us fully incarnates the entire human promise. As individuals, we are idiosyncratic and real rather than normative and ideal. The fully actualized, universally erotic human being exists only as an impossible ideal or an archetype. But the ideal may help by giving us a map that points in the direction of our becoming.

To judge that a motive, an act, a style of life has become perverse means that some virtue that was perfectly appropriate in some (usually earlier) context has become untimely and therefore unbalancing. To cling to Mother or Father is a prerequisite for health in a small infant, but to remain passively dependent beyond childhood is to suffer from too much of a good thing. We travelers in time have never been this way before, so we have a tendency to try to extend into the unknown future the virtues that served us in the past. We are always responding to fresh situations with yesterday's solutions. We never pass evenly through the stages of life, as philosophers would have us do to keep their theories neat. At any so-called stage we are ranging over the entire map. The child is already practicing to be an adult and foreshows in its innocence the wisdom that comes to fruition only in autumn. Each adult juggles mature and infantile motives, adjudicates between "rebellious emotions" (as Wilhelm Reich puts it) and appropriate feelings.

To the degree that we are faulted, we are motivated by our fear of deficiency rather than our trust in sufficiency. *Our love proceeds more from trying to fill the hole than by allowing the whole to fill us.* We become obsessed with what is missing rather than what is given, with the past rather than the present, with the wound rather than the gift. What we call "love" becomes searching (in vain) for what (we imagine) we lack—a father or mother who would love us enough. The vacuum forms the icon of our desire. The more we force a lover, a wife, a husband, a child, a job, a cause, a thing, or a drug to try to fill the void, the more that "loved" one becomes a misplaced focus for eros, an idol that will inevitably disappoint us, and which we will come to hate.

Thus, fellow perverts, no one of us has or will ever be entirely finished with the promise or pain of childhood. In large measure, becoming a lover involves coming to know the unique and common ways in which eros has been twisted in us, knowing the faulted child, and all the devious ways we have tried to fill the hole in our heart. Eastern religion calls this the task of unveiling the illusions of Maya and seeing the laws of one's karma. Western religion speaks of repentance, turning the mind around. Psychoanalysis presents us with a secular technique to make the unconscious conscious. No matter what language or discipline we adopt, the task is to become aware of how the childhood fault remains, to see how our character or persona covers up the infantile motives that remain in the recesses of the unconscious. Again and again we must return to the interface between our original and our faulted childhood, to hold our hope and our disappointment simultaneously in our awareness. Then we begin to see how thoughtless habits convert our splendid hours into dull routine, how our love relationships repeat the scripts of unfinished dramas we once played with Mother and Father, how our tiresome efforts to succeed, to perform well, are futile efforts to win the approving smile from "the face." To understand our faultedness is to see a double vision, the heads and tails of our identity: (1) our character type, personality style, defense mechanisms, addictions, neurotic patterns are the result of the perversions of eros—an outward and visible sign of an inward and invisible dis-grace or dis-ease; (2) the essence of who we are *is* eros, grace, ease.

The healing of eros, the unfolding of the story of the person, moves in a circle. The spiral rather than the arrow inscribes the geometry of the spirit. The more deeply we move into freedom, into novelty, into a chosen future, the more we must keep the gates of the sanctuary of the past open.

THE ANHEDONIC CIRCLE AND THE BONDAGE TO PAIN

When we think of erotic perversions, the fetish comes to mind. If a man is sexually aroused only by the sight and touch of a woman's shoe, or a woman only by a man who smells of garlic, it is clear that eros is somehow displaced. "Normal" people are a bit repulsed, amused, and titillated by the more bizarre fetishes. "Weirdos" and "freaks" are a comfort to the moderate. The joke about the man who gets stimulated by smelling bicycle seats reassures those of us who have only heterosexual obsessions that we are in good erotic health. So what if we are only "turned on" by women with large breasts, men who are tall, handsome, and wealthy, or someone who makes us feel superior, or inferior?

The faulted character of childhood makes fetishists of us all. By the time we reach maturity, few of us retain the ability to feel passionate love for a member of the same sex (homosexuality!) or even for people who are very different from ourselves, the old, the ugly, the unusual. We cling to our class, our clan, our look-alikes. We come to desire the stereotyped beauty of the models of masculinity and femininity that are presented to us by the media—love goddesses and sex symbols. The healthiest among us retain a narrow circle of family and friends where love is permissible. We seldom feel that erotic excitement mixed with wonder that young children experience in seeing a flower, a rock, or a rocking chair.

The roots of our perversity—twisted, violent, or missing bonds —are easy enough to uncover, nearly impossible to untangle.

Let's begin with a perversion so common that we consider it the normal condition of human beings—*anhedonia* (the insensitivity to pleasure, the incapacity for experiencing happiness). An anthropologist from another galaxy studying the ways of earthlings would probably look at our habit of warfare, our propensity to chronic anxiety and worry, our tendency to be motivated by guilt and shame, our obsession with work, our creation of stress and psychosomatic illnesses, and conclude that the human race has a love affair with pain. It is a rare person who is able to tolerate three uninterrupted days of happiness! We are most deeply threatened not by the fires of hell, but by the pleasures of paradise. Clearly, the earth is rich enough in resources to allow us pleasure, prosperity, and peace. Instead, we choose superfluous suffering. We manufacture surplus pain in quantities far greater than would be imposed upon us by our biological nature. In truth, we are not *homo sapiens,* the wise species, but *homo analgesia,* the species that can remain insensitive to pain or pleasure without the loss of consciousness.

Why do we choose to be anhedonic? The reasons are complex and multiple. Throughout this reflection on becoming a lover, we will be untangling the perversities, freeing eros from its attachment to pain. For the moment, we must be content with taking a first step that will not explain the *"why"* but will show *how* we receive our anhedonic dispositions.

Let's go back to our first education in pleasure—the encompassing arms of our parents. A lush smorgasbord of experiences are homogenized into the single experience of bonding that takes place when a child is lovingly held: the mutual pleasure parent and child feel; the tacit knowledge of security and belonging that is communicated by the syncopated heartbeats; the mystical union of flesh and flesh; the visceral knowledge that the world is succoring, filled with the milk of human kindness.

Now consider what happens when no loving arms educate us in kindness.

A parable. In a now-famous experiment, Harry and Margaret Harlow took infant rhesus monkeys and isolated them in cages where they could see other monkeys but could not touch. Movies of the small animals show what would seem to be broken hearts. As the isolated monkeys grew into physical adulthood, they were withdrawn and lethargic. They rocked back and forth like institutionalized children. Often they cruelly bit themselves. If placed in a cage with another monkey raised in solitary confinement, they showed immediate fear; the moment they touched, a fight began. Long deprived of contact, they were now phobic, terrified of what their organisms craved, exiled from the pleasure of touch. When given the opportunity, most would not mate. Mothers who did mate were child abusers, ignoring, biting, and sometimes killing their young.

Drs. James Prescott and Robert Heath took the experiment a step further in looking for a physiological cause for the conduct. Did isolation and the lack of touch change only the behavior of monkeys or did it affect their brains? Their research suggests that the cerebellum (which coordinates movement) was undeveloped because it had not been stimulated by the normal rocking and cuddling the infant receives from its mother. And, if the movement center is poorly developed, what effect would this have on the emotional centers of the limbic brain? Was there, Prescott asked, a relationship (obvious to any poet) between the capacity for motion and emotion? Heath discovered pathways between cerebellum and limbic brain.

Prescott's and Heath's work[1] suggests one part of the answer to the mystery of anhedonia and our perverse love affair with violence and pain. If the dendrite chains in the limbic brain are dependent for their development on stimulus from the cerebellum, then infants who are deprived of rocking and cuddling will not develop the neural apparatus necessary for an easy experience of pleasure. Since there are fewer available pleasure centers to stimulate, the deprived person will develop an insatiable need for pleasure and a difficulty in experiencing it. "Think of these people as similar to diabetics," suggests Prescott. "As long as the diabetic gets his regular supply of insulin, everything is fine. Deprive him of insulin, and all kinds of physical and emotional disturbances may result. In a similar way, a child deprived of physical closeness will develop an extraordinary need for affection later in life, which is unlikely to be fulfilled in the real adult world. This person often lapses into periodic violence."[2]

Prescott has gone on to make a cross-cultural study that shows a correlation between child-rearing practices, sexual and sensual tolerance, and physical violence. It turns out that societies that provide children with a high degree of touch, cuddling, and carrying, and that are permissive of a wide range of sensuality and sexuality in later life, are the least prone to interpersonal violence.

This parable helps us understand the vicious circle of anhedonia: deprivation of bonding creates erotic poverty; erotic poverty gives rise to violence; violence further inhibits eros. We can't make love on a battlefield. The less care we receive, the less we are capable of giving. Steele and Pollack[3] studied child abuse and found that parents who abused their children were themselves abused as children, were deprived of physical affection, and had poor sex lives. Female child abusers were nonorgasmic.

The circle of deprivation, pain, violence helps us understand a second common perversion that normal people like to keep in the closet—sadomasochism. "S and M" or "B and D" (bondage and discipline) conjure up dark and dirty images of men beating women, handcuffs and ropes, whips and leather, pornographic violence, the Story of O. The small minority who actually practice the ritual giving and receiving of pain, who frequent the shops specializing in the paraphernalia of torture, who pay others to beat and humiliate them, are often baffled by their own conduct. One man I interviewed, who regularly paid one hundred dollars to a professional "mistress" to beat him, asked: "Why do I do this? It hurts. It humiliates me. Each time I swear I will never do it again. And yet when I get the money together I always go back. I don't ever have a sexual climax, but in some way it relieves me. Why?" The sad answer to his sad question lies in the distant past, with parents who were abusive. The one thing a child dreads more than pain is being abandoned. Hence, when a baby is bonded to cruel parents, it comes to associate the only kind of conditional love and security it has with the pain it receives. To the abused child, painfully bonded, the motto of life becomes the dreadful choice Faulkner posed at the end of "The Old Man": ". . . between nothingness and grief, I will choose grief." The masochist returns to pain because it is psychologically linked to the only security he knew as a child. It is better to be punished than be ignored. Pain becomes the perverse signal that somebody cares. To the abused child, humiliation and pain are familiar. When, in later life, abused girls become battered wives, it is not the pain they desire but the family.

In *Pornography and Silence,* Susan Griffin unmasks the sadomasochism that permeates the normal life of our culture. In pornography, the woman, reduced to the role of body, is humiliated and subjected to violence, seen as an object, desecrated. To understand this strange obsession with pornography and violence, the ritual of S and M, we must see that the sadist and the masochist are one being who feels and who would not feel. The sadist wishes to dominate, punish, humiliate that part of himself—feelings, needs, sensations—that links him to the knowledge of his own body. Since he associates this type of knowledge with the vulnerability, dependency, and helplessness he felt as a child bonded to his mother, he seeks to control and deny his own eros by dominating the woman, who is always symbolically his mother (and Mother Nature).

When we look with an eye to symbolism, we see that the sadist controlling and humiliating the masochist is also enacting the same dramatic conflict that marks all of us who live within the western myth. It is the old civil war between

| | | |
|---|---|---|
| man | and | woman |
| mind | and | matter |
| spirit | and | body |
| culture | and | nature |
| reason | and | feeling |

Thus the anhedonic circle becomes vicious. In the measure that our myth has valued masculine achievement over feminine being, it has woven a punishing set of rationalizations into its views about birth, child care, touch, and sensuality. A generation ago, my mother heeded the best medical advice and listened in agony while I cried and waited to feed me until the schedule said I should eat. Nudity and fondling within the family were forbidden by Puritans and orthodox Freudians because they supposedly invited incest. Generation after generation we produce children who are poorly bonded because their parents were terrified of their own sensuality. Gradually, the body politic increases its disposition toward obsessive sexuality (the compensation for the dearth of touch) and violence.

The abnormal or severe cases of erotic deprivation serve as a parable that allow us to preview what the future holds if we do not recreate a social order rooted in familiarity and intimacy. Selma Fraiberg points out in *The Magic Years* that babies who have been deprived of maternal care and placed in sterile institutions where they receive routine tending do not find pleasure and excitement in exploring the world around them. A loved child develops "a hunger for sensory experience as intense and all-consuming as the belly hunger of the first months of life." But the deprived child who receives no pleasure from its first human object expects none from the world outside its body. "Such babies remain, for an alarmingly long time (and sometimes permanently) on the psychological level of the young infant. The body and the body-need remain the center of existence for them."[4] In mapping the stages of life, we will see that *any fundamental need that is not satisfied at the appropriate time arrests the psychological and physical development of the person at that stage.* Thus many "adults" remain children, still crying out for absent arms.

The implications of what we now understand about bonding are clear and threatening because of the radical social critique they imply. Our capacity for knowledge and love are inseparable. IQ and EQ are intertwined. We can never be at home in the world without developing that type of consciousness that depends equally on cognition and compassion. When we lose touch, the world ceases to make sense. Since trust and adventure, love and understanding, develop together, the arms of mother and father, the bosom of the family, are necessary to create a fully erotic (i.e., motivated) child. Reinhold Niebuhr once said that nothing of significance could be accomplished in a single lifetime. We cannot fabricate compassion. Lovers are grown, not made; and the process, like farming, takes generations of care. An erotic philosophy is seminal, not technological; it pays attention to planting, tending, nurture; it creates a family, a community, a place, an ecology within which a child may enjoy the luxury of innocence and security so that it may grow strong enough to explore.

## POSSESSION AS AN EROTIC SUBSTITUTE

The psyche cannot tolerate a vacuum of love. In the severely abused and deprived child, pain, dis-ease, and violence rush in to fill the void. In the average person in our culture, who has been only "normally" deprived of touch, anxiety and an insatiable hunger for possessions replace the missing eros. The child, lacking a sense of welcome, joyous belonging, gratuitous security, will learn to hoard the limited supply of affection. According to the law of psychic compensation, *not being held leads to holding on, grasping, addiction, possessiveness.* Gradually, things replace people as a source of pleasure and security. When the first gift of belonging *with* is denied, a child learns that love means belonging *to.* To the degree that we are arrested at this stage of development, the needy child will dominate our motivations. Other people and things (and there is fundamentally no difference) will be seen as existing solely for the purpose of "my" survival and satisfaction. "Mine" will become the most important word.

Myth, philosophy, and psychology have all warned that "the spirit of possession" (as Gabriel Marcel called it) is one of the major illusions to which human beings are prey. Long before the advent of capitalism, the tantric philosophers said that the first barrier to be overcome on the journey toward enlightenment was the tendency to grasp, "thingify," and turn life into something that could be possessed. In their colorful symbolism, the sacred-sexual energy that moves consciousness in its pilgrimage could become blocked at the lowest level, which they identified with a psychic center in the anus (see Appendix A). This ancient insight that linked a psychological disposition with a physiological constriction was later expressed by Freud, who discovered a correlation between character and anatomy and christened the three types of personality anal, oral, and genital. He agreed with the tantric philosophers that the anal-compulsive person was arrested at an infantile level of erotic development. Erich Fromm, following Freud, found a link between "the hoarding orientation" and a philosophy of materialism. Hoarders, who as children were treated as things rather than people, see reality as a series of it-it relationships, the world as an accidental interaction of mindless particles, history as a prison of cause and effect. Their lifestyle is one of holding tenaciously to their money, ideas, position, ideology, or religious dogma.

THE THOU AS IT: LOVE AND SEX AS POSSESSION

A possessive style of life turns all it touches, all it thinks about, into property. It experiences eros only as a form of ownership. Love and sex are modes of having and holding.

Only a moment ago in western history, after the death of the religion of the Goddess, sex became a subcategory of property rights. Women, slaves, and land were all things that men might own. Marriage was a sanctified social arrangement for producing children and sharing labor. As recently as Victorian times, sex was officially a wife's duty and a man's right. Until a few years ago, women's magazines were still encouraging women to cultivate their sexual skills so they could hold on to their men. In our more liberated times, most educated people have turned away from the view that marriage is an institution for one and a half persons, and consider a woman's right to personal and sexual satisfaction equal to the man's. With the emergence of women's liberation, the pill, and multiple orgasm, men have been alerted that they had best polish up their sexual skills to keep their women from wandering. In their slightly more equal version of the epoxy theory of sex, the Drs. Masters and Johnson counsel both partners that their separate but equal sexual unguents are necessary to form "the pleasure bond."

At the most blatant level, possessive love turns the other into an object. In the vernacular, a woman or an entire sexual act is called "a piece of ass." Nothing makes clearer the Freudian contention that there is a link between anality and possessiveness. The anal or obsessive-compulsive personality makes rigid separations between the clean and the dirty, love and sex, mothers and whores, good girls and bad girls, tenderness and excitement. Love is clean and dull; sex is dirty and exciting. Good old boys may grab a piece of ass from a black-lace tramp, but they marry a white-clad virgin and go mad with jealousy if she looks at another man.

Finally, the link between the possessive orientation and sadomasochism becomes clear. Both sadist and masochist agree to a contract in which they are reduced to things. The masochist asks

Reduce me to a thing; use me, let me become base matter, a piece of shit in your hands, a slave. The master-slave drama allows both partners to participate in the fantasy of ownership and objectification. There is perverse comfort in being a thing. Things, after all, do not have to bear the burden of consciousness, anxiety, and free will. They make no decisions, share no response-ability, know no guilt. To turn the self into a thing is to return to the safety of being Momma's or Daddy's little girl or boy. It is a confusion of possession with belonging, a parody of the surrender that religious mystics called "being possessed" by the Holy Spirit.

### OCULAR EROS AND THE QUEST FOR APPROVAL

As the child's mouth finds the nipple, its eyes rise and behold that it is beheld. The primal ocular bond between mother and child is forged. Again and again the eyes meet in the ambience of the pleasure of nursing. By the second month of life, the infant acknowledges the erotic relationship with a smile. As the child begins to travel beyond the range of touch, the contact of the eyes continues. Mother and Father watch over us, bathe us in their countenance, keep us safe. We learn to watch their eyes, their smiles, to monitor whether we have fallen from their graces and may tumble into danger. The disapproving eyes and frowns mark the dirty, the dangerous, the forbidden, the region of taboo, guilt, and shame. The approving smile rewards us with self-esteem and pride. We bring a small gift, a crumb found on the rug, a bit of torn paper, to Mother and bask in the "thank you" of her eyes. So long as we gain the approval of the eyes of our overseers, all is well. When we grow and venture beyond the range of our parents' vision, we find, to our surprise, that they are omniscient, still watching over us. Conscience, "the watching institution," the introjected eyes of the parents, still looks over our shoulders approvingly or disapprovingly. If the watching eyes smile more often than they frown, we will gradually learn to trust our instincts, to continue our explorations into the unknown, to gain confidence in our abilities and judgments. Basking in acceptance, we will learn to explore our own desires even at the risk of occasional disapproval; we will move smoothly from the dependency of childhood into the counterdependency and adventure of the rebel.

But if the watching eyes are cold, disapproving, judging, strict, if the conscience is harsh, filled with impossible oughts and don'ts and shoulds and shouldn'ts, then our capacity for ocular intercourse, the eros of the eye, will be displaced and perverted. Instead of seeing, we will seek to be seen; instead of caressing the leaves of a quaking aspen or the sculpted hollow of flesh, we will always be looking into the mirror of another's eyes, searching for a sign of approval. The eye will never be filled with the delight of seeing because of its insatiable quest for approval. Our own eyes will be self-consciously focused inward on the court of conscience, where we are vainly trying to present our case in a good light so we can get a verdict of "not guilty."

Zen and Gestalt therapy both recommend techniques of sensory awareness to help us escape the maze of mirrors. Pay attention to what is present this instant before your eyes, the texture, form, design, hue of the bowl of mixed fruit on the table . . .

The hidden psychological assumptions that provide the motive for the addiction to approval are as follows: To be is to be seen; I only exist as a reflection of the opinions others have about me; if I "lose face" I lose myself; if I do not please others I must be wrong.

Exotic and common varieties of this perversion abound:

The exhibitionist reveals the taboo parts, hoping to gain from the audience the acknowledgment of the reality and goodness of the genitals that was withheld by Father or Mother. Look, he says, I have a penis. I am a man. Look, she says, I have breasts, a vagina, I am a woman. Status seekers are careful to wear the correct clothes, be seen in the right places with the right people. They measure their worth by conspicuous consumption of the recognized tokens, change their habits to conform to what is in style. Fame seekers want approval from the eyes of the public. In theatrical and sexual performance, the other is turned into an audience. The persona is the mask we wear when we are in public. If it is so tight we cannot take it off, it prevents the self from seeing. Most often, the mask is frozen in a smile, it presents itself in a way that will guarantee its acceptance.

Perverse, twisted, gnarled. We all leave childhood with wounds. In time we may transform our liabilities into gifts. The faults that pockmark the psyche may become the source of a man's or woman's beauty. The injuries we have suffered invite us to assume the most humane of all vocations—to heal ourself and others. In daring to feel our own brokenness, we gain the courage to listen to the cry of others. And only by coming to love the gnarls may each of us, as Howard Thurman, the great American mystic, said, "be true to the unique grain of our own wood."

Limping, we proceed on our journey toward wholeness. With gratitude and anger we leave childhood behind and rebel against all that has been given and imposed upon us.

# 4.
# The Rebel

For love to exist, there must be two beings who move toward each other but never entirely become one. Loving is a continual dance between bonding and returning to our boundaries, coming together and going apart. Thus eros is not all urgent "yes," yearning to be one flesh, encompassing arms, harmony within the bosom of nature. The prodigal impulse calls us to turn against mother and father, motherland and fatherland, to go out into the strangeness of history and create something that has never yet been. Without the sacred "no," the power to negate, the courage to oppose, the audacity to cut ourselves off from the past, there would be no freedom, no spirit, no love. The urge that moves us toward at/one/ment with matrix and patrix will always be in tension with the impulse that moves us toward in/dividuation.

To gain our freedom, we must use the knife of de/cision. We come to a fork in the road, either/or. We must choose. We cut ourselves off from fantastic adventures on untaken roads in order to commit ourselves to a single course of action. To say a single "yes" we must say "no" a hundred times. Thus Nietzsche could say: "I love the great Nay sayers for they are the great "yea" sayers."

The first, and hardest, "no" is the de/cision to sever our ties with home, to endure the alienation that inevitably comes from leaving all that is familiar. Our temptation is to remain in safety, beyond tragedy. But if we do, all the delightful virtues of childhood will become twisted into dependent vices. Instead of becoming responsible, we will be reactionary; instead of creative, conservative.

To create we must first learn to destroy. No new structure can be built without destructuring the old. The moribund structures of the psyche and the polis that squeeze the life out of us must be resisted. We must do battle with dragons guarding treasures and maidens they do not enjoy and tyrants who promise us security if we will sacrifice our freedom. Deadly taboos must be broken and replaced by codes of right and wrong that we make our own. Without the force of rebellion, love becomes a sickly sentiment, a mortar that holds together the status quo. Since this world is not all it might become, those who are faithful to the promise of the future must have the courage to topple the idols. The nice people who are too polite to struggle for freedom of the spirit become the myrmidons of yesterday, the servants of habit, the guardians of tyranny.

To sustain love, a man and a woman must continually be marrying and divorcing, moving *with, against, away from,* and *beyond* each other, saying "yes" and "no."

To sustain a creative relationship with myself, I must affirm what is young and wise and hopeful in my experience against all the blackmailing tendencies of my antiquarian superego that would have me feel guilty and anxious whenever I depart from the old ways. I must retain the power to negate irrational fears, repressive authorities, and break out of the prison of habit.

Like the god Janus, the rebel faces in two directions, negating the old in order to affirm a vision of the new. Thus the rebel is a challenger of authority; a rude iconoclast; an impudent breaker of taboos; a devotee of the sacred "no"; a destroyer of structures that have become claustrophobic, repressive. At the same time, the rebel is a dreamer; a romantic; a visionary; a creator of hope for a new order.

THE LOVING AGONY: SMALL REBELS, EARLY WARS

The rebel impulse emerges early in the healthy personality. Our earliest cry is a protest against the felt dissatisfactions of existence. With powerful lungs, the baby makes its likes and dislikes known. It demands the comforts of touch and food. Crying, which is neurologically designed to sound like the rasping of fingernails on a blackboard, is a powerful instrument of persuasion, a forceful argument, a voice of the incipient will.

## The Rebel's Psyche

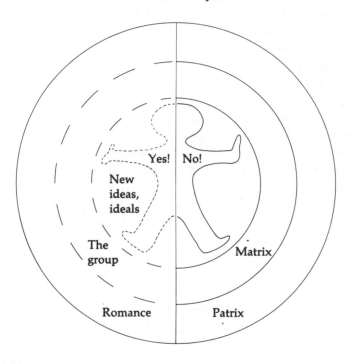

At best, the harmony of childhood does not last for long. Even before a baby can move around independently, a contest of wills develops. The loving agony begins (the Greek *agon* means contest, or game). Mother or Dad wants to wipe baby's face. Baby doesn't want its face wiped. Yes! No! Anger. Tears. Mother is tired and puts baby down for a nap. Baby feels abandoned, screams its protest. The time comes for toilet training and the battle of the sphincter begins. Inevitably, the freedom of the baby to have, do, and be exactly what it pleases will be challenged. The battleground will develop around food, or bed, or toilet.

All parents know and dread the approach of what has been called "the terrible twos." In the second year, as the child begins to gain some independence, it begins to do just the opposite of what its parents want. "No" becomes the most frequently heard word in its vocabulary. Even if it wants a cookie, it may well say "no" just to establish its right to independent judgments. While this stage is irritating to parents and arouses anger, it is necessary to the child's development. Fraiberg says:

> The chief characteristic of the second year is not negativism but a powerful striving to become a person and to establish permanent bonds with the world of reality. We must remember when we speak of the "negativism" of the toddler that this is also the child who is intoxicated with the discoveries of the second year, a joyful child who is firmly bound to his parents and his new-found world through ties of love. The so called negativism is one of the aspects of this development, but under ordinary circumstances it does not become anarchy. It's a kind of declaration of independence, but there is no intention to unseat the government. . . . Many years later, in adolescence, he will do the same thing. He will declare his adolescent independence by opposing, on principle, any views upheld by his parents or members of their generation.[1]

HIDDEN REBELLION: LATENCY AND THE FORMATION OF THE PERSONA

Throughout childhood there is an alternation between harmony and agony, bonding and rupture. At some times, there is open rebellion; at others, seeming conformity. But all the while the rebel impulse is growing, biding its time, developing strategies.

One day I climbed down from Father's lap, where I lay basking in the bass resonance of his voice, and girded my will to test the authority of the giant. To protest the law that dictated that small boys forsake their enthusiasm at six o'clock sharp and report for supper, I began a hunger strike. No! I will not eat! My jaw tightened, my breath shortened, my muscles drew in to armor my body for combat, ready to stand against the enemy. My first challenge was ignored. I survived my fast for a day or so (sustained by a store of candy I had secreted for such an emergency). On the third day, my parents decided I would eat. My father held my nose until I opened my mouth and Mother shoved in the spinach. I surrendered to superior power. But the anger fed my will to individuality, and a civil war began that was not to end until I passed adolescence.

Another day, I was taking a nap on a sultry afternoon in Florida. I wasn't sleepy. An eternity of solitary confinement in a crib loomed before me. I was ordered to sleep. Instead, I found a miraculous toy that changed shapes and produced delightful sensations when fondled. Immersed in my secret resources, I did not hear Mother approach. She removed my hand from my delight and said, "Nice boys don't do that." The rebel knowledge deepened in me. To keep the security of her love, I would pretend to be a "good boy"; but I would secretly treasure my desires and pleasures, my sensuous "bad boy." To protect my growing sense of self from parents' eyes, I had no choice but to live in duplicity, lie, create the facade.

By about the age of six the child learns to be a secret rebel. Early in life, we develop a set of attitudes and behaviors that allows us to deal more or less harmoniously with the inevitable civil war that develops between our deepest desires and the superior will and power of our parents and other authorities. The child begins to construct an ego, personality, a system of defense mechanisms or character armor. Each of us learns to survive within the family and society by making a compromise between our deepest eros and the laws, rules, and mores.

The process of forming the mask of personality is largely unconscious: (1) Conflict arises between parent and child; (2) the child decides it is too painful and dangerous to resist the will of the powerful and loved parent; (3) the child splits its consciousness and faces simultaneously in two directions. The outward-facing persona is modeled after the image of masculinity or femininity that is represented in the parent of the same sex (i.e., the child *identifies with* the father or mother, adopts his or her style, or at least one that is acceptable and pleasing). The inward-facing consciousness keeps alive a dialogue with the secret self, the feelings, desires, and dreams that must be hidden from others. So long as there is communication between persona and self, so long as the child remembers its own dreams and the knowledge of what price is paid for love, the duplicity does not degenerate into a "pathological" form of schizophrenia. The civil war goes on, the person is normal, the rebel hides and bides its time through the years of latency.

ADOLESCENCE, ANGER, AND OPEN REBELLION

With adolescence, the rebel comes out of hiding and dares to challenge the authorities. With bursting pimples and self-consciousness, the adolescent throws questions and challenges like hand grenades into the established order of things. Why can't I? Who says I can't? What right do you have to tell me? Obedience changes overnight into systematic disobedience, resistance, and rebellion. Nothing in the world of the Giants remains unchallenged. The budding self bursts through polite constraint, doubts everything (except doubt), takes the opposite side in any argument, steps carelessly on sacred tradition, provokes conflict, demands "freedom now" (and continuing support), resents past limits and restrictions, decries the hypocrisy and stupidity of the elders, breaks taboos.

Healthy adolescent rebellion is such an irritation to adults that it is often difficult to see the conflict as birth pangs for a new mode of eros. Yet, in adolescence, three love affairs are beginning: with the self, with the new community, with the romantic-sexual partner.

The self that has been slumbering awakens. As hormones push the body toward physical maturation, the adolescent feels the stirring of the promise of autonomy.

A new conscience, which is the untasted potentiality of the self, calls the rebel. The old conscience, which is the hidden injunctions of the parents, the coercion of shame and guilt, grows weaker.

In order to get an image of the future self the rebel adopts a new hero and a new set of ideals. Some heroic figure—John Wayne or John Lennon, Isadora Duncan or Jane Fonda—becomes the new model for the authentic life, the icon that focuses eros, the pin-up and incarnation of the dream, and allows the adolescent to articulate the identity of the secret self. Yes, I will be like _____. Not like Father or Mother.

My adolescent dream was horses and cowboys. Throughout my high school years, I wore cowboy boots (in Wilmington, Delaware!), devoured the western books of Will James, and studied how to dehorn bulls and rotate crops. Finally, graduation day came and I left for the West in my Model A Ford. Father gave me his blessing and a warning I didn't understand: "Remember, west of the Mississippi there is no law, west of the Pecos there is no God." Mother tied a silver butter knife to the rear view mirror of my car to remind me of the importance of my manners. I was interested only in going beyond the frontiers of the known. For a season I wandered, working on wheat harvest, carnivals, ranches, with men who didn't wash often and women who didn't mind. I drank beer, and for the first time felt at home in levis and cowboy boots. But some itch in my mind was not scratched, some vistas not opened, some questions not silenced by long days of pitching hay and mending fences. When I decided to follow my questions wherever they might lead, I returned to the East, to college, to a new ideal of the life of adventure. In time I chose new heroes— poets, philosophers, D. H. Lawrence, Nietzsche, Gabriel Marcel, Albert Camus, Kierkegaard, rebels of the mind.

To open up the space for freedom, adolescents slash at the bonds of family. Simultaneously, they form powerful new bonds with chosen friends, peers, a gang, a fraternity or sorority, buddies, mates, best friends with whom they share forbidden thoughts, feelings, dreams. Together they banish the loneliness and create a counterculture, a band of rebels who criticize parents and the stale values of the authorities. They sing the praises of free expression, all the while conforming to the norms and fashions of the clique or gang. Style rigidly dictates the insignia of adolescent member-ship. Bobby sox, Beatle cuts, or punk regalia are the uniform of the day; the jitterbug, the frug, or slam dancing the required dances.

ROMANCE AND THE LOVE OF IDEALS

Meanwhile, the gonads are preparing the elixir of transformation. Eros, which once bonded us close in family, now uses its black magic to cast a spell that lures us through strange pleasures to new responsibilities. Testes and ovaries clothe their urgent demands in the rituals of courtship and the illusions of romance. We rush toward sex and fall into love.

Ideally, the passage between adolescence and adulthood is lubricated by sex play. Boy meets girl, or girl meets girl, or boy meets boy, and they touch shyly. When sexuality is first budding, exploration is pre-moral. We reach out to others and taste the feedback of our senses. Does it feel good or bad, pleasurable or painful, appropriate or inappropriate? Sexual exploration is a variety of the sensual adventure without which we would develop no first-hand knowledge of the world. Without erotic outreach, the mind would not grow. When exploration is prematurely inhibited by "don't touch," "dirty," "thou shall not," we never have the freedom to recognize the shape of our native desires. Sex is a way of knowing, a cognitive adventure. Without sexual experimentation, our judgments will be prejudices, rules automatically taken over from our parents or peers. *What appeals to us is our erotic vocation, a calling as necessary to the full life as a vocation to work or to justice.* We can only make informed choices about our more permanent love partners when we know what kind of persons smell, taste, feel "right" to us. Adolescence is the appropriate time for playboys and playgirls. Erotic play comes before seriousness, delight before commitment. Our best hope for the development of "mature" sexuality lies with our full enjoyment of the moratorium for sex play without consequence or long-range promises. Care-ful play.

Romance goes hand in hand with rebellion. Passion feeds on the ideal. The rebel's heart opens to a new dream, a new love, an ideal society, or a lover who will sweep away the petty compromise and repressive "oughts" of the old generation of authorities. A young woman falls in love with modern dance in the fervent belief that spontaneous expression will replace the conceits of ballet, and the world will move freely and beautifully. A young man discovers socialism and passionately argues for a new social order that will eliminate greed, competition, and war. Most adolescents fall in love with some plain John or Jane who is immediately transformed into the ideal. Clandestine meetings and secret pleasures (carried on within the parentheses of space and time hidden from the authorities) heighten the pride rebels have in their inordinate and illicit love. Sweet romance dissolves the old identity and wraps the new psyche within a community of mutual adoration. A passion, awkward as a colt's legs, carries the rebel toward the future, toward inevitable disillusionment, and a new love affair with mature power.

Since the romantic impulse is central to the healthy development of the rebel, central to the western ideal of the individual, and, in its perverse form, a central addiction of American culture, we need to look more closely at the phenomenon.

Why do we invest so much of our eros in the quest for a singular affection? The romantic myth presents us with a puzzle that must be solved if we are to set eros free from its adolescent captivity and allow it to grow into maturity. We need to demythologize romantic love to understand why, in Whitehead's terms, our expectations for fulfillment through a single relationship are a type of "misplaced concretion"; or, in biblical language, an idol; or, in psychological language, the erotic instinct becomes twisted into an addiction. What is this modern-day holy grail called romance?

Let's listen to its voice in the lyrics of commonplace songs, in the popular poetry, and the clichés that express in unsophisticated language the unconscious longings our minds are often embarrassed to confess.

Love is destiny and grace, not work or accomplishment. It promises that "some enchanted evening, you will see a stranger across a crowded room, and somehow you'll know." "You are my destiny." It invites us to get out of control, and surrender to an overwhelming surge. "Can't help loving that man of mine." Helpless but happy, like a child, responsive but not responsible. "You made me love you, I didn't want to do it." We can lay down the burdens of moderation, reason, all of the hard virtues we struggle to achieve, and be refreshed by passion when "That old black magic has us in its spell!" A sweet violence tears us out of our routines. Dionysus makes us drunk and blind with ecstasy. We are beside ourselves, outside our normal egos.

Love is mystery revealed. "Ah, sweet mystery of life at last I've found you." The secret is hidden in the heart. Home is where the heart is. Our hands may labor, our brains invent, but the world is made into a hearth only by the opening of the heart. The heart may be open or closed, hard or tender, broken or healed, bitter or sweet, despairing or hopeful, but without it there is no path, only empty space and whirling atoms. When we feel empty, void, desolate, the vacuum is always in the heart. Nihilism is cosmic loneliness. Nobody cares.

Love gives us a purpose. "Love is nature's way of giving, a reason to be living." But the purpose is never an abstract plan, never a blueprint of universal reason. It comes as breath, or spirit. "You are my inspiration, Margie," or as illumination intimately given in the love-light in the other's eyes. The wisdom of the love song tells us that the place we will find purpose and meaning is in what is idiosyncratic, unique, individual, unrepeatable, fragile, personal, exceptional. The abstract eye of science that seeks objective truths, statistical probabilities, verifiable facts may show us universal patterns, but it never satisfies our hunger for a purpose for the individual life.

Love destroys isolation. "Now, I'm no longer alone without a dream in my heart, without a love of my own." A character in a play by Gabriel Marcel says, "There is only one suffering, to be alone." The blues in the night tell us that darkness and depression are the same as isolation. Finally, the only cure for mood indigo is the valentine, the passionate heart. Trouble, pain, can be tolerated so long as we are side by side.

Love is adoration. "How I adore you. My life I live for you, my wonderful, wonderful one." I worship the ground she walks on. Somehow, in the presence of the one we love, we feel humbled, not quite worthy, as if we had been chosen for a great honor. Hushed, silent, we speak in whispers, aware that we have been caught up in something larger and more powerful than either of us.

Love is exclusive. Lovers are fascinated by each other, have eyes only for one another. "Only you and you alone beneath the moon and under the sun." "You are my one and only, my everything."

In romance, eros does not calculate or make limited contracts. It is no "arrangement," no open marriage of liberal minds. It asks and offers everything, withholds nothing.

Love is eternal. "Till death do us part." "Forever, my love." "Our love is here to stay, not for a year but ever and a day." Love understands the lament of St. Augustine: "Anything that ends is too short." Romance enchants us with the promise that "love is a song that never ends."

Love demands sacrifice. "I would gladly spend my life, waiting at your beck and call. Everything I have is yours. . . ." Sometimes, it borders on masochism: "Abuse me, misuse me . . . I'm yours till I die." Or turns us into slaves.

Love is uncritical acceptance. Unconditional. She could do no wrong in his eyes. "How can you tell if you are in love?" I once asked my father. "Well, if the Queen of Sheba walked by and you are in love with somebody else, all you will notice is that she has big feet," he replied. Love does not try, or need, to improve the other. Seeks no alteration.

Love finds the all in the one. This man is all men to me. All the qualities of woman are suddenly incarnate in Jan Lovett. When I fall, some Beatrice promises to guide me into the paradise of love.

The modern romantic myth, like the fairy tale, promises that the loving pair will live happily ever after.

The slightest bit of realism shatters the myth. Romantic love lasts between ninety days and a year. In the harsh light of proximity, the illusion begins to fade. The gentleman turns chauvinist. The shining knight is really interested in conquest. The fair maiden is more chaste than caught, her magnolia heart conceals a manipulative will. Or both are romance junkies who must fall in love every three months to avoid both intimacy and the threat of being alone. Or they marry and discover that it takes years of struggle and care to get beyond facades and games and establish authentic intimacy.

When the illusions of romance are so regularly and predictably shattered, why does the impulse remain so strong, the myth so resilient?

ROMANTIC DISILLUSIONMENT: THE BROKEN HEART AND THE QUEST FOR
UNCONDITIONAL LOVE

Beneath the drama of romance and disillusionment, something
momentous is happening. In the cocoon of adolescent romance,
eros is preparing for its second great metamorphosis. The rebel is
weaned from love of the familiar by the romance with a particular
stranger. But before eros can be freed to fly, the new attachments
to the one and only love (who has replaced the family) must be
shattered. Falling out of love is as necessary as falling in.

By falling in love with a person, an ideal, a cause, we leave
pragmatism and security behind, release our hold on what is safe,
move beyond the circle of self. Our heart "goes out" to another.
Calculation of self-interest is abandoned as we yield to desire. *It
is this awakening of the instinct for adoration that is the hidden motive power
of romantic love, and the reason it must shipwreck.* The heart is opened by
being broken.

Listen again to the language of romance, and the reason for its
failure becomes evident. "I adore you. My life I live for you." The
language of the love song is cryptotheological. The lover is the
icon of the divine, the incarnate symbol of what will heal and
satisfy us. A moment's reflection shows us that the unconditional
love sought in romance is not available from any mere mortal. The
intensity of the demand for an adorable object builds into romance
the certainty of failure. No person can be worshiped without the
certainty of disillusionment. In romance, we encounter the existential paradox, the erotic koan that drives us to search more
deeply into the nature of our primal desires: We demand something of each other we cannot fulfill; romantic passion invites its
own frustration.

Why do we play this trick on ourselves? Philosophers from
Plato to Augustine to Hegel have said that the path of the spirit
involves a progressive series of disillusionments. Passion is necessarily blind because we are fragments of an incomprehensible
totality. We err because we are mortal and our perspective is
limited by time, space, and culture. The stages of life involve a

progression toward a more adequate knowledge and love of the whole. We begin with the particular and move toward the universal. In the platonic tradition, love begins in darkness. We are embedded in the matrix, the cave, the mother, the fertile womb of becoming. Gradually, we ascend into the sunlight of knowledge by climbing the ladder of eros. We practice loving in the narrow confines of the family before we blossom out to include strangers. In romantic love, we focus an inordinate amount of love on a single person in order to discover the limits of loving. When we reach the point of inevitable frustration in interpersonal relationships, we may begin to suspect that our primal desire is for something metaphysical. The man or woman we desire so ardently is a trickster who brings us closer to the realization that human beings have an insatiable longing that cannot be satisfied *by any* sexual attachment. Sex is one of the many disguises of eros.

Through romance, we catch the first glimpse of how the world might look through the eyes of the heart, we sniff the first scent of the full human potential. The impulse toward adoration and communion, although misplaced, is real.

For a moment our alienation ended and was replaced by a sense of belonging. Consciousness discovered it was not isolated, but joined in an intersubjective nexus. The gestalt of isolation shifted and we grasped the interconnection of life. In love we are rebonded. The body relaxes. Blood flows freely through every artery and vein. Character armor softens. The defense mechanisms we have honed to protect ourselves against the hostile world vanish. We move harmoniously within a strange environment. Compassion replaces paranoia. This psychedelic moment, which is at the heart of the romantic vision, opens a vista, however briefly, to the higher kingdoms of consciousness. To adore opens a door beyond the self. The inspiration to become a lover comes in a flash. The journey requires a lifetime. In its third stage we must leave the defiance and dreams of the rebel behind and explore the path of the adult.

# 5.
# *Rebellious Emotions and Twisted Adolescence*

THE HISTORY AND POLITICS OF REBELLION

The emergence of the rebel impulse that allows the adolescent to begin to define the self over against the authority of parents and society, and is then blended in with other impulses to build toward a fully resonant life, depends on the way rebellion is accepted. The healthy rebel must hone the will; cultivate the personal power to challenge authorities; become comfortable with anger; break old taboos and define new limits; fall in love with an ideal; and rebond to chosen friends and lovers. But, like fire, rebellion once loose is hard to contain. It is awkward. It makes us uncomfortable. Consequently, society rarely encourages or appreciates rebellion. The spark is often extinguished for fear it might consume all law and order. In permissive segments of society, parents shortcut adolescent rebellion by refusing to be committed to any values against which the young might rebel.

The recognition that rebellion is a necessary impulse within the psyche and the body politic is largely a modern western idea. The sacred "no" finds its charter in both the Judeo-Christian and the Greek strands of our tradition. The Judeo-Christian myth begins with Adam and Eve being expelled from the Garden of Eden for daring to disobey God and insisting upon their right to taste of the fruit of the tree of the knowledge of good and evil. They, like Prometheus, made the tragic decision to transcend the limits of blind obedience, to challenge the plot set by the Author of their lives. Although the biblical God consistently demands obedience, he is paradoxically most fond of the rebels—David, Job, Jeremiah,

Isaiah. Christian theologians spoke of the "happy Fall," recognizing that without disobedience there could be no responsibility, without alienation no healing. Prometheus the heaven stormer, and the wily Odysseus, who constantly oversteps the limit into unseemly pride (hubris) are the archetypal heroes.

From such rebellious heroes, the western spirit has created a new ideal for human life: the individual. Each person has, in theory, the right and obligation to create a life without precedent, an individual path, a unique pattern. (In fact, until quite recently, the majority of women, slaves, children, peasants, and workers has been denied any real opportunity for individuation by the repression of government and the exploitation of the privileged.) Nevertheless, the ideal remains and provides some sanction for the rebellious emotions, some acknowledgment of the importance of doubt, iconoclasm, and the smashing of taboos.

Recognizing the necessity of rebellion for the healthy psyche, western culture has created a period in the life cycle after childhood but before maturity in which there is a moratorium from adult responsibility. Adolescence is a stage of life that was largely unknown before modern times. In traditional tribal societies, boys and girls went directly from childhood into adult status. Rites of initiation, such as the bar mitzvah, ushered the thirteen-year-old budding adolescent into the duties and privileges of warriors. Boys were made into men by painful ordeals that often literally etched the myth of the tribe on their skin with ritual scars and wounds. With first menstruation, girls were forced to assume the status of junior adults and became the property of their husbands. In Indian and Chinese cultures, truth was handed down from one generation to another. The disciple did not question the wisdom of the guru or elder, nor did the son aspire to a position above that of the father. The caste system effectively stifled the rebellious emotions and created a static, conformist culture. Characteristically, in eastern spirituality anger and rage are seen as problems to be overcome by the cultivation of meditative calm rather than as emotions that must be acted upon in the political arena.

Tolerance for the rebel will always be correlated with allowing the moratorium of adolescence; cultivating doubt and curiosity; challenging the certainties of the past; the growth of scientific inquiry; individualism; political self-determination. Where the rebel is repressed, there will be dogmatism, ideology, enforced conformity, a tyrannical elite or Grand Inquisitor governing a conforming mass, the curtailing of philosophical and scientific inquiry. The degree to which the rebel stage of the human pilgrimage can be fulfilled and transcended depends on the political context within which the psyche develops. In a political situation where tyranny reigns and rebellion is not tolerated, few men and women will have the luxury of going beyond the stance of the rebel. Where authority represses freedom, rebellion becomes the hard work of love, which is necessary because love, freedom, and spirit are inseparable. As Che Guevara said: "The true rebel is motivated by love."

One cannot adjust to the tyranny of the left, right, or middle without destroying the spiritual ecology necessary to the blossoming of the full human promise. Tragically, there are situations in which armed resistance and strategic violence may be the only way of keeping eros alive. As Dietrich Bonhoeffer (the Christian theologian who participated in a plot against Hitler's life and was executed by the Nazis) pointed out, the criteria for the loving use of violence are hard to make clear. The very notion is dangerous because it opens the floodgate to every sociopath. In principle, we can say that loving violence is never exerted against authorities who are surrogates for parents against whom one did not rebel at an appropriate time. It is never used indiscriminately. It is not blind, spontaneous, or unconscious resistance to father figures. It may be used, if at all, only by those who have passed beyond the psychological stage of adolescent rebellion and are moved by compassion.

The political context created by the western myth has resulted in a disparity in the psychological development and expression of the rebel stage between men and women. Traditionally, rebellion has been more tolerated in men than women. Boys will be boys, and pranks and mild delinquency were expected of every red-blooded youth. But girls were supposed to be sugar and spice and everything nice and not too aggressive or outspoken. Sexually active boys were just doing what comes naturally, but the same behavior earned a girl the reputation of being fast, bad, and dirty. The natural impulse to rebel was long squelched in women. Hence many women who have fulfilled their adult roles are only now discovering their rage. Because it has long been denied, it is fiercer and more challenging to the status quo than male rage, which is mostly focused and expressed within normal channels—sports, war, condoned violence, alcohol, rapacious attitudes toward woman and nature. In all liberation movements, the mixture of rebellious emotions, adolescent rage, prophetic challenge, and aggressive compassion is difficult to disentangle. An understanding of the variety of ways in which the rebel impulse becomes twisted may help us deal with the inner rage we feel in this time of the breakup of our old myths, the disintegration of our traditional identities and roles, and the disappointment of our hopes for fulfillment.

THE PERVERSIONS OF REBELLION

Look around at the faces, postures, dress, and behavior of a random sample of "adults," and you get the impression that many who have chronologically reached adulthood are psychologically still in adolescence. Watch salesmen at a convention get drunk, tell dirty jokes, and try to impress each other with locker-room talk. Listen to a well-dressed woman talk in the high-pitched, hysterical voice of a sixteen-year-old girl.

Carl Jung described the personality of those arrested in adolescence as the *puer eternis* or the *puella eterna,* the eternal boy or girl, the Peter Pans who decided never to grow up. They are easy to spot by their incongruous youthfulness. They may be charming or irritating, playful or rebellious, but above all they are young. Often their faces are unlined. We admire them, until we sense their secret. Like Dorian Grey, they have never dared to move into psychological maturity, never really left childhood.

There are at least three fundamental ways in which the rebel impulse may become perverse, three detours that lead away from full adulthood: (1) the Adversaries form a negative identity, exhibit an excess of rebellious emotion, get caught in a stance that always positions them *against* others; (2) the Pleasers, Nice People, and Sentimentalists are deficient in the power to say "no," and hence follow the path of least resistance; and (3) the incurable Romantics, Idealists, Playboys, and Playgirls seek to prolong the adolescent dream of endless possibilities, and hence live in a moratorium from commitments.

## The Adversaries

A passionate life is a continuing dialogue between self and other. And all real dialogue, according to philosopher Karl Jaspers, is a "loving combat." To become who we are we must learn to wrestle. Push-pull. Yes-no. Love must be muscular, to enter the contest, to endure the agony, of the clash between points of view.

But, sadly, parents, guardians, and authorities often squelch the first trace of rebellion. "Don't you dare contradict me." They demand unquestioning obedience. They react to the young rebel's "no" as if it were an insurrection that must be controlled at any cost. When the authorities are too rigid and insecure to embrace the rebellious ones, either the spark of individuality will be extinguished or the repression will act like gasoline thrown on the embers and inflame the situation.

In the adversarial personality, the bad boy or bad girl continues to play out the drama of adolescent rebellion. Defiance becomes a way of life. The adversary will always be linked in an antagonistic relationship to some authority. If you live out of a negative identity, the only time you will feel alive is when you are in conflict or combat. Others will always be cast in the mold of the enemy against whom you must struggle. Eros will be reduced to a mode of warfare, life to a battle. You will be aroused by the prospect of violence. If you are "normal" you will limit your love for violence to lawful competition, fighting with your spouse, and voyeurism—a regular ritual bloodbath on TV or in the movies. Your daydreams will be filled with schemes for conquest, plans for achieving what psychoanalyst Karen Horney calls a "vindictive triumph" over others. Even if you don't win, you can achieve a victory by being drunk, drugged, or in disgrace. You will show "them" you can't be bossed around. Perhaps you will think of suicide as a way to get even, to pay them back for not caring. By failing, you may disappoint the expectations of the authorities and thus win.

The adversarial personality comes in a wide variety of types.

Anarchists, radicals, and prophets politicize their need to stand against the authorities. They divide the world neatly between the oppressors and the oppressed, the wicked and the innocent, chauvinists and victims; and they, of course, stand righteously against the establishment, the power-elite, and the ruling class. They cherish anger and outrage as politically necessary emotions. Usually, their visions extend no further than winning liberation from the oppressors, destroying the structures created by the authorities.

By definition, the conservative mass of society and the ruling class always try to cast the motives for rebellion into doubt. The rebels are angry children who must be disciplined by the benevolent parents. In Russia and China, they are eliminated or sent to camps for "political reeducation." In the more democratic countries, they are hounded, investigated, and often entrapped by government agencies or vilified by the press.

In truth, determining the motives of anarchists, radicals, and prophets is difficult, at best. In some perpetual rebels we can recognize a lingering adolescent character structure. In the great reformers, prophets, and critics, the impulse to compassion outweighs all obsessive needs to remain in an adversarial stance toward life. As Albert Camus said, the true rebel is motivated by outrage against the diminishing of human life. No doubt, in every political rebellion, many of the participants see the authorities as surrogates for parents. Nevertheless, political tyranny must be resisted, prophetic judgments uttered. The most just and necessary rebellion requires the energies of both mature and immature rebels. History seldom allows us the luxury of unambivalent motives or simple actions.

Criminals fit more neatly into the character type of the arrested adolescent rebel. The criminal is not *outside* but *against* the law. On a tour of Alcatraz I was appalled by the strict conditions the authorities forced on the prisoners. As I was becoming angry (how could "they" make men live in little iron cages!), my perspective suddenly shifted and I saw that both prisoners and authorities were trapped in the cops and robbers game. Both were captive to the same system, players in the same illusory drama. The punitive fathers, unable to show tenderness, were still punishing the rebellious sons who had to go to extremes of crime in acting out their anger and disappointment. The adult criminal is usually, psychologically speaking, still a juvenile delinquent trying to express a need for attention and care from an absent or abusive parent.

## Resentment and Paranoia: Involuted Rebellion

The adversarial stance may be either overt or covert, either inward or outward in its direction. We easily recognize as adversaries the loud and visible prophets, rebels, and reformers. But the spirit of rebellion may be expressed covertly against both self and others. When appropriate out-rage is not expressed, it turns to in-rage.

Nietzsche identified resentment as the emotion of hidden revenge. Those passive persons who have not been en/couraged to rebel secretly envy those who have, and become frozen in a negative emotional style. They seem to carry a grudge against life. Resentment is a form of emotional prejudice. Even before an experience presents itself, the resenter has judged that it will be disappointing. Their stance says, "I have been cheated." "Life is guilty until proven innocent." The pervasive low-level hostility of resentment is based upon the hidden assumption that reality, other people, and the depths of the self are not to be trusted. Resentful people adopt the lifestyle of the cynic. By always expecting the worst, they create a self-fulfilling prophecy, and are seldom disappointed. Acts of simple kindness seldom penetrate their character armor.

Paranoids show us the logic of the adversary taken to its extreme. The paranoid stands on an ever-shrinking island, with very few allies, in a raging sea of enemies. He is convinced that "they" are out to get him and every event that occurs only proves the conspiracy. In the paranoid mind, anger has been denied and projected onto the others, aggression has been disowned and attributed to the enemy.

## The Pleasers: Nice People and Sentimentalists

If the adversarial personality is a reactionary prolongation of the style of "bad boys and girls," the pleaser's mask wears the perpetual smile of the good boy or girl. Pleasers are the "yes" men and "yes" women. There is nothing vivid or dramatic to say about pleasers because they are by definition neutral, grey, unobtrusive. They never gave their parents or teachers any trouble. Their employers can count on them to cooperate, not to rock the boat or have any moral convictions that will upset their superiors. Pleasers aspire to be well-adjusted, well-liked, comfortable, anonymous, nice.

Since pleasers make up a large part of any mass society, we seldom identify them as perverse. After all, they don't cause trouble. They make up the ranks of the good Germans, good Russians, or good Americans who do not question authority or protest against the quite reasonable plans their leaders have for social reforms, war, or final solutions. Without them, the machinery would not run smoothly, the boss's mail wouldn't get sorted. Within the corporate world, they make up what Earl Shorris has called "the oppressed middle," the middle-managers who enjoy "the comforts of fearful people" and pay by submitting to their superiors' definitions of happiness and success and their totalitarian rule. But their acquiescence, passivity, and lack of courage to protest is what allows genocide and the triumph of what Hannah Arendt described as "banal" evil. So, from the perspective of the health of the body politic, their deficiency of the Promethean spirit, their willingness to do anything they are ordered to do by superiors, is a polite pathology. They make up the mass/ochists who make possible the sadistic designs of "bad" men.

Beneath the smiling mask, we can see the injury that results from a deficiency of rebellion. The nice ones are never quite real. They lack self-definition, self-confidence, because they have never created boundaries and limits for themselves by making decisions. Having never dared to break the taboos they suffer from shame. Their sins are ones of omission rather than commission. They "have left undone those things they ought to have done," most especially deciding for themselves what is good and evil. Being impotent because they have never dared to assert themselves, they continually play the blame-game. They are innocent and powerless and, therefore, others are always to blame when things go wrong. In their world, the only authorities are God, the church, the Bible, the government, the boss, and what the neighbors think. They have yet to bite the apple of consciousness. The price they pay is high, although not often visible. Their repressed negativity erupts as ulcers, gut reactions, boredom, depression, suicide, and, occasionally, murder. Notice how frequently the newspapers, when interviewing the neighbors of the latest mass murderer, report: "We don't know how he could have done it. He was such a *nice* boy. Something of a loner, but everybody liked him." Repressed rebellion seethes beneath the pleasant facade, but eventually breaks forth in violence.

If the nice people can be said to have a philosophy of life beyond accommodation, it is sentimentalism. *Sentimentalists* take the rebel's dream of perfection, strip away its sexual-romantic overtones, and proclaim that the future has arrived and we already live in the best of all possible worlds. For sentimentalists, love is the panacea for every ill. They firmly believe that if only everyone would think positive thoughts and avoid "negative" feelings, there would be no personal or political problems. These healthy-minded optimists embrace cliches: Think positively. Stay on the sunny side of the street. Look for the silver lining. Give out happy vibes. In essence, the world is already perfect; so if we ignore the supposed imperfections, they will disappear. Evil and suffering are illusions— maya. The real world is governed by love. Therefore we should ignore conflict, and rise above anger. As one sweet soul (with terminal cancer) told me: "Whenever anyone does anything that might make me angry, I just send him pink thoughts." They see the adversarial rebels as troublemakers, political turmoil as the result of outside agitators, and illness as caused by bad thoughts.

The price of positive thinking and sentimentalism is high. We cannot live by love alone. In the real (as opposed to the ideal) world, a tender heart needs to be balanced by a tough mind, good feelings by a willingness to struggle for justice. The "bleeding hearts" who want love without anger, relationship without conflict, harmony without contradictions, are forced to create an illusory world of unambivalent love inhabited only by the pure of heart (i.e., themselves and other children of light). It is not accidental that such perfect persons (who never question their own motives, or suspect their hidden ideology or self-interest) make others feel tainted and guilty. Every sentimental sermon is served with a side-dish of guilt. In their presence, honest doubt is named cynicism, anger is called evil, and ambivalence is castigated as craziness. Sentimentalists *are* too good to be true. The example of their refusal to see how love and hate are always locked in embrace gives us fair warning that an honest lover will always be too true to be merely good.

### Incurable Romantics: Phantom Lovers, Pornographers, and Idealists

Romance, so sweet in adolescence, turns sour when we try to prolong it into a philosophy for mature love. When we are green and lithe as willow branches, we dream of the ideal—the perfect woman, the perfect man, the utopian society. Unblooded in the arena of politics or compromised by the necessities of adult life, we fall in love. We know we can make all things new and beautiful, endless love, an alabaster city undimmed by human tears. Everything seems possible. And then, as suddenly as it began, the love song ends. The romance dies. But we find we have become addicted to the music, and we go out searching for someone to sing to us again. The true addict falls in love with love, becomes an incurable romantic, prolongs the adolescent expression of eros beyond the moment of its appropriateness.

Phantom lovers are romance junkies who habitually fall in love, repeat the cycle of quest, conquest, and disappointment without ever examining the illusions built into the romantic idea of love. They are excited only in the expectation but never in the actuality of any relationship. Every actual lover is judged by the standard of a nonexistent, ideal, phantom lover—the real thing, the platonic archetype of man or woman—who is just over the next horizon. Love addicts never doubt their own sincerity or lovability. Nothing is the matter with them. It is always the other person who is to blame. "If only she weren't so critical, and had larger breasts." "If only he were more demonstrative and responsible." "Some day he'll come along, the man I love." Romantics are committed to the ideal of grand passion and disdain any compromise (compromising is the essence of the adult). They want to be swept away. Love should be easy, spontaneous, effortless. Incurable romantics never face their own illusions, never see that impossible idealism is a hidden form of cruelty that makes any relationship with a flesh and blood person impossible.

The perversity of incurable romantics becomes clear when we see that they are essentially voyeurs. They never get beyond the plastic facade, the attractive surface of the other's persona. Their eros is aroused more by the image than by the flesh, more by the idea than the actuality of the other. Their mode of loving is pornographic rather than carnal. Like the voyeur, the phantom lover looks but remains distant; desires only the perfect unblemished anybody, the youthful platonic form on which time has not yet written; sees in the ideal the hope of escaping the actual world of change and death. By contrast, a carnal, mature, lover touches, tastes, and seeks intimacy; desires an imperfect somebody, with faults, crowsfeet and stretch marks.

Pornography and romance excite passion from afar. The stimulus is visual—a performance by actors. When we meet as persona and persona, the action takes place between two masks in a theater. We hope to excite each other by the attractive surfaces.

The pornographer, the voyeur, and the romantic follow a similar principle—keep your distance and stay in control. All are stimulated more by absence than by presence, more by the visual than the tactile, more by the fantasy than the reality of the other, more by the superficial than the profound. Sexual desire is only aroused by a "beautiful" exterior, like that of Sophia Loren or Warren Beatty.

Carnality is love between embodied persons. It lives by touch rather than sight, by proximity rather than distance. If, or rather when, I cannot reach beneath your surface, or when I am unwilling to share your chaos, or pain, or strength, there is no we, no compassion, no feeling together. Only I and I. Distant persons "I-ing" one another from afar. The appeal of pornography is in its magical promise (always broken) of passion without involvement—you can be shaken by ecstasy without touching another embodied human being. Little wonder most pornography is used to excite masturbation. Without embodiment, the self never breaks out of the circle of the I—the eyes.

There is a time in the rebel stage of life when it is appropriate to look rather than touch, to keep distance rather than make commitments. In fact, our capacity to be deeply engaged with another person is vintage wine that requires time to mature. As Jung says, in the first part of our lives we fall in love with the archetype of the opposite sex as it is dimly reflected in the other person. In matters of sexual attraction, we begin as Platonists—we love the image more than the reality, the archetype more than the flesh and blood. At first we fall in love with a thinly disguised reproduction of father or mother (or anti-father or anti-mother). The ideal form is the source of arousal, the image and fantasy of the person we desire stimulates our juices.

Sometime in our early adult years, the voyeuristic and pornographic illusions pale, we grow tired of love affairs between archetypes and attractive masks. The performance gets boring. Iconic sex is not enough. The myth of romantic love is worn thin. We want to drop the pretenses and know and be known by another. We discover that it is only in Hollywood that love begins in sufficiency. Only among celluloid gods and goddesses (or perhaps among the rare compassionate and erotic saints) is love a spontaneous sharing of the bounty of perfection. For all mortals, wounded by inadequacies and left hungry by unrequited longings, love begins in shame, guilt, fear, and unrealistic hope. Actual persons enter life maimed by the failures and triumphs of their parents and society. There are no virgin births and therefore no people who are not marked by hidden guilt and shame, by inhibitions and fears of abandonment. By midlife, if we have dared enough erotic folly to become disillusioned, we want a lover who is patient enough to wait for fears to emerge and dissipate, wait for shame to melt and frigid flesh to know its own warmth, wait for confusion to ripen into clarity, wait for the laughter that will free us from too much seriousness.

As we get older, it takes more to stimulate us. We want a conscious relationship of self to self. The outward beauty is not so important as the touch, taste, smell, and conversation of the beloved. Complexity of consciousness and richness of experience are the aphrodisiacs. We come to love the wounds our lover has sustained in honorable combat, the gnarls that mark the storms that have been weathered, and the scars that give silent testimony to suffering born with dignity.

But we are getting ahead of our story. Let's return.

The idealist is a romantic whose eros has been invested in a political vision, in a quest for a phantom body politic. The species can be found in profusion any sunny Sunday giving speeches in New York's Washington Square, talking earnestly in North Beach coffee houses in San Francisco, in the environs of any university, or in the ranks of leadership of most radical political movements. The idealist rarely survives in social service agencies, corporations, hospitals, prisons, local politics or other institutions that deal with the nitty-gritty.

The twentieth century has shown us that nowhere are the perversions of eros so dangerous as among idealists and ideologues. Hitler's frustrated adolescent dream of creating an ideal city evolved into the effort to create a pure German Reich. The ritual of purification of the Aryan blood led inevitably to "the final solution." Stalin's gulags, the Chinese purges, the Cambodian genocide, the Vietnamese bloodbath—all were designed by idealists with a vision of a perfect society, a five-year plan, a sacred mandate to preserve the democratic way of life. Idealists, like pornographers and romantics, are excited by the image of perfection rather than the smell, touch, and taste of intimacy. Their chief erogenous zone is in the cerebral cortex, not in the limbic brain or in the nerve endings.

## Playboys and Playgirls

Playboys and playgirls remain in the moratorium of adolescence by adopting a philosophy of play and gamesmanship. Our language diagnoses their condition: We do not say play*men* and play-*women*. Since our youth-adoring culture has lately held up players and gamesmen as models for the "cool" or authentic life, we need to look closely at what happens to eros when it is reduced to fun and games.

The philosophy of gamesmanship has recently been applied to every area of contemporary life. New-age business executives (never production line workers) explain seriously that business is a game in which the goal is beating the competition and profit is the mark of winning. Economics has become "the money game." Pop-psychologists tell eager players how to dress, shake hands, meet the eyes of a rival, master the art of one-upsmanship in order to win at the power game. In the Pentagon, nice men in uniforms play war games and invent scenarios for limited and unlimited nuclear "exchanges." Educators hope to solve their problems with learning games. Gurus teach the inner game of tennis and enlightenment. Oh, so easy. And, of course, eros has become the love game, or the sex game.

The metaphor of the game is a natural vehicle for the expression of an adolescent philosophy of life. The game, like adolescence, takes place in a moratorium from responsibility. It is governed by an arbitrary set of rules that preside over a make-believe world. With the game we can choose to play or not, quit when we want, or change the rules by common consent. Games refresh us precisely because they are a respite from the real world, from tragedy or death, and from the serious limits of moral commitments and vows. The player is pre-moral, amoral, or extramoral. Gamesters grant themselves the perpetual adolescent privilege of refraining from making moral decisions that would force them to take adult responsibility for the consequences of their actions. In the money game, they play the market without considering whether speculation in economic futures is creative or destructive for the psyche or the body politic. (What effect does gambling or income earned without producing useful goods have?) The war gamesmen sit like Olympian gods and never consider the morality of playing war games—whether, for instance, the very playing of the game increases the level of military spending and escalates paranoia. Gamesmen, like adolescents, live in a subjunctive world of endless possibilities, arbitrary rules, and enemies—the other team—which must exist in order for the game to continue and a winner emerge. The very notion that people can be divided into winners and losers is a polite form of sadomasochism, a gentle way of setting up a situation in which one person can defeat another, a device for allowing a superior to triumph over an inferior. In back of the rhetoric of the gamester hides the nice adolescent's unexpressed rage and need for revenge.

Among the playpeople, the romantic myth is dead and sex has been reduced to fun and games. An honored line of philosophers from the Kama Sutra to Henry Miller to Hugh Hefner have stated the rules. The first rule is that the purpose of sex is to maximize sensation and minimize feeling. Sensational sex involves at least two sets of highly sensitive and trained sexual players whose aim is to give and receive pleasure. Their relationship is amoral in that it does not necessarily demand any commitment or deep feeling, except in so far as "love" is necessary as an aphrodisiac to heighten sexual sensations. "If," as Dr. Alex Comfort, the author of *The Joy of Sex,* tells us, "you can only get high quality sex with love," then love is justified. But the point of the game is pleasure, not deep involvement. Playboys and playgirls, according to the *Playboy* philosophy, are committed to observing only a single rule: Whatever is mutually pleasurable to two or more consenting adults is right. If it feels good, do it.

The *Playboy* Advisor, Jim Peterson, explained in a letter his view of sex:

> The old-style model of sexuality took the judge out of the bedchamber and put him on the altar. If you were married and intended to have children, sex was not a sin. Which is not the same as being good or pleasurable. A wife's duty was to lie there and think of England. Nowadays, sex is permitted outside of marriage, deprived of an ethical context (Is it good?). The act becomes something else. A gentle sport. An activity with self evident rules. The new question: Am I good? Did I win? Did you come? . . .
>
> What are my models? The closest thing would be what you call "gentle sports." Athletes and Big Sur prophets alike have commented on the state of grace they achieve in a game: the loss of self in concentration, or fascination. A natural athlete can do no wrong. He transcends technique and becomes one with the game. He is an outlaw, but he is honest. He is no saint, but he is divine. And he has bad days, but is not discouraged. . . .
>
> The gentle sport metaphor assumes some rules. What is a game but structured play, a pattern for concentration. Passion is not chaos, it's not a bad metaphor. It assumes rules (not roles). There are rules, biological ones. Like chords, they make possible the song. A game contains endless variety. The best played encounters may be scoreless. So learn to play.

The problem with trying to prolong adolescent sex-play into a style of adult sexuality is that it rapidly becomes gamey and repressive. A perverse fate has overtaken playboys and playgirls. By accident, they have created a monster, a new tyranny, a rigorous set of rules about how the game of sex should be played, a new "cool" ethic, and a style of sexual gamesmanship. Advocates of sport-fucking would do well to heed the warning that is implicit in Huizinga's classical work on play. In *Homo Ludens* (man as player), Huizinga begins with the intention of dealing with fun, and ends by treating only games and contests. The same lesson can be learned by watching Little League: Fun and pleasure, when organized into a game, is changed into competition. The game of love has turned into a new form of contest, an *agon,* to see who can produce the most orgasms. Since everyone is now expected to perform like a pro, there is a new anxiety. Do I know the positions, the strategies, and moves well enough, and can I perform with sufficient grace under pressure to score a touchdown in the final minutes of play? Am I capable of multiple orgasms? Can I find the "G-Spot"? Added to the new performance anxiety there is a new set of conditions about who is permitted to play the sex game. By implication, playmates and playboys, like the gods and goddesses of Greek mythology, must always be young, beautiful, well-endowed, and without inhibitions, shame, or guilt. The fat, ugly, lusty, middle-aged people who grace the paintings of Breughel would not qualify as centerfolds. Unfortunately, few actual persons can reach the airbrushed, idealized standards of beauty, performance, or grace of the mythical playpeople. Most bodies are misshapen by injuries, labor, or age.

A purely sensational approach to sex misses the paradox of pleasure. Human beings are not young forever, do not live in the perpetual moratorium of the game, and cannot isolate present sensations from associated feelings. We are multidimensional. Therefore pleasure is greatest when sensation (present awareness) feeling (past associations) and intentions (future expectations) are unified in a single act. If all parts of the self are allowed to participate, everything feels better. A sensational approach tries to isolate a sexual relationship in the here and now. Playmates don't ask about the future or the past. For them, life is supposed to be a series of one night stands, serial moments of pleasure, episodes of sensation. The moment is everything. But when two people are pleased with each other once, they want to be pleased a second and a third time. Carnal knowledge creates a desire for recognition. When we have known each other intimately we want to remember the stories we have told together. A satisfying sexual relationship naturally expands from sensation to feeling to intention. I enjoyed you so much yesterday that you please me more deeply today and I want to be with you tomorrow. The path of pleasure leads us to the door of commitment, adult sexuality.

# 6.
## The Adult

In time, cupid must grow up. Rebellion and romance ripen into mature love. Innocence is traded for power. Young minds and bodies harden and the amorphous fantasies of what might be must conform to the limits of a single possible life. Love is not strawberry fields forever. We learn to wait, to work, to weave patient threads of care, to husband and till the land, to bake bread, to change diapers. As love grows into commitment, it is often called upon to sacrifice immediate pleasure, forego the spontaneous impulse of passion, and pledge the fidelity from which hope blossoms. Eros must finally put on work gloves and an apron.

Erik Erikson, in summarizing the eastern ideal of maturity and comparing it to his own, says of the man entering the householder stage of life:

> He settles down to marry, he is encouraged to devote himself to *Artha,* the "reality" of family relations, of communal power, and of productivity. The Manusmriti declares, "He only is a perfect man who consists of three persons united—his wife, himself, and his offspring." Much of this corresponds to our assumption that the rarified intimacies of young adulthood will ripen to a capacity for true intimacy which is a fusion of indentities. This, in turn, is the basis for that sense of care which crowns what we call Generativity and becomes a source of strength for all who are united in procreation and productivity.[1]

Love, in the noontime of our lives, is a homesteader, laboring to build a house, to manage the economies of the hearth, to put down deep roots in familial soil, to tend a piece of earth that is defined by well-made fences. The husband's art requires the limits and boundaries of marriage and the dedication to family and work. When eros puts away childish things and chooses to procreate, it must weave a nest solid enough to cradle the young. It takes a hard-headed man and a pragmatic woman to create shelter. But it takes more than that. The dyad must be surrounded by the clan; and the clan swaddled in the rule of the tribe; and the tribe must construct a single system of myth and ritual that forms the chaos of human experience into a coherent cosmos.

We like to think love is simple, a child resting in a mother's arms, or the flesh of two lovers melting into a wordless pool of pleasure. But it is not so. Mature love is shaped, informed, and forced to conform to the mores and laws of culture. It is housed within the institutions of marriage and the family. It follows the rules of kin and clan that dictate who may be loved, when and how, and which strangers must be met with enmity. An adult must learn to live *among* kinsmen and allies, *within* the rule of law and custom that creates civility, and be willing to make whatever sacrifices are necessary to protect loved ones *against* enemies.

## THE MAKING OF AN ADULT: BIOLOGY AND CULTURE

The definitions of "adult" and "mature" mirror the uneasy blend of biological inevitabilities and cultural inventions that make up a human being. The word "adult" (from *adultus,* the past participle of *adulescere,* to grow up) suggests that we, like flora and fauna, naturally bud and blossom before fading. But while maturity is a matter of biological inevitability among plants, humans come to adulthood only by a process of cultural nurturance and education. Thus our definitions of maturity also usually signify that one has reached some social milestone, such as wearing long pants, being marriageable, or of voting age. The more psychologically oriented definitions stress the achievement of control, effective interpersonal relationships, internalization of moral standards, and so on. Norman Cameron's definition is typical:

> What are the psychological criteria of adulthood? They are the disappearance of the turmoil, uncertainty and conflict of adolescence, the

## The Adult Personality

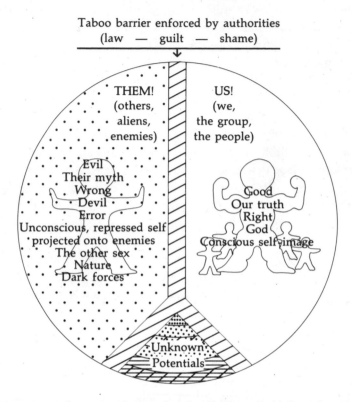

Taboo barrier enforced by authorities
(law — guilt — shame)

THEM!
(others,
aliens,
enemies)

US!
(we,
the group,
the people)

Evil
Their myth
Wrong
Devil
Error
Unconscious, repressed self
projected onto enemies
The other sex
Nature
Dark forces

Good
Our truth
Right
God
Conscious self-image

Unknown
Potentials

appearance of emotional control and general predictability, the establishment of self-confidence and self-respect, a willingness to accept
adult responsibilities even within the framework of thinking and judgment.[2]

Unfortunately, such sensible definitions overlook the most obvious and significant determinant of "maturity." It is culture, not
nature, that gives us the content of adulthood. Each society assigns
its *own content* to the definition of adult status. *Adult status is won by
internalizing the central myth of a culture, adopting its official symbols of status,
playing a recognized role, tailoring one's consciousness and conduct, one's loves
and hates, to fit the tribal or group mores.* A naked Kalahari Bushman and
a well-suited American business executive express their manhood

in different ways. But the cultural process that leads one to invest his pride in a penis shield and the other in a fistful of credit cards is identical. The world over, more or less adolescent children are made into adults by the elders who initiate them into the myth and mysteries of the tribe and the roles they are expected to play. Each culture superimposes a character, a persona, a mask, a definition of adulthood upon the unadorned biological humanity of its children. It is the nature of the human animal to be unnatural. We are not fully human beings, but cultural animals whose potential has been foreshortened so that we may be Germans, Navajos, Scots, Gypsies, Poles. Our consciousness is parochial; our eros is constricted to fit neatly within some tribal-mythical image of man or woman.

RITES OF PASSAGE: SEVERING THE BONDS OF CHILDHOOD

Nowhere do we see more clearly the way culture carves, imprints, and in-forms us than in the traditional rites of passage that mark the initiation into adulthood.

In tribal societies, males are expected to graduate into manhood sometime between twelve and sixteen years of age. Ordinarily, the rites of passage are ordeals that involve fasting, beatings, knocking out teeth, scarification (the myth is literally carved into the body), removal of a testicle, subincision of the penis, or sacrifice of a finger. Often, initiates are expected to prove their courage by killing an enemy or a wild animal. The main purpose of the ordeal is to mark the transition between nature and culture, to sever the relationship between the mother and the son, to prepare the boy for the role he must play as husband and defender of the tribe. Individuality must be sacrificed to the group. The incipient warrior must harden, learn to endure pain without complaint, live without flinching in the presence of death, kill without guilt. The boy must be taught to despise the soft and sensual ways of women. The Gallas of Northeast Africa amputated the mammae, since only women should have breasts. Marine drill instructors insult the recruits by calling them girls or pussies.

As the boy is severed from feminine virtues, a new heroic ideal of masculinity is introduced. Stories and songs of the brave acts of ancient warriors provide a model for what a man should be. Odysseus, Geronimo, General Patton become the tutors of masculinity. Our myth-making machine—television and the movies—shows us such models as John Wayne in *The Sands of Iwo Jima*. As Sergeant Streiker, he is dedicated to making fighting men out of recruits. They hate him until they get into battle, when they find he has trained them well. The recruits prove their courage under fire, and Streiker gets killed just as they are raising the flag over the hill. They watch the flag, see Sergeant Streiker's body, and the new leader (the reluctant hero throughout the story, the softy who wants his son to read Shakespeare rather than the Marine handbook) takes the leadership of the platoon and repeats the rough liturgy of the Sergeant. "Saddle up and let's get back in this war." Fadeout to the music of the Marine hymn.

Women's initiation rites, even when they involve painful ordeals such as clitoridectomies, are designed to inculcate the domestic rather than the martial virtues. Usually around the time of the onset of menstruation, the girl is taken into a circle of women and taught the virtues proper to her gender and the duties she must perform as a wife and mother. Almost universally, women have been expected to assume the major responsibility for the young and the domestic chores so that the men might be free for hunting and protecting the tribe from its enemies.

As tribes have become nations and have come to be governed by the western myth, the rites of passage have also become secularized. Nevertheless, they still operate powerfully. Boys and girls still must accumulate the tokens of maturity—driver's license, the loss of virginity, registering for the draft, graduation from high school or college, the right to vote and drink, a job, an apartment away from home, credit cards, debt, marriage, an automobile, a home. In modern society, much of the process of initiation is informal and haphazard and takes place in schools, through the media, in business, in factories, and other institutions. But it still produces a character type that is recognizable. More than a century ago, de Tocqueville made observations about Americans that still hold true, and which show how well our informal rites of initiation work. As a nation, we are individualistic, pragmatic, careless about tradition, ahistorical, concerned with appearing nice, extroverted, restless, technological optimists, inventive, aggressive, self-righteous, wealthy. This character type creates an unconscious norm to which we conform and by which we judge ourselves. Quiet, unambitious introverts, poets and dreamers, and others lacking the particularly masculine cast of the ideal American temperament, are reminded in a thousand subtle ways by our myth-making machine that they are less than they should be. They are invited to attend shyness clinics, to take courses in how to win friends and influence people, to develop their vocabulary, to learn to speed read, assert themselves, improve, make money in their spare time, build their bodies, get ahead, become winners, make a killing in real estate, pull their own strings.

## MYTH AND NORMALITY

Every society, including our own, is informed by a central myth. Therefore the notion of myth has an exact meaning we must understand if we are to grasp the nature of adult or normal consciousness. To repeat the definition offered earlier: Myth is the system of basic metaphors, images, and stories that informs the perceptions, memories, and aspirations of a people, provides the rationale for its institutions, rituals and power structure, and gives a map of the purpose and stages of life. *Lived myth always involves the polis, and therefore provides the content of the definition of maturity.*

To understand how myth in-forms and limits consciousness, let's begin with its most primitive and simple expression. Mircea Eliade reports that every tribe has some way of symbolically affirming that its territory is the center of the world, its people the chosen people, its ritual a path to the sacred. The aborigines of Australia, for instance, practice this mythical discipline of living at the center by driving a world-pole, or *axis mundi,* into the ground.

According to the traditions of the Achilpa, in mythical times the divine being Numbakula cosmicized their future territory, created their Ancestor, and established their institutions. From the trunk of a gum tree Numbakula fashioned the sacred pole and, after anointing it with blood, climbed it and disappeared into the sky. This pole represents a cosmic axis, for it is around the sacred pole that territory becomes habitable, hence is transformed into a world. The sacred pole consequently plays an important role ritually. During their wanderings, the Achilpa always carry it with them and choose the direction they are to take by the direction toward which it bends. This allows them while being continually on the move, to be always in "Their world" and, at the same time, in communication with the sky into which Numbakula vanished. . . . For the pole to be broken denotes catastrophe; it is like "the end of the world," reversion to chaos.[3]

Throughout history, various peoples have had more elaborate ways of affirming their centrality and sanctifying their way of life. At one time or another, the temple, the basilica, the holy mountain, the ark of the Covenant, the Gothic cathedral, have all functioned as the *axis mundi* that made the sacred visible for a people. Around these centers there grew up cults, cycles of stories and legends, daily and seasonal rituals and liturgies that dramatized the myth.

Inevitably, since it sanctifies the power structure and provides the principles for the organization of society, the central myth of a culture is political. In the strict Marxist sense of the term, *myth is always allied with ideology.* Those people and castes who enjoy the privileged positions find the rationale for their power in the myth. In a theocratic society, the priestly function is exalted. The theology of the Goddess celebrated the priority of the feminine and sanctified the position of the priests who served the Goddess. Medieval theology justified the divine right of kings. The western myth celebrates the superiority of manpower and puts the values of the marketplace at the center of life.

In the modern world, political centers such as the Kremlin and Washington, D.C., have replaced sacred places such as Mecca and Jerusalem as power spots. Banks, laboratories, corporations, and factories have taken over the place the cathedral once held in a city. They now define the nature of reality, provide definitions of the good life and status symbols that trigger our desire, and claim to be the creators of meaning and value. Thus, no less than that of the aborigines, the life of modern people circulates around an *axis mundi* and is informed by a myth.

Many will protest. "Money is no myth. Science is no myth. Government is no myth. Our lives are organized by secular principles, by pragmatism, democracy, etc." But, as we have suggested earlier, living mythical-political systems are invisible to those who live within them. The problem of myth and consciousness is reflected in the old saying: We don't know who discovered water, but it wasn't a fish. Myth is the sea of commonly accepted assumptions that are not questioned by the majority of those living within a system. To the average, normal member of a society, the myth is what is natural and obvious. To the believer, it is indisputable that Jesus is Lord, that Mohammed is the Prophet, that money can buy happiness, that science will solve our problems, or that capitalism will dig its own grave. You can usually tell when you are in the presence of mythical belief by the clichés, well-worn phrases, time-polished metaphors, and unquestioned proverbs. The Hopi Indian knows that Earth is Mother and Sky is Father as certainly as the average white Anglo-Saxon Protestant (WASP) knows that this is the land of opportunity and that genius is 1/10 inspiration and 9/10ths perspiration.

The men and women who do not accept the consensus view of reality—shamans, outlaws, madmen and madwomen, artists, prophets, lovers, the odd ones—see how normality is constricted. They give us the answer to the puzzle. They know who discovered water. It was a *flying* fish. The moment the fish broke the surface, it must have said to itself: I have been swimming in something that is thick and heavy, I think I will call it "water." It is only from the perspective of the outlaw and lover, which we will explore shortly, that we are able to see that mythically informed normalty is a form of mass hypnosis that systematically limits both IQ and EQ.

MYTH AND THE BODY: THE SOCIAL REORGANIZATION OF EROS

The mythical system determines not only the way we think but what, whom, and how we will desire. To become an adult, we put aside the purely biological drives of the body and accept a new set of social motivations. The flesh is imprinted with the vision of the body politic, the individual gives up uniqueness in exchange for membership. Whether the urgency in the loins will be expressed in homosexual or heterosexual ways, in monogamy, polygamy, or promiscuity, depends on society. Before a Sambian male may graduate from youth to adulthood, he must practice ritual homosexuality for a number of years, "eat the seed" of the warriors who rank above him in the social hierarchy. Each society's definition of the good life is incarnate in its heroes and heroines. Whether we will make love like "little women," Lady Chatterly's lover, the sensuous woman, stick to the missionary position (but never on Sunday), revel in oral sex, or remain celibate, depends upon the models of sexuality given us by our society.

In becoming adults, we consent to a body transplant, to the mythical in-formation of our biological bodies, to erotic incorporation. Society colonizes us with its metaphors, implants within us a model by which we interpret our longings. For instance, in Goddess-worshiping cultures, the world was perceived as the body of Goddess—Mother Earth. The movement of the stars was her pulse, the seasons were her body rhythms. Men and women lived within the world-body of the Goddess and experienced their sexuality as a part of her sacred fertility. Later, in the Christian context, the Church became the body or bride of Christ within which the believer lived. Men were enjoined to love their wives as Christ had loved the Church. The body became the temple of the holy spirit. Within the body of Christ, all members had a function. The genitals were to be under the governance of the "higher" powers.

A body doesn't just meet a body coming through the rye. In songs and dreams, lovers may be overwhelmed by passion beside some sleepy lagoon. We may dream of "Jeannie with the light brown hair, floating like a vapor on the summer air"; but, in reality, a body is more likely to meet a body in an office in Philadelphia or in a bordello in New Orleans. We are not situated in Utopia, and our bodies are always shaped by some social, political, economic, historical and familial context, by the ways in which power and money are gained and distributed. When a modern body meets a body, the values of the marketplace will not be absent. Passion must always contend with political realities.

When Plato dreamt of a Utopia, he cut one pattern to fit cosmos, polis, and psyche. Reason was to govern the cosmos; philosophers were to govern the state; and the mind was to govern the body. What Plato could propose as an ideal, Marx and Reich have shown is a sinister reality. The body politic imposes its values on the carnal body. The economic and political order creates a hierarchy of values, a vision of the good life, and a way of structuring time and utilizing energy that shapes the individual body-mind. (Note: Even the word "value" is an imposition on our experience that is taken from the economic order.)

Thus we cannot divorce the effort to renew passion from politics. The way our privates behave is a matter of public policy. Uncle Sam is watching you and so is General Motors. The man who comes home exhausted because he has been taught to believe without question that his male identity is based on nine-to-five loyalty and the giving of his best energies to the corporation has made a decision about his sexuality. He sacrifices his corpus to the corporation. His chosen method of expending energy and structuring time disallows afternoon dalliance with his wife or lover.

But eros is kairotic, not chronological—it is governed by body-time, not clock-time. The woman who is trained to be accommodating and servile has been ideologically rendered incapable of being a tigress in the bedroom. In corporate society, where time is money, success belongs to those who can maintain a high level of drive. The man or woman on the go must always be ready for fight or flight. Overstimulation of the adrenal glands (with consequent exhaustion of the spirit) is the price of our incorporation within the male womb of the modern corporate society. It is not difficult to guess the effect that constant competition, overstimulation, and stress have upon our capacity for sexual delight. Kinsey reported that the average American male had an orgasm two and a half minutes after beginning intercourse. Some experts have questioned his data, and have suggested that a more accurate figure might be five to six minutes. The point is moot. Either way, it is speedy compared to the hour-long rituals of lovemaking that are practiced by tantric lovers. We are unlikely to find a lover with "slow hands" (as a recent popular song says) when we live in the fast lane.

Deeper still. A society that trains us to specialize in making, doing, performing, and producing neglects to educate us in wonder and appreciation. The true erotic impulse springs from the desire to touch, smell, listen, appreciate. Sexual desire is only one minor division of Eros, Inc.

The gentlest and most insidious way we are dominated by the body politic is by the official visions of the good life that are implicit in advertising and propaganda. Happiness is a new car, a color TV—fill in the gap with your own "freely chosen" artificially simulated desire. Security is a perimeter of ICBMs surrounding all "hostile" nations; a large insurance policy; knowing your underarm deodorant will keep you spring-fresh throughout the day; being well-liked (poor Willy Loman); having a good job. What we "should" desire creeps silently inside us and replaces what we really desire. We begin to structure our time and energy to achieve what we "desire." We take jobs, make compromises, and settle down for the long wait, for the arrival of the future that will bring the reward of happiness we so justly deserve for our sacrifice of the pleasures of the moment. The process is so slow we scarcely notice the substitution of plastic for flesh. We forget how the body sang when it ran free; how it rejoiced in stretching, rolling, skipping, dancing, walking, eating, loving, bouncing, leaping, resting.

Gradually, the body begins to change to protect itself against the intrusion of joy or sorrow. It armors itself against the threat of playfulness and spontaneity. Physiologically, the creation of a "body armor" (Wilhelm Reich's term) involves a process in which muscles shorten, thicken, and lose elasticity. Connective tissue joins adjacent fascial envelopes and makes an unresponsive mass out of muscles that should operate with democratic autonomy. A postural set and a style of restricted movement develop and become habitual. We become "set in our ways," rigid. Henceforth free emotional and physical flow is no longer possible. The working body is complete when it is thus armed against those emotions that would threaten the primacy of the work ethic and the pattern of delayed gratification upon which it rests.

The final step in tracing the logic that links the body politic to the carnal body is understanding the relation of body structure and sensation. The body politic creates desire. Desire governs action. Action creates structure. Structure governs sensation. For example: In a competitive society, aggression is a primary value. Aggression is manifested physiologically by the changes that prepare the body to fight or flee. The adrenalin level rises, breathing becomes shallow and rapid, the striking muscles in the neck, shoulders, and upper back become tensed for action. Great release is experienced when the prepared body goes into action. It feels good to hit, to wrestle, or push. However, when aggression is not expressed in physical action, tension remains within the body. Muscles on constant alert lose their resiliency and become chronically tense. A state of preparation for offense or defense is not conducive to dalliance. The current medical name for this condition is "stress," and we are told it is the primary culprit in cancer, heart attack, and other dis-eases that are most prevalent in western culture.

Pleasure involves both tension and relaxation. The sex act is a good model. For the maximum enjoyment, the body must be able to retain a high charge and then discharge this energy. If muscular and psychic structures are too flabby, desire cannot become strong; if they are too rigid, it cannot be completely expressed. In either case, pleasure is severely limited. Emotion involves motion. Wherever chronic rigidity and tension or atonic flabbiness exist, a body will lack the capacity for the rhythmic motion that is the essence of pleasure.

Thus, in the end, if we love our flesh we must go beyond the adult citizens' view of the world and make a revolution. Turn every body around. We need a body politic that is created to satisfy the desires of the carnal body. Until this period in history, civility and carnality have been at war. Humankind has sacrificed much of the life of the body to satisfy the demands of the state. The world has now become too dangerous to be governed by ideologies and allegiance to nationalistic values. We need to get back to the earth, to our carnal beginnings, to rediscover what we really desire. We need a new carnal body politic, a compassionate corporation, a cosmopolitan community. Only one motto can make the politics of the future safe for flesh-and-blood people: All pleasure to the people.

IMMORTALITY THROUGH MARRIAGE AND MEMBERSHIP

Initiation into adult status signals a radical change in our erotic life. Gone the days of carefree play, trying on personas, daydreams of alternative lives, the romance with ideals as pure as they are untested. If a society allows adolescent sexual experimentation, adulthood usually marks the end of careless love. Time to settle down, to marry and produce children.

Why give up youth, spontaneity, the will-of-the-wisp, to take up the responsibility of a household?

At the moment, marriage (although championed by the Moral Majority) has a rather bad press. Many consider it an obsolete institution that can only be understood from the perspective of sexual politics. Radical feminists claim that men, being physically stronger than women, formed a conspiracy and invented marriage as a way of capturing the exclusive sexual rights to a female and enslaving women. According to the sort of man who reads *Playboy*, women invented marriage as a way to contain the wandering affections of the naturally promiscuous male and to ensure that they would have somebody to bring home the bacon and protect their young.

Both explanations demean marriage and the intelligence of men and women. The universality of marriage and its continued popularity (94 percent of us try it) suggest that the practice endures because it offers more satisfaction than dissatisfaction, and that it is erotically superior to any alternatives that have yet been found.

Certainly we all lament the passing of childhood. Passage from one stage of life to the next always involves a small death, grief for what must be given up. But the healthy person is drawn forward into responsible adulthood because it is more exciting and fulfilling to master a skill, play a role, become a citizen than to remain in the playful but impotent stage of make believe. We desire ripeness. Society offers us something better than childhood and "dreaming innocence," in Paul Tillich's phrase, more moving than casual passion and one night stands. Marriage is a discipline that takes us nearer to the heart of reality than romance.

Adulthood and marriage offer us pleasures of potency and seminal sexuality that are greater than the pleasures of play. A game may be fun, but procreation is joy. We enter a new stage of life when we ask the questions: What is coming to birth in and through my life? Our relationship? Life itself? With the emergence of seminal sexuality, male and female bodies are no longer mere instruments for sensual games but find their deepest pleasure in the expression of a mysterious power and purpose.

Plunge into the paradox of pleasure and you discover that the pleasures of intentionality and purposeful action are more profound than those of pure sensation. I have asked many people to describe their most exciting sexual experience. To date, the most frequent candidate for pure ecstasy was the occasion when a man and woman decided it was time to create a child between them. "I remember," one woman told me, "the night when I threw away the diaphragm and we said to each other as we began making love: 'This could be the time! Wow!' " Or, as a man told me: "I had been to the Turkish baths and was tired. So I went right to bed. Several hours later, my wife slipped in beside me and immediately we were aroused. We began to make love and then remembered she wasn't protected. But we were on the third floor and the damn contraceptives were downstairs. We were almost ready to have another child anyway so we went ahead. I can hardly describe the power, the mystery, and the pleasure we both felt. The moment we climaxed we both knew we had conceived. I could feel my sperm joining with her ovum. Afterwards we lay still for a very long time. It was as if a thunderstorm had just passed through us. . . . Our son is now nineteen and I still remember that moment."

At the bottom line, sexual pleasure is nature's way of enticing us to reproduce the species. Eros wants history to continue. Desire is a trick to get us to keep the evolutionary experiment going. There is a "biological" imperative contained in every sex act. Sex is an election arranged so the genes and chromosomes can cast their vote about the outcome of history. Desire is the evidence that our bodies are building a kingdom that transcends the moment. Our deepest pleasure is inseparable from fertility. Our most unshakable security lies in the knowledge that we are bonded together in a fruitful universe. Something larger than we can know or understand is moving us.

Initiation, adulthood, and marriage also signify that the individual has entered into a social body. Although marriage may present the most satisfying form of sexual expression for a majority of people, it is not designed primarily for sexual pleasure or companionship, or, indeed, even as a relationship between individuals. Traditionally, marriage has been understood not as a culmination of a romantic urge, but as a uniting of families.

> No anthropological specialist maintains that marriage is a pair-bond, cemented by sexual imprinting. For the majority of humanity—and possibly for all of it before modern times—marriage is less an alliance of two people than an alliance of families and larger networks of people. . . . In most preliterate societies marriage is "not erotic but economic" . . . motivated by the desire to attain adult status and recognition in the community, to have a household of one's own, to have children, to gain an economic partner, and to acquire sexual rights.[4]

Marriage and membership establish communion as the primal human reality. The lone ego, which we have come to think of in western philosophy as the starting point for knowledge, the first and last truth about the psyche, is an abstraction. I am I only within the context of a family and a community. Marriage and the other disciplines of citizenship establish compromise—co-promising—as the adult form of loving. Identity and motivation are shifted from the singular to the plural. What is most important to the fulfillment of life is not what *I* want, but what *we* want. The bond within which we live and move and have our being as adults is created by mutual vows. The social contract is not based on a cynical compromise that we make because without the laws of civility we would be enemies to each other; rather, it is based on the visceral knowledge that we would die without communion with our own kind. The singular life, as we are discovering now that western individualism has destroyed the basis of community, leads to alienation, anomie, and apathy. The motive power for the individual life, paradoxically, is inseparable from community.

Within the ambience of the group, it is not intense passion that is valued so much as orderly care, not wild encounters with strange loves, but quiet kindness. Society tames us, teaches us to keep our Dionysian impulses in control (except during Mardi Gras, Fasching, orgies on the Sagittarian moon, and occasional affairs). It is not prudery that leads the tribe to domesticate eros, but the observation that it is patience, day-to-day kindness, basic trust, and competence that makes for a full life. For cooking, one wants embers, not flames. For a bountiful harvest, seed must not only be sown but cultivated. Stability is the precondition for the development of intelligence and love.

If we were immortal, perhaps we would not need membership or marriage. We might frolic like playboys and playgirls and tickle our nerve endings. But since we do die, we need some reassurance that something to, with, or within which we belong abides. We cannot live without the trust that we will live on. The desire for immortality is deeper in us even than the desire for pleasure. The history of culture is the story of the ideas, objects, and institutions in which men and women have invested their hope for immortality—religions, books, symphonies, causes, quests.

But by far the most common and convincing way we have of affirming our abidingness is through our children. I look at my children and see a crooked smile that once played across the face of my father, a set of jaw that reincarnates my mother, the almond shape of the eyes that is mine; and I know with visceral certainty (beyond all the disclaimers of the mind) that together we partake of something that death does not destroy. We invest our eros in marriage and family because something within our instinct to love is not satisfied with anything that is not perennial. Marriage is designed to give us a chance to fall out of love, to abandon fleeting romantic intensity, and to create something that withstands the acids of time. The vow—for better, for worse, richer or poorer, in sickness and in health, till death do us part—signifies the birth of a type of love that is not dependent upon attractive facades or pleasing personalities, or the satisfaction of conditions (so long as you don't gain more than five pounds or start to snore). It is rooted in the recognition that we are fundamentally moved by a desire to procreate rather than to experience momentary pleasure. And procreation (whether of a child, a book, or a social movement) always involves more than the single ego.

In adopting the myth and the roles that go with adulthood, we are rewarded not only by the tangible immortality of marriage and children but by membership in the ongoing entity of the tribe or nation and identity with its symbolic immortality project. As Ernest Becker has shown in *Denial of Death* and *Escape from Evil*, the mythology of every tribe and nation locates it at *the center* of some divine scheme or cosmic order. Each tribe has a manifest destiny or a messianic role to play in history. Even formally atheistic societies, such as Russia, are religious. Becker puts it this way: "Culture itself is sacred, since it is the "religion" that assures in some way the perpetuation of its members. Culture in this sense is always "supernatural," and all systematizations of culture have in the end the same goal: to raise men above nature, to assure them that in some way their lives count in the universe more than merely physical things count."[5]

Thus the promise of adulthood, of belonging to the body politic, is in form identical with the promise we found implicit within romantic love. *In romantic love, the beloved who is adored is the icon of the sacred. In adulthood, the group becomes the icon of the sacred.* Unconsciously, we expect social membership to satisfy our longing for an adequate object for unconditional love. The sacrifices we make of our individuality in order to belong are based on the belief that the tribe is the everlasting body within which we will find satisfaction of our desires and security.

Why the promise of normality is doomed to fail, why eros must go beyond the horizon of myth, take leave of the social dharma and the virtues of the householder and become an outlaw, becomes clear when we look more closely at the perversity of normality.

# 7.
# The Perversity of Normality: The Wound of Culture

The notion that normality may become perverse seems strange. After all, the norm is the yardstick. If the average adult is not the model for sanity, if the majority is neurotic, how do we decide who is healthy? And who decides? The idea of a supranormal stage or mode of life raises visions of Nietzsche's superman (which Hitler misused with grotesque results). The arrogance of the "spiritual elite" who claim the right to transcend the norm is fearful.

Yet the problem is unavoidable. As we have seen, each culture fills the definition of adulthood with its own content, its own myth. So, if there is nothing higher than adult status, we are left with complete cultural relativism and must conclude that whatever is sanctioned in a given culture is right, and what is tabooed is wrong. It is right to commit genocide if you are an Indonesian in Timor, or a Communist in Tibet, but wrong if you are a Quaker. It follows that there is no *human* nature, no *human* values, no transcendence of our parochial perspective, no escape from character, persona, roles, myth. And we are all left with the moral schizophrenia that Lt. Calley expressed so vividly in his defense of the massacre at My Lai: "I'll do as I'm told to. I'll put the American people above my own conscience, always." Yet the formation of the League of Nations, the United Nations, the Nuremberg trials, and the trial of Lt. Calley are all testimonies to the effort to discover a binding moral law that transcends tribal or national law and a form of conscience that is more than obedience to the consensus of the mores of the tribe. If we have obligations extending beyond the duty we have to our in-group, then the psyche cannot rest with the achievement of adulthood.

To go beyond adulthood, we must first see how adult character becomes perverse.

### EROTIC CRIPPLING: MYTH, LOVE, AND HATE

The making of an adult is a complex process that systematically cripples, reduces our consciousness, our compassion, and our potential to love. The de/cisions required for maturity exclude from care all except family, friends, and fellow citizens. The circle of love is small, the circle of hate is large. Tribal consciousness is formed more by negation than affirmation, more by fear than by wonder, more by dis-ease than by health.

For a moment, let us return to the world of the child who has not yet been radically informed by culture. There is, of course, no time, even *in utero* when culture is not in some degree influencing our biological or spiritual potential. In theory, however, let us say that a child begins with 100 percent of its IQ and EQ intact, which we will symbolize by a full circle:

**100%: Erotic and Intellectual Potential**

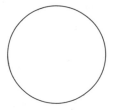

If a child was not conditioned to suspicion, fear, and hatred, it might develop an abundance of erotic attachments to family, strangers, animals, things. It might, as Buddhism suggests, naturally love all sentient beings and develop an empathic consciousness of a kind we glimpse only in those rare individuals we call saints or enlightened beings. Data shows that children raised with a great deal of touch, sensuality, and affection do not develop a taste for violence. We can make a reasonable theoretical leap to suppose that our potential erotic capacity is far greater than most adults suspect. We can hardly imagine a human being who retained 100 percent of his or her erotic capacity; but we can see the process by which culture cripples us all.

## Consensual Paranoia: The Tribe versus the Enemy

The first requirement for adult status is that we divide our love and multiply our hate. Normal consciousness begins with a division between those who are to be loved and those who should be hated, between us and them, kin and strangers, the tribe and its enemies. We begin the process of acculturation by dividing the circle, amputating 50 percent of our EQ:

**50%: Them, the Enemy, versus Us, the People**

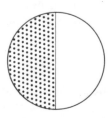

As nearly as we can tell from historical and anthropological evidence, most of the world's people have lived in tribes and nations ruled by *consensual paranoia*. The corporate identity of "the people" was dependent upon having an enemy. The number of tribes who have lived by a mythology of peace, such as the Hopi, the Tassaday, or the Pygmies, is very small. Normally, social cohesion is maintained by projection and paranoia. We deny our own aggressive, destructive, hostile impulses and attribute them to an enemy. Ernest Becker, in studying the roots of evil, puts the matter this way:

The thing that man wanted most was to be part of a close and loving ingroup, to feel at peace and harmony with others of his kind. And to achieve this intimate identification it was necessary to strike at strangers, pull the group together by focusing it on an outside target. So even . . . the sacrificial ravages of the Nazis could be approached in terms of neutral motives or even altruistic ones: love, harmony, unity . . . the Agape motive. Man wants to merge with a larger whole, have something to dedicate his existence to in trustfulness and in humility; he wants to serve the cosmic powers. The most noble human motive, then, would cause the greatest damage because it would lead men to find their highest use as part of an obedient mass, to give their complete devotion and their loves to their leaders. Arthur Koestler . . . recently reaffirmed this: it is not aggressive drives that have taken the greatest toll in history, but rather "unselfish devotion" hyperdependency: combined with suggestibility. . . .[1]

The mythic mind is obsessively dualistic. It splits everything into polar opposites. Even when a flesh and blood enemy is absent, reality is cast in the form of a cosmic, sexual, or religious drama, or a morality play, a conflict between:

| | | |
|---|---|---|
| Light | and | Darkness |
| the Sacred | and | the Profane |
| God | and | the Devil |
| Good | and | Evil |
| the People | and | the Enemy |

The cosmic battle between good and evil is acted out in rituals, sports, and sexual relationships, and especially in warfare.

Considerable psychological sleight of hand is necessary to make people kill without suffering overwhelming guilt. Mythology always includes a justification for killing the enemy. It makes killing and dying a sacred act performed in the service of some god or immortal ideal. Thus the creation of propaganda is as old as human history. Truth is the first sacrifice we make in order to belong.

It may be that one of the earliest human inventions was the image of an enemy. And shortly after that came the weapon, for killing. Typically, propaganda changes the enemy from a human being into a demon, an incarnation of evil, a stain that must be wiped from the earth. The human face, which might be loved, is changed into a loathsome thing, an animal. The Jap becomes an ape, the Nazi a blond beast, the American a capitalist pig, the communist an atheist, the Jew a vermin. By contrast, the majority of names tribes have invented for themselves mean simply "the people," man or human. The Carib of South America, for instance, say, "We alone are people."

## The War Between the Sexes

The second requirement for normal adulthood that further cripples eros is that men and women are viewed as radically different, as semi-enemies to one another. Because the world is dangerous and filled with enemies, males must be hardened and formed into warriors to defend the tribe. This means they must also be on guard against women. The more the identity of the male is rooted in the warrior ideal, the more a society will degrade women and cast the relationship between the sexes as a form of warfare. The warrior, whether primitive or sophisticated, will see the woman as an inferior to be conquered, raped, dominated. In discussing the Sambia of New Guinea, Gilbert Derdt puts the matter succinctly:

> A society of warriors tends to regard women unkindly, and Sambia attitudes have carried this emphasis to its furthest reaches in the relationships between men and women. Harsh even by the standards of New Guinea where sexual differences are sharply contrasted, the rhetoric and ritual of men represent women as polluting inferiors a man should distrust throughout his life. Men hold themselves to be the superiors of women in physique, personality and social position. Indeed, survival for individual and community alike demands hard, disciplined men as unlike the softness of women as possible. This dogma of male supremacy permeates all social relationships and institutions. It forms the bedrock on which are based warfare, economic production and religious life. . . . Men idiomatically refer to women as distinctively inferior and "darker" species than themselves. The sense of this cast one hears constantly in the cliché, "Women are no good," or still worse, "Women have that vagina, something truly no good."[2]

In other words, "normal" sexuality is based upon a culturally condoned form of sadomasochism. The male is expected to dominate and degrade the female, and the female has learned by long experience to win by losing, to wield power in the passive-aggressive manner of the masochist. Robert Stoller goes so far as to say that a whisper of hostility is the key element in creating (normal) sexual excitement: "Hostility overt or hidden, is what generates and enhances sexual excitement, and its absence leads to sexual indifference and boredom. This dominance of hostility in eroticism attempts to undo childhood traumas and frustrations that threaten the development of masculinity and femininity (gender identity)."[3]

The following newspaper item shows, in the most gross manner, the war between the sexes that underlies the western myth:

> Feminists lost their third Swiss court battle Friday when the country's Supreme Court ruled that Swiss soldiers using a life-sized *Playboy* centerfold for target practice were not offending women's dignity. The court said a model who posed nude for *Playboy* magazine "cannot be regarded as representative of all women." Further, the court ruled, the Swiss Association for Female Rights lacked legal justification in taking the issue to court because there is no proof that it can talk for all Swiss women.[4]

Further evidence that sex is routinely considered a polite form of warfare, that eros is perceived as a disguised agent of thanatos even among the proponents of sexual liberation, is found in the popular sex manuals. They abound with military language and metaphors of conquest. Take, for instance, *Sex and the Single Man*, by Albert Ellis. Ellis tells men to observe the traits of a woman they want to win and to plan an appropriate campaign to bed her. First, we must put aside certain dangerous illusions that will prevent seduction. Ellis tells us forthrightly: "You are not here primarily to achieve something wonderful during your lifetime, to be of great service to others, to change the course of the world, or to do anything else but (in one way or another that you find particularly appealing) to enjoy yourself."[6] Having our self-centered goal

firmly in mind, we may now proceed to the advice about how we
are to win a reluctant lover. You will note the language has a
certain similarity to General Patton's discussion of how to conquer
the Desert Fox.

> Thus you slip your hands underneath her brassiere or down the top of
> it, without literally removing it. And you can get to a girl's genital
> region without necessarily removing her skirt, slip, or panties. In fact,
> if you insist on your attempts to get at her breasts or genitals by fully
> undressing her, you frequently will defeat your amorous ends: for she
> will then forcibly stop you from going further, and that will be that.
> If, on the other hand, you get to her vital erotic zones while her clothes
> are still mainly on, and you massage and kiss these zones effectively
> until she becomes truly aroused, she *then* will offer no resistance what-
> ever to taking off her clothes completely, and may even voluntarily do
> so herself.[5]

The notion of sex as warfare and conquest has, until recently,
been more popular among males than females. The female of the
species, however, has lately discovered and asserted the right to
aggression, thus escalating the battle between the sexes. Helen
Gurley Brown gives combat advice to the female warrior in *Sex and
the Single Girl.* For the single girl, marriage is "only insurance for
the *worst* years." Men are "lambs to be shorn and worn" and are
necessary, but the smart girl will keep plenty of them around to
fulfill her needs.

> It is harder to like men generously and selflessly when you're single.
> They are, after all, the enemy! One kindly smile from you, they think
> you're sweet on them. It's true, there has to be quite a lot of unrequited
> liking on your part for a while, but then men stop being suspicious and
> allow you to collect them as sons and lovers.[7]

The successful single girl (never woman) must turn her whole life
into a strategy for capturing the man or men she wants. Being sexy
is a woman's greatest weapon, and "the smart woman in any
culture packages herself to please her particular clientele." Being
sexy is charming:

A charmer has her antenna up and her valves open at all times. With sensitive radar she detects what the other person wants to hear and says it. And she senses what he doesn't want to hear and refrains from saying it.[8]

Charming people (like paranoids) are *"thinking ahead all the time."*

Ellis and Brown are noteworthy because both blatantly articulate a common approach to sex. Under the facade of charm, style, and the "normal" roles men and women play is the view that sex is conquest. A man adds notches to his "gun." A woman baits "the tender trap." Beneath the surface, there is warfare between the sexes. The male of the species is concerned with maintaining personal power—potency. The female is taught wiles and strategies to manipulate so that she may seem feminine, gentle, and yielding and still control the situation.

For most people, the warfare is civil, and there is fun in the hunt. The lion and the lamb do lie down together, for awhile at least. Love occasionally graces the battlefield. As in medieval wars, there are holidays when hostilities cease. But for some, the injuries sustained by the continual climate of suspicion and competition are too great. The distance between man and woman grows until it can only be bridged by violence. To the man for whom all women are enemies, rape becomes the only way to simultaneously express both hatred and need. For the woman to whom sex is a battle in which she cannot lose control, the *fantasy* of rape relieves her of the responsibility and guilt for surrendering and allows her both to yield to an overwhelming force and to enjoy the joy of surrender. Among those who are severely wounded by the battle between the sexes, sex becomes exciting only when it is surrounded with suggestions of violence. As Larry Flynt, the owner of *Hustler* magazine, discovered to his profit and sorrow, pornography appeals most to those who like their sex liberally sprinkled with violence. Blood and gore are the real aphrodisiac for the warrior. Hemingway noted in *Death in the Afternoon* that blood and the proximity of death seem to revive the satiated libido.

In our calculus of normality, we are thus forced to conclude that the most frequent adult role assignments, which forbid male tenderness and female toughness, bring paranoia into the heart of the relationships between the sexes and reduce our erotic capacity by half. Since half of those people falling within the circle of friends, family, and fellows we were permitted to love are of the opposite sex, our EQ has been reduced to 25 percent:

**25%: Them, the Enemy, versus Us, the People**
**Women, Caretakers, versus Men, Warriors**

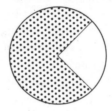

## The Taboo Against Tender Men and Fierce Women

The division between the sexes is also a division within each sex. We are all born with various levels of both male and female hormones and with the capacity for the full range of virtues that is usually assigned to the different sexes. Nowhere is it written in our biological makeup that men may not be tender nor women fierce. Yet, as we saw earlier, most rites of initiation are aimed at inculcating sexual specialization and destroying psychological androgyny. Thus men are forbidden to love one half of their nature —that which is soft, intuitive, sensual, bodily, nurturing. Women are denied muscular intelligence, rational thought, forthright wilfullness, the exercise of power, and the taste of victory. It is an oversimplification of physiology, but not wholly untrue, to say that adult males are produced by crippling the right hemisphere of the brain, and adult females by crippling the left hemisphere. Normal role divisions are a form of *consensual schizophrenia*.

In the modern secular world, we have replaced the quaint mythologies of conflict between male and female gods—Zeus vs. Mother Earth—with abstract terms, but the ancient battle still rages. Now the opposition, and the schizophrenia we impose upon ourselves, is between:

| | | |
|---|---|---|
| the masculine | versus | the feminine |
| logos | versus | eros |
| consciousness | versus | the unconscious |
| intellect | versus | intuition |
| ego | versus | libido |
| duty | versus | desire |
| work | versus | play |
| science-technology | versus | religion-art |
| reason, mind, spirit | versus | emotion, matter, body |
| abstract, quantitative | versus | immediate, instinctive |
| objective knowledge | versus | sensuous, personal feeling |

Since we are forbidden by our social conditioning to love more than one half of our own psychological capacities, our EQ is once again cut in half. It now stands at 12 1/2 percent of our full potential:

**12-1/2%: Them, the Enemy, versus Us, the People
Women, Caretakers, versus Men, Warriors
Feminine Traits versus Masculine Traits**

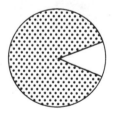

## The War Against Nature

The western myth imposes a further limitation upon the arena within which we may exercise our capacity to love. The nonhuman world, which was once filled with burning bushes, bountiful harvests, bison who sacrificed their lives to feed the people, and other signs that some caring presence was homogenized into nature, has now been reduced to an "it," an infinite system of mindless particles governed by probability, not purpose. Nature, once Mother, has now become a storehouse of resources to be used as we wish to manufacture the machines and consumer goods that are supposed to make us happy. At best, we consider nature an "environment," a kind of zoo without walls, a park in which the scenery must be preserved for backpackers and other voyeurs, or property that may be owned and utilized, a rural factory for agribusiness. The more we see nature as something external to ourselves, the more alien "she" becomes. And the more threatening, the more she must be conquered. When we automatically assume we have the right to probe, slice, rearrange, or harness and control nature, we lose the ancient view that human beings form a community with all sentient beings.

Thus our erotic potential is again reduced by half. The elements —air, earth, fire, and water—and our fellow creatures (except cats, dogs, and other pets), have been banished from our circle of love. Our EQ now stands at 6 1/4 percent of its original capacity:

**6-1/4%: Them, the Enemy, versus Us, the People**
**Women, Caretakers, versus Men, Warriors**
**Feminine Traits versus Masculine Traits**
**Nature, Uncontrolled, Feminine, versus Man, the Controller**

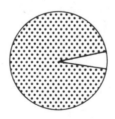

## The Homosexual Taboo

One final item remains in our calculus of the diminishments of normality—homosexuality. As we all know, in Socrates' time in Athens, comrades in arms were literally comrades in arms. The warrior mentality automatically creates homosexual groupings within society. Men form their most significant bonds with other men, women with women. As Robert Brain has shown in *Friends and Lovers,* the warmest bond in most cultures has been not romantic love, but friendship, such as that between David and Jonathan. Pals, bosom buddies, mates, chums, comrades, companions, alter egos have in times past celebrated and ritualized their love, taken blood vows, sworn undying loyalty to each other. Friendship has always been considered erotic, even when custom dictated that there be no "homosexual" expression of love. But, as often as not, close friendships crossed over the firm line we have now drawn between homosexuality and heterosexuality.

As modern society has become homophobic, it has also become philiaphobic. Homosexuality is so feared, especially among "real men," that friendship is rendered difficult. After hearing of the loneliness of men in the course of my many years of leading groups, I have concluded that modern men avoid friendship with other men for fear that any tenderness might be a sign of homosexuality. We dare not touch each other, dare not allow the facade to slip, dare not confess that we are vulnerable, lonely, tired, not in control, that our relationships with women have not given us the intimacy we need, that we fear letting loose of our competitive relationships with each other.

If we allow that modern society grants women slightly more permission for homoerotic feelings than men, we may calculate that the taboos we place on friendship reduce our EQ in slightly different proportions. For men, 3 1/8 percent remains. For women, let us estimate 4 percent:

In constructing this calculus of the systematic diminishment of

**3-1/8%—4%: Them, the Enemy, versus Us, the People
Women, Caretakers, versus Men, Warriors
Feminine Traits versus Masculine Traits
Nature, Uncontrollable, Feminine, versus Man, the Controller
Women versus Women, Men versus Men**

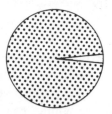

EQ that accompanies becoming a normal adult, we should remember that 3 1/8 percent and 4 percent represent the proportion of our potential that remains *before* we begin to calculate any of the atypical and special injuries we suffer from abusive parents, special hardships, tragic losses, betrayals, and so on. At best, normality exiles us from most of the power and pleasure, the promise of knowledge and love, that is our innate birthright. Our humanity remains eclipsed.

THE ADULT CRISIS: THE UNDECLARED CIVIL WAR

Normal adult character organization is a form of interpsychic warfare between the reigning ego and the guerrilla forces of the repressed anti-ego. The dark and forbidden qualities are disowned and projected onto an enemy, the opposite sex, or nature. We are protected from the knowledge that evil is our own shadow by a taboo barrier between the ego and anti-ego, a kind of Berlin wall that keeps us unconscious. The "authorities" (church-state, mores) with their extended surveillance system of conscience (the watching institution), censor our dreams, our thoughts, and our actions. They enforce the consensus by the blackmail emotions of guilt, shame, and anxiety that threaten us with abandonment and punishment the moment we move toward the forbidden territory. Thus the adult ego struggles to accentuate the positive and eliminate the negative, to live up to the idealized self-image and refrain from doing evil. Being absorbed in the battle between the light and the dark, the adult only rarely (in peak experiences) glimpses the myriad of potentialities that lies beneath the personality in the rainbow of the unknown self.

The systematic diminishing of our potentiality in the socialization process sows the seeds of the crisis of adulthood—the midlife crisis. Our membership and role in society are purchased at the cost of ignoring what is unique, idiosyncratic, amoral, antisocial or asocial within the self. Assuming the mask of personality, constructing a character, starting a family, and making a living requires the major amount of our attention and energy during the first half of life. But sometime near the midpoint, the civil war begins to take its toll and a dis-ease begins to grow within us. At first we may be depressed, life loses its zest. And then we become anxious. The potentialities we have sacrificed begin to surface. The repressed vices and virtues return and begin to force their way into consciousness. Gradually a new vocation, a dim awareness of all the unrealized promises of the self, the voice of the future, begins to make itself heard. Something calls to us to break out of our shell, to abandon our cocoons, to leave the security of personality-position-prestige and begin the solitary journey to the center of the self. Before us opens a new path into an unknown future, excitement, and terror. If we choose to go on the journey, as Dante said, "midway in life we enter a dark wood"; or, as the mystics said, we go into the dark night of the soul.

A majority of people in most cultures in normal times will choose to remain at home within the security of the mythic consensus and the appointed roles. They will avoid solitude, flee from self-knowledge, and remain asleep within the mutual hypnosis of the accepted social order. They will decide to kill or die to preserve the tribe rather than risking living alone. The majority will abort the opportunity of the midlife crisis and make the second part of life a repetition of the stale patterns of the past. As Nietzsche said: "If one has character one also has one's typical experiences that reoccur again and again."[9] They will choose repetition, compulsion, predictability, conformity, and the illusion that "this is how things *really* are" rather than the insecurity of what is new and uncharted. The majority choose to develop their personalities rather than to explore the self or allow the self to be re-created by the spirit.

It is hard to calculate the price we pay individually and culturally for our habit of prematurely ending the journey of the human spirit.

Until modern times, life expectancy was short. Old age began at forty and only exceptional individuals lived long enough to have a midlife crisis. A few shamans, mystics, lunatics, and witches, often with the aid of hallucinogenic drugs, traveled beyond the normal consensual reality; but most people remained within the circle of unbroken myth.

Although few individuals experienced any considerable disease with their parochial consciousness, cultures as a whole often seem to have a midlife crisis and to have committed corporate suicide rather than break out of their mythology. When we look at the magnificent ruins of ancient civilizations, such as the Mayan and Aztec temples and the cities of the Xian period in China, it is hard to avoid the conclusion that most cultures die midway through their natural life span. Their inability to adapt to changing conditions is rooted in the rigidity of their mythology, not in their lack of pragmatic or technical means of solving the problems that beset them. On Easter Island, for instance, the activity of producing the large stone gods became such an obsession that little creative energy was left over for solving practical problems. Mythology and ideology blind and paralyze the group mind. In recent times, we have watched Hitler destroy Germany rather than abandon the Nordic myth of Aryan superiority; we have seen Stalin murder as many as twenty million of his own people to create ideological purity; we have watched Pol Pot commit genocide on the Cambodian people to establish a mythical form of rural communism. And we watch America beginning to bankrupt its economy and imagination by producing arms rather than exchange the myth of American democracy versus communist aggression fo the realities of a world of declining resources, rising expectations, rampant nationalism, and a frightening plurality of power. As have past civilizations, we face the imminent danger of suicide because of our refusal to transcend our mythic horizons.

Every modern society that is in-formed by the western myth maintains its myth not only at the price of possible nuclear or ecological suicide, but by creating a psychology that reduces its citizens to beings whose dignity is defined by their productive capacity and whose journey is declared finished at the point of retirement from labor. Unlike ancient cultures that revered their elders, honored philosophy (the pursuit of wisdom is no game for the young), and dignified old age as the apex of life, modern societies see the aged as obsolete. We worship youth. Our psychology has defined the goal of "maturity" as the construction of a strong ego and a productive social personality. With the possible exception of Erik Erikson and Lawrence Kohlberg, we have scarcely any developmental theory that has the slightest clue what Rabbi Ben Ezra meant when he said, "Grow old along with me, The best is yet to be. The last for which the first was made. . . ." A large part of the despair, loneliness, and confusion of those individuals now undergoing midlife crises is that they have no map that suggests post-normal, post-adult stages of life. Our official maps warn us that beyond the ego lies the edge of the earth, demons, madness, immorality, and death.

In truth, the journey beyond normality is hazardous and full of extremes. But those who decide to stay safely at home risk the boredom and depression that haunts the sedentary spirit. The dis-ease created by identification with the persona may show up in many ways;

For example:

Abandon the quest for your unique self and you will live with the fear that others will abandon you. Your infantile shame will become permanent because your unexplored self will be embarrassed in the presence of the facade you have created.

No matter how much you eat, how many things, or how much

money and power you accumulate, you will secretly feel empty, small, and alone. But you will not allow others to know this shameful secret.

To avoid the void you will (a) keep busy, work, strive always to reach a higher goal; (b) fill the emptiness with entertainment, (vicarious living), recreational eating, drugs, or sex; (c) if mild remedies fail, you may resort to the stimulus of violence or illness; or (d) surrender to passive acceptance. At all costs you will avoid *experiencing* boredom.

No matter what your age you will feel old, exhausted, and at least slightly depressed, although you may keep functioning dependably in your job, your marriage, your role.

You will feel that your life has lost meaning and that you are, somehow, a stranger to yourself.

You will remember times earlier in your life when you had passion and enthusiasm, and will wonder what happened to it.

You will find your horizons shrinking, your body growing more rigid, your sense of adventure drying up.

Your life will seem to settle into a pattern of repetitions, a rat race, the same old anxieties, addictions, habits, and pleasures.

You will wrestle with unwanted fears of death, probably by cancer.

Those who decide to undertake what has always been recognized as the heroic journey into the heart of the self (and beyond) will have many ancient heroes and heroines as guides. They will also be undertaking the journey at a particularly propitious time in human history since our culture is also at the point of its midlife crisis. The western myth is crumbling as the result of its own success. The love affair with the machine and secular potency has brought us to the brink of self-annihilation. Now we must change our basic understanding of the purpose of human life or go the way of the Mayans. Alongside the dominant culture, an alternative culture is emerging. Feminism, the ecological movement, the new physics, the antiwar movement, appropriate technology, humanistic psychology, are the tip of the iceberg of the new myth that grows stronger as the energy crisis and the arms race bring us to the consciousness that we are at an end of the old paradigm. We stand at the edge of understanding the myths, the roles, the political forms that have in-formed our psyches.

The midlife crisis presents us with questions few individuals and fewer cultures have ever had the luxury and necessity to ask themselves: Are human beings more than culturally conditioned, myth-bound, ideological puppets who are bound together by communal paranoia? Do we have the capacity to transcend our programming? Are we condemned to exhaust our substance in interpsychic conflicts, struggles between the sexes, warfare between nations? Is there within us the power-potential-promise to transcend our captivity? Can we create a form of social consciousness based upon compassion and inclusion rather than exclusion? Are we creatures of the spirit? Are we free to become . . . ? Is there life after normality?

# 8.
# The Outlaw

## INDIVIDUATION: LOVE AS THE LAW OF THE SELF (AUTONOMY)

Love makes the law and then breaks it. God, Being, Nature—all speak with a forked tongue. Speaking through his lawyer, Moses, the Great Legislator laid down .the Torah, the commandments. Speaking through his prophet, Jesus, the Great Lover revealed that Spirit is always going beyond the law. Nature teaches the same. lesson. The evolution of life proceeds by an oscillation between regularity and deviation, the rule and the exception, order and chaos. Generations of chimpanzees dutifully wore their hair long and shivered in the trees until some deviant naked ape stood on its hind feet, played with fire, and took up residence in a cave. Each species follows its ancient mores until an individual emerges who tastes the apple, finds a superior way, and forms a new dynasty. Nature is never on the side of mere survival. It restlessly moves to create novelty and complexity. It provides just enough order for us to calculate the probabilities and enough deviation so we can never predict the future with certainty. There is something wild and lawless at the heart of creation. Being is law-abiding. Becoming is an outlaw. Being-becoming-itself is both.

As human consciousness is moved by eros to become as inclusive and powerful as it may, it continually breaks free of yesterday's dogmas. The majority, the folk, abide. They move as one body to the rhythm of the tribal drum, repeating the ancient dances and rituals as exactly as they can to ensure that they will not lose the magic passed on to them by their fathers. The mass, like the normal ego, is conservative. Its law is a repetition compulsion. Its aim is to avoid the novelty and terror of history. Its code of good and evil is sanctified by the authorities. Then along comes an exception, an individual, a breaker of rules. Prometheus steals the fire. Adam and Eve eat of the fruit of the tree of the knowledge of good and evil. Buddha destroys the caste system and reveals the way to extinguish suffering. Socrates discovers dialogue and dialectic as the instrument of eros. Jesus smashes the law of tribal morality, invents forgiveness, and propounds the notion that we should love our enemies. Copernicus, Newton, Darwin, Marx, Freud all insulted the ego of their times and expanded the world.

At first the outlaw is declared a heretic, an atheist, an enemy of the people. But when it becomes clear that the exceptional one is the bearer of the genetic promise of the future, he or she is recognized as a hero and becomes the center of a new cult. After the fact, the authorities praise the courage, the creativity, the genius of the law breaker. The hero who took the lonely journey beyond the norm is proclaimed a certified exception, a demigod who is to be admired, even worshiped, but not imitated. The priests of the new cult move fast to contain the spirit, to make clear to the majority that only the divinely ordained one was justified in breaking the rules. In the second generation, as Max Weber said, the spirit is bureaucratized. The authorities of the tribe repair the hole in the myth.

But things are never the same. Each time the charismatic individual smashes the tribal consensus, human consciousness is expanded. The pool of knowledge grows, and with it the potentiality to love.

But enough apology for the outlaw principle. It is scarce comfort to any person now setting out on the journey beyond adulthood to know that nature sanctions the risk and that some past heroes survived. Permission for the outlaw quest cannot be given by any authority, nor can it be justified by any scientifically verifiable theory of creativity, history, or human nature. The decision to become an individual, to allow oneself to be moved by the deepest impulses of the self rather than the social consensus, can only be made with fear and trembling. It is, by definition, a lonely decision. It necessarily involves anxiety and self-doubt. At first it will seem awkward, embarrassing, unnatural, and will require a high degree of painful self-consciousness. One will stumble and fall often. Frequently, the path will disappear into the brambles. The outlaw will often wonder whether asserting the right to know, to taste, to experience, to judge is not an act of arrogance. The individual's way always is an unbeaten path. It is, as the Katha Upanishad says, "the sharpened edge of a razor, hard to traverse"; but to one who listens to the still, small voice of the erotic conscience, it is also the "gateway to the great liberation." The way is always a fearful risk because it leads so far beyond the boundaries of "normality." Søren Kierkegaard used the model of Abraham's decision to sacrifice his son Isaac to explain that the task of becoming an individual always involves "a teleological suspension of the ethical." Some telos, goal, or good that is higher, wider, more loving than the consensual love-hate of the tribe calls us to undertake a dangerous journey beyond the old definitions of good and evil. To become an outlaw, I must decide that my personal experience rather than the mores of the tribe is the authority upon which I will base my judgments. In a bold act of self-love and self-trust, the outlaw proclaims the individual to be higher than the universal.

## THE MOTIVES OF THE OUTLAW

At first glance, it is easy to confuse the outlaw with the criminal. The name "outlaw" conjures up images of Robin Hood, Bonnie and Clyde, psychopaths, criminals, and con men. Because so few of us in polite society have fully acted out our rebellious impulses, we have a lingering romance with rogues and law-breakers. The lives of Robert Vesco, Charles Manson, Gary Gilmore, and other colorful criminals intrigue us. Through them we vicariously live out our antisocial impulses. But there is a crucial difference between the criminal and the outlaw. The criminal is a perverse rebel who acts out *against* the law, a subnormal person who is unable to care enough about others to bear adult responsibilities. The outlaw is a supranormal individual who cares about others too much to accept the limitations on eros that are imposed by normal life. Thus the outlaw quest moves *outside* and *beyond,* not *against* the law.

## The Outlaw Self

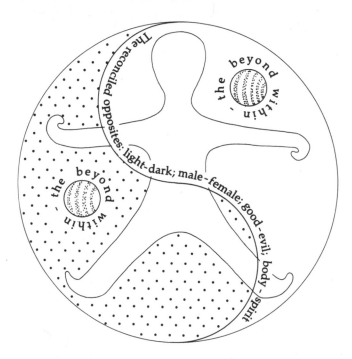

While the rebel is an antinomian, merely rejecting the established, the outlaw is motivated by a quest for autonomy, self-government. The difference between the rebellious mind and the outlaw mind can also be seen in the distinction between antisocial, sociopathic violence and *civil disobedience*. Outlaw consciousness inevitably leads to some form of civil disobedience. A change in identity brings with it a change in the way we see, feel, think, and act. But, clearly, the prophetic protests of Gandhi, Martin Luther King, Daniel Ellsberg, Dorothy Day, the Berrigan brothers, the women's movement, Anatoly Sakarov, Amnesty International, and Solidarity are *not* rooted in any undigested psychological need to rebel, but in a passion for justice, dignity, and freedom. The trans-moral conscience of the outlaw is the inner voice of a universal community that is struggling to be born.

To become an outlaw, I must stand out, dare to become a first person singular, refuse to take refuge in the corporate "we." I must turn inside-out, become inner-directed rather than other-directed. I must turn my back on the consensus and begin an inner journey into the unknown interior, the *terra incognita* of my self. The adventure is inward bound—the discovery of the nature of consciousness.

The criminal uses the knife against others; the outlaw uses the knife to separate the persona from the self. The outlaw uses the warrior's sword to cut through his own character armor to destroy the defense-mechanisms that have kept him imprisoned within the citadel of personality and role. He uses the knife to de/cide, to in/dividuate, to cut himself off from the unconscious life of the majority. The outlaw is the conscious warrior who makes use of aggression to break down the walls, barriers, and boundaries that artificially separate and alienate. As Norman O. Brown says:

> The truth concealed from the priest and revealed to the warrior: that this world always was and is and shall be ever-living fire. Revealed to the lover too: every lover is a warrior; love is all fire.[1]

THE INVISIBILITY OF THE OUTLAW

If we wanted to film the outlaw in action, at what might we point the camera? The child we might photograph in arms. Rebels are always highly visible. Because they need antagonism, they can always be found resisting authorities; their lives are the stuff of documentary movies. A day in the life of an adult would show the details of a man or woman going to work, tending children, saluting the flag, watching TV, buying tomatoes, and so on. But the outlaw?

If we were in traditional India, we might film the outlaw stage in the development of consciousness by focusing on that point in the life cycle when men made a transition from the householder life of action in the world to the contemplative stage. Our camera would show a middle-aged man, having set his economic and domestic affairs in order, taking leave of his family and putting on the robe of a mendicant and taking up a wandering life free from attachments. We would follow him as he begged for his meals, made spiritual pilgrimages to sacred places and renowned gurus and holy men, sat in meditation, and practiced austerities in a cave in the foothills of the Himalayas. We would see him practice the different disciplines of consciousness—breath control, repeating the holy syllable Om, performing acts of devotion to his chosen gods, assuming the acrobatic postures of hatha yoga. If we were to ask him what he was doing, he would tell us he was trying to break through the veil of illusion, dispel maya, and break the cycle of his karma.

In the western world, it is more difficult to make the outlaw stage visible because it has never been officially recognized, ritualized, or given institutional form. In Buddhist countries it is expected that every adult male will spend some time in a monastery learning the art of contemplation. But within Christendom, the practice of retreat and contemplation has been considered a special vocation. The contemplative way, radical reflection on the self, like heart surgery or elevator repair, is considered a vocation to be practiced by specialists—monks, nuns, and philosophers. The avverage person is expected to remain in the active life, unless he or she is unfortunate and unstable enough to have an old-fashioned nervous breakdown or a midlife crisis. Then it is permissible, with the help of a psychotherapist, to probe the depths of the self and ask some radical questions about one's identity.

The most frequent solution to the cinematographer's problem is to show the outlaw quest as a highly dramatic hero story that can be made visible by using allegory and metaphor—a quest for the holy grail, a plunge into the underworld, the ascent of a mountain, a battle with demons, a dreamer awakening. Joseph Campbell in *The Hero with a Thousand Faces* has shown how, universally, the myth of the hero is used to depict the psychological process of gaining self-awareness. In shamanism, the initiate symbolically died, was dismembered, and the spirit took flight with the wild gander. In the earliest known epic, Gilgamesh dives to the bottom of the sea to find the elixir of immortality. In the *Odyssey*, Ulysses, like the prodigal son, goes to a far country, is lost, and has many adventures before returning home. The pilgrim and the knight in search of the grail always undergo many hardships. Alice goes down the rabbit hole, through the looking glass world of the ego. The adventurers in *Mt. Analogue* try to ascend a strange mountain that is not in normal time or space. Don Juan teaches Castaneda how to stop the world, to disrupt his ordinary routines, in order to enter the separate reality.

The problem with focusing our attention on dramatic heroes is that it mystifies outlaw consciousness and leads us to believe it is a special capacity or gift that belongs exclusively to an elite. Ordinary people can't be expected to follow the lead of spiritual genius. Hero tales suggest the price of courage is beyond the ordinary budget. They tempt us to disown the common capacity of the human spirit to transcend normality. It is the vocation of each person to become unique. The normal crises of the life cycle bring each of us to that anxious point where we are invited to step outside the framework of our myth and become conscious.

Therefore, even at the price of losing the poetry and drama, we need to demystify and democratize the process of achieving personal power, individuation, and the adventure of consciousness.

The miracle of consciousness is so mundane and wonderous, so simple and complex, so common and rare, that if we were to film it we might see nothing more spectacular than an ordinary man or woman sitting quietly alone in a room, lost in thought. The only hint of action might be the play of muscles as a frown of puzzlement gave way to a smile of insight. As Hannah Arendt has suggested, the most virile form of action may involve nothing more than thought. The words of Cato she quotes may characterize the true radical action of the outlaw's struggle to become conscious: "Never is he more active than when he does nothing, never is he less alone than when he is by himself."[2] Many of the greatest explorers of human consciousness have been nearly invisible to their peers, their exploits unsung. We can never tell by appearances, often not even by behavior, how much freedom of consciousness a person has won. A quiet woman who has overcome the terror of having been abused as a child, raped as an adolescent, and has learned in spite of everything to take the risk of intimacy may have escaped the prison of her character much more than such flamboyant outlaws as Frank Lloyd Wright or Norman Mailer.

Frequently, outlaws hide on purpose, learn to use masks and disguises to protect the sanctuary of their solitude from hostile observers. Nietzsche, perhaps the greatest philosopher of the outlaw consciousness, said:

> Everything profound loves the mask. . . . It is not the worst things of which one is most ashamed: there is not only deceit behind a mask— there is so much goodness in cunning. I could believe that a man who had something fragile and valuable to conceal might roll through life thick and round as an old green thick-hooped wine barrel: the refinement of his shame would have it so. A man whose shame has depth, encounters his destinies and delicate decisions too on paths which very few ever reach and of whose existence his intimates and neighbours may not know: his mortal danger is concealed from their eyes, as is the fact that he has regained his sureness of life . . .[3]

Much as it may frustrate the moviegoer who demands dramatic models, we must try to describe in a nonmetaphorical way the skills and disciplines necessary to expand consciousness beyond the agonal dualism of the adult mythic mind.

### THE WITNESS SELF: DIS-IDENTIFICATION, DIS-ENGAGEMENT, AND DELIBERATION

Outlaw consciousness is born the moment I drop out, stop the world, cease being an actor identified with the mythic roles I have been playing in society. Change begins when I do nothing except observe. The wisdom of the railroad crossing: Stop. Look. Listen. Meditation is the healthy form of voyeurism: My self watches my ego.

For the adult, all the world is a stage and the personality is the mask one wears to play the assigned role. The outlaw quietly takes a seat in the back row of the theater of the mind and watches the dramatic conflicts created by the unconscious contradictions that rule the personality. I watch myself alternately playing the role of tyrant and victim, sadist and masochist, guilty and innocent. I watch my moods swing back and forth in the neurotic cycle between omnipotence and impotence. I watch the games I play, the habitual postures I adopt—one-up, one-down. I watch how I use charm, status, bluff, money, lies, power, sex, persuasion to manipulate others and get what I want. I watch the costumes, manners, tones of voice, muscle-sets I adopt when I play the role of father, teacher, lover, friend. And I watch how I ease and dis-ease, heal and sicken my self. Above all, I pay intricate attention to the differences between my private and my public selves. (A prime time to catch yourself putting on your personality is in the moments between sleeping and waking. As my friend Howard Thurman once said to me: "Never get into or out of bed in a hurry. Before you go to sleep or when you have just wakened—simmer. Look back over the day. Think about who you were in your dreams. Let your mind roam forward into your intentions for the day.")

But won't self-observation make me horribly self-conscious? Soon I will be like the centipede who tried to figure out how he walked and got so confused that he tripped over his own legs.

No. Self-awareness and self-consciousness are entirely different. When I am "self-conscious," it is really someone else's eyes that are watching, judging, and criticizing me. And I always fail to come up to the standards of the watcher. When, for instance, I am playing tennis, or making love, and I watch my moves to see whether I am playing correctly, it is the eyes of the authorities that are judging me. As Fritz Perls said, this kind of self-consciousness is a mild form of paranoia. The watchers are the prosecuting attorneys in the court of the infantile conscience. I am judging my self by norms that are exterior to my experience. It is these eyes that must be put out if I am to make sense of and remain in touch with my true self. And when we fail to find symbolic ways of destroying the watchers by becoming our own true witness, then the parents or authorities are sometimes literally killed. A recent mass murderer in Santa Cruz killed his mother and ate her eyes. The boy in *Equus* put out the eyes of his gods—the horses.

The self-awareness that grows out of the habit of witnessing is *nonjudgmental.* I look at my actions, my feelings, my experience with soft and compassionate eyes, from a great distance as if I were God or a novelist. The chief rule of the witness is: Judge not. Do not identify with or against anything you observe. The witness must be amoral, a pure phenomenologist. The courtroom of civil conscience must be closed for a time. There is a time when the outlaw switches from contemplation to trans-moral action. But in order to stop the reactionary patterns of thought and behavior that make up the personality, there must be a prior time of inaction.

As I gain skill as an objective and compassionate witness, my identity gradually shifts from my persona to my self. In place of the old compulsive, preprogrammed reactions, I find a growing ability to pause between the stimulus and the response. I cease being merely a biological creature who reacts automatically to steak and potatoes, the lure of immediate sex, or the invasion of my territory; I deliberate and choose what is most desirable. I am no longer captive either to my impulses or to the judgments made upon me by my society. In the newfound silence, I find the freedom to disengage from my old self-images and addictions.

### ADDICTION AND THE TRANSFORMATION OF DESIRE

If there is a single question that is the guiding star of the outlaw's quest, it is: "What do I really desire?" I awaken from the trance that culture has cast over me with the realization that I have been chronically dissatisfied. My life as an adult netted me the standard satisfactions, and yet I lack a sense of fulfillment. Still empty. The culture promises me that if I do, buy, eat, consume, strive, work, my desires will be satiated and I will be happy. But I notice that the carrot of happiness has been dangled in front of me, just beyond my reach for as long as I can remember, and I have never gained on it. It is always still just a step beyond me. And, what's worse, I have been hypnotized by the promise so that I keep going for it, stay in the harness. The moment I turn my eyes from the carrot and ask the radical question about my true desires, I step out of the harness and begin to wander freely in search of what will satisfy my hungers.

The path that leads from the persona to the self, from the adult to the outlaw, consists of learning to distinguish between false desire and true desire, or superficial desire and profound desire, or obsessive desire and free passion, or addiction and the hunger for Being-becoming-itself, or illusory needs and real needs.

One of the easiest ways to pierce through the confusion that surrounds the problem of desire and see how far culture separates us from our deepest desires is to look at addiction. However, it won't help us to pull the usual trick and study those bad people who are drug addicts. The polite majority regularly deludes itself and hides its own erotic crippledness by focusing attention not on the phenomenon of addiction, but upon the officially disapproved substances— the "bad" drugs. If we can limit the problem to chemical dependency upon heroin or alcohol, we can ghettoize the addicts and comfort ourselves with the illusion that the rest of us are normal.

The greatest addiction of all is to our personality—our routines, roles, rigidities. If we were to list the addictions of those who live in modern society in order of popularity, the lineup would be: competition, striving, stress, work, violence, status, food, sex, romance, cigarettes, alcohol, marijuana, hard drugs. If we add the propensity to suffer whether we need to or not, the list is broad enough for us all to find our favorite addictions.

The test for addiction is simple, in theory. Review in your mind those substances, activities, and persons upon which you habitually depend, and contemplate what would happen if any one of them was taken from you.

Next, monitor the panic, anxiety, nameless terror that rises when you think about life without _____ (fill in the blank). Whenever an *inappropriate* quantity of terror or sadness arises, you are in the presence of your addiction. The trick, of course, is to decide what is appropriate. To contemplate losing one of your family, or some person with whom you have a satisfying intimate relationship, triggers a healthy fear. To contemplate being without romance, tobacco, alcohol, sugar, coffee, pot, an automobile, money (beyond what is necessary for survival), or _____ should not produce terror. It is the quantity of fear that gives the clue to the presence of the addictive orientation.

Notice the obsessional character of your need. In back of the outward calm with which I pour the drink, take the fix, count the money, protect the status, make the sexual connection, a small terrified voice cries out: "I need it. I have to have it or . . ." The end of the sentence is lost in chaos. The need is so strong that an illusion is created that it must be fulfilled, or the very existence of the self is threatened. Since addiction roots in infantile needs and fears, any time we tamper with it we restimulate our fear that without mother we will die. The addict never dares run out of a supply of smack, work, or money, because the unspoken sentence is: I must have it or I will die. Addiction is the idolatry of the ego. The addict sets up a false center around which life revolves. Getting the fix is the ritual of the day. Goethe once defined sin as what you can't stop doing. In this sense, addiction is sin because it is a capitulation to the tyranny of a false, idolatrous desire.

In the presence of our addictions, we are not free to ask what we really desire. Eros is silent. The addiction floods us with the noise of its demands, the plans for its satisfaction. There is no interval for deliberation. The urge strikes us, and there is an automatic connection between stimulus and response. I "want" a cigarette and reach for it without thinking. I do not pause to reflect, weight my various desires, and adjudicate them. "Would I rather have the cigarette or the pleasure of breathing easily?"

Addiction destroys love as well as freedom. A lover is willing to be moved. The addict clings to the status quo. The addictive substance is a security blanket, a crypto-mother or father, a fetish. The more it disappoints us, brings us pain, the tighter we grasp it —or, more accurately, the more it holds us in its grip. It always promises a satisfaction it does not deliver—love, adventure, self-esteem. (Notice the implicit promises of sex, adventure, and status that are contained in the advertisements for tobacco, liquor, and automobiles. Black Velvet suggests that liquor is quicker, Dewar that it gives distinction. A man belongs in the desert with his Camel, or riding free with a Marlboro.) The addictive substance is the one certain satisfaction in a capricious world. Home, family, health, friendship may collapse, but the addict holds fast to his habit. Unmoving.

The cure for addiction lies in developing the witness self. When I pause in the presence of my grasping need and do not take a fix, I become capable of surveying a larger field of my desires; then I can decide freely which I will satisfy. Yes, I would like a drink, but I want to remain clear-headed. Yes, I would like to go to bed with you, but I have promises to keep and miles to go before I sleep. The illusion of addiction depends upon keeping the multiplicity of our desires unconscious. When I invite all that I am into awareness I realize that no one substance, activity, or person has the capacity to satisfy me fully. I leave aside the security of the fix and begin the adventure of falling in love with the multiplicity of the self and the world.

DIS-ENCHANTMENT: DEMYTHOLOGIZING PERSONAL HISTORY

In the process of forming an ego, I was bewitched, en-tranced, and enchanted by my culture. Transformation begins by studying trance-formation. Søren Kierkegaard said that the only way we can be released from the enchantment, the siren song of the myths, is to play the music through backwards. To break the spell of the ego I must recover my personal and political history, I must de-mythologize the private, family, and public myths that have informed me. The process of cultural in-formation is reversed by a process of *un-formation*. I must be willing to become dis-illusioned with my images of myself.

The ego, the neurosis of normality, the adult identity, the tribal mind, is a case of repetition compulsion caused by the repression of awareness. The self must re-member the dangerous knowledge that has been exiled in the unconscious. Castaneda's advice (via Don Juan) to "erase personal history" has led a generation of young people into silly rituals of wrestling with spooky enemies, searching for spirit allies and mysterious power spots, and ignoring the personal, familial, and political struggles that must be engaged in order to win freedom.

To know myself I must begin to discriminate between my essence and my accidents, my self and my persona, my "raw" experience and my in-forming myths. And although I must make the effort to distinguish between the content and the form of my life I cannot ever completely separate them. There is no virginal "I," no essence of the self that has not been in-formed, no *tabula rasa*. Nevertheless, when I dare to look at the myths that have informed me, I expand my potential, stretch my eros, free my self. Each part of my story that I recover decreases the power my ego and external authorities have over me and increases the authority of the self. By demythologizing my personal history, I learn to author-ize my self. Midway in life's journey I must pause and re/collect my history. The promise of my future will not be kept unless I begin to write my autobiography. I share my story to invite you to take your story playfully.

For instance:

I might begin my psychological striptease, demythologizing my personal history, by looking at what's in a name—Keen.

The Keen clan had its myth. We were keen, sharp, perspicacious, and superior by dint of hard work and good business sense. Granddad and his brood were known for sharp trades and firm beliefs. It was said that they were frequently wrong, but seldom in doubt. Dad half escaped the mold. He was too sensual and emotional, loved wandering and playing the fiddle too much to make a good merchant or preacher. He lived more freely than his brothers and sisters, but paid the price of feeling that he should have been more successful.

The McMurray clan, my mother's people, were educators and leaders in the church. They were among the best people in any Presbyterian town and took pride in good food and serving the less fortunate. Mother drank deep of Scotch virtue, but not whisky, and had the Calvinistic love for religion and true doctrine, rightly defined and fundamental.

As I search for my original face, I must remember the myths of the Keens and McMurrays, and gently try to remove them from *my* consciousness like the restorer of an ancient painting lifts layers of paint from an old canvas. Who would I have been had Dad been French and Mother Polynesian? What if I had been a Goldberg, a Kakalski, a Smith? How would my mind and body have been different? My desires?

My place within the family inscribed another layer of myth on my consciousness. I was the second-born son. Research has shown that birth order has a definite effect upon personality. Number twos, like Avis, try harder but do not always succeed as well as number ones (who have seniority and the natural right to lead). Second children are more introverted, more aware of the unspoken tensions in the family. They are less overtly aggressive, but always ready to steal the birthright of number one by the use of charm and "understanding." They are natural mediators.

As I fumble around trying to repair a simple carburetor on my lawnmower (I would rather use the push mower), I know I am all thumbs because of the family script. I hear the often-told stories that assigned me certain virtues and denied me others: "Oh, Sam is like his Dad, sensitive but not mechanical. Lawrence [my brother] has always been a mechanical genius. When he was two-and-a-half years old he took the lawnmower apart and his Dad couldn't put it back together. Finally, Lawrence took over and got it back the way it belonged." Imagine my surprise at age thirty when I was tested for a factory job and found I was in the upper 5 percent in my ability to see mechanical relationships. How different would life have been had I put together pieces of steel rather than chains of ideas?

To recover my personal history, I might go through my life year by year. I recall the stories told and retold around the dinner table, the heroes whose virtues were applauded and the villains whose wicked, wicked ways were condemned. Would I be writing a book about eros had not my sensual nature been so encouraged by Dad's example, and my sexual explorations so discouraged by John Calvin? I recall especially the stories about my earliest years that my parents told. "Sam was always asking questions. At four he listened to the Bible story about Moses and the burning bush and asked, "Didn't God make the whole world?" "Yes," Mother replied. "Then if Moses took off his shoes because he was standing on holy ground, shouldn't we always go barefoot?" I wonder, was the philosopher's quest/ion always stirring in my blood even before I was in-formed by my parents' hopes and beliefs?

Let me jump from personal to political myth. By accident or predestination, I was born a WASP, which placed me automatically among the privileged. As we all know, WASPs are more equal than others. We are naturally endowed (by "In God We Trust," who ordained that the accumulation of capital—the sacred $—was the sign of grace) with all the qualities that make for success. We are trustworthy, loyal, helpful, friendly, courteous, kind, obedient, cheerful, thrifty, brave, clean, and reverent. And, yes, I naturally became an Eagle scout, along with General Westmoreland, Gerald Ford, and General Bonesteel III. Quite without knowing it, I was in-formed by the unofficial myth of white supremacy, which, though forbidden by law, nevertheless remains etched in the American psyche. By osmosis I took in a scheme of unconscious valuation that assumed that virtue declines as (1) we go from north to south (people who inhabit warm countries are lazier than Northern Europeans); (2) skin tones get darker (browns and blacks are definitely lower on the scale of civilization than whites); (3) height decreases (westerners who tower over orientals are naturally superior); (4) the use of muscles increases (head work is more valuable than bodywork, intellectuals are more valuable than laborers. People who, like the blacks, have rhythm and love to dance, have bad morals. A swinging pelvis bakes no bread); (5) the love of smell and strongly spiced food increases (cleanliness is next to godliness); and (6) the love for bright color increases (the best people dress in grey or black. Tweed at best).

How can I begin to think who I would be were I stripped of my WASP credentials and prejudices? Once upon a fevered hallucination, I thought for a long time that I was an old black woman, a sharecropper in rural Florida dying in poverty. When I awoke and came to myself, I was both glad and ashamed to be a WASP.

The process of education added several layers of mythical information to my psyche. Along with the mystical properties of money, the value of education is unquestioned. Knowledge is power. And schooling is the path to knowledge. By the time I graduated from Harvard and Princeton, I knew about explanatory power: Whoever has the fastest tongue and the most convincing explanation wins the minds, and eventually the hearts, of others. I learned to trust in words and cultivate the gift of gab. The better I got at my discipline, the more of an expert I became. Recently, I have wondered what kind of mind I would have if I had *not* learned to read so early, had *not* been introduced to so many abstractions so young, if I had cultivated what Aldous Huxley called "the non-verbal humanities"—the art of listening, smelling, touching, dreaming, silence, moving. Schooling unconsciously taught us all a dogma that has not yet been questioned. As my fifteen-year-old nephew said, "The main thing schools teach you is to take life sitting down." The sedentary, urban, abstract, professionalized modes of thought that characterize my educated mind are part and parcel of having been schooled. How different the balance of my senses, my metaphors for life might have been had I been raised as a Hopi. Without my BA STB ThM MA PhD, I might now be a rancher rounding up horses rather than ideas.

Maleness forms another layer of my myth and character armor. Anatomy certainly had something to do with my destiny. But the genderal assignments that were grafted onto the biological fact of my maleness taught me some foolish lessons about "being a real man." Men don't cry. Control yourself. Be a winner. Real men, like Clark Gable, Clint Eastwood, Joe Namath, Alexander Haig, and Ronald Reagan have no self-doubts. They think positively, are always potent, and keep women in their place—which is above men on the pedestal and beneath them in the pecking order and the bedroom. Subtract the cockiness from me and who would I be? How do I separate my self from the mythology of gender?

My mask is tinted with the red, white, and blue. I am an American. From my earliest memory, I have pledged allegiance to the flag and to the republic for which it stands. One nation under God, in whom we trust to bring the Pax Americana to the world. I remember the time before the myth was tarnished when we still believed America was a sacred crusade and we killed the Hun and the Jap to protect freedom. And, in spite of the atrocity of Vietnam and our continuing nuclear folly, I still shiver a bit when I hear, "Oh, beautiful for spacious skies, for amber waves of grain." Because I have worked on wheat harvests in Kansas, and ranches where you couldn't see the nearest neighbor, and have traveled from coast to coast a score of times. I feel this country as part of my body. How different I would be had I not grown up in a country with an open frontier, space for the individual to grow, and a high degree of freedom. For, as Hannah Arendt says, it is even harder to think freely than to act freely under the conditions of political tyranny. Who would I have been if I did not have the freedom to think, to criticize, to propose changes?

Finally, my body-mind has been deeply in-formed by the western myth. Without second thoughts, I have had a promiscuous affair with machines. Early I lusted after and consummated my desire for a Model A Ford roadster, later a red convertible. I pop up toast, fly the friendly skies of United, filter the world through TV, thank God for X-rays and microtechnologies that probe my body for signs of illness. I move through time to the cadence of the clock that cuts my days into minutes and hours. The fear of the bomb has polluted the atmosphere of my mind and done violence to my hopes since August of 1946. My fortune rises and falls with inflation and depression. I am addicted to money and to buying what I need to survive. Making a living has consumed much of the energy of my adult years. And when some sacred green and windswept spirit, some intimation of the eternal significance of my time, moves through the heart of my self, it must still battle a positivistic turn of mind and a mean-spirited secularism that denies the existence of the holy. Being modern, I am half machine and must struggle to remain in touch with my flesh. And yet I do not know how I would survive without technology. The demon and I live in an uneasy marriage.

And so on. The process of peeling away the layers of familial, economic, political, and religious myths that have in-formed my image of myself is endless. Demythologizing the personality is a task of a lifetime, and is never complete. Consciousness is always involved in escaping from past limitations. The religious hope for complete enlightenment—a form of consciousness free from every trace of myth—is an illusion. Next year I will find that this year's identity is too small to encompass my experience. Guru Bawa, a wise and holy man from Ceylon who now makes his home in Philadelphia, once said to me: "Truth is too large for us to grasp. We are like men rowing a boat. We make progress toward the truth if we keep pushing illusions in back of us."

## METANOIA: REPENTANCE AND THE REVOLUTIONARY MIND

It is by turning, turning, turning that we come round right. Freedom is a circle dance in which we turn away from the persona and toward the self. It is a matter of conversion. The great Hassidic mystic, the Baal Shem Tov was said to have been an ordinary man until the day he "turned around and walked out the back door of his own mind."

The adult mind is rooted in consensual paranoia. The outlaw's chief discipline is the opposite of paranoia—*metanoia.* Metanoia is repentance, reowning the shadow, turning around, having the flexibility to adopt many different perspectives.

There are many ways we may talk about metanoia.

The ancient maps that chart the stages of human life recognize that midway we must begin a long process of purification and repentance. Before we enter paradise, we must spend a season in purgatory.

In the old religious language, repentance involves the confession of sin. "We have all sinned and fallen short of the glory of God." However, confession and repentance aren't feeling sorry for peccadillos, but seeing how we have been captive inside the machine of personality, a prisoner of ideologies, an automaton manipulated by defense mechanisms. The evil we previously objectified and assigned to exterior agents—devils, communists, capitalists, chauvinists, faithless lovers, the system—must be discovered within. We can no longer divide the world between good and evil. The line between saints and sinners runs down the middle of my being. As Pogo said, "We have met the enemy and he is us."

In psychoanalysis, the patient wins a new freedom only after an agonizing process of transference, projecting infantile feelings of dependency and rage onto the therapist, and then re-owning the projections. It is the work of years, perhaps a decade.

In the tantric scheme (see Appendix A), purgation, the work of the fifth chakra, depends upon taking the warrior energy and weapons and turning them against the ego. Before we can become enlightened, we must express all our hidden thoughts, dare to face our projections. We must take responsibility for the devils and demons we have created by our own disowned tendencies for evil, as well as for the angels and saviors in whom we invest our own power for goodness.

Metanoia means the end of power politics. I make unilateral initiatives. I break down the defense mechanisms that keep me from life. I destroy my propaganda machine that automatically casts me in a favorable light and others in the shadow. I disestablish my Pentagon.

Metanoia is hazardous to once-born healthy-minded adults. Normal people follow Satchel Paige's advice: "Don't ever turn around, something might be gaining on you." When I turn, I find that something is gaining on me—death, the darkness, the "negative" emotions I have run from for a lifetime. But, to be twiceborn, I must face my own hostility, my fear, my rage, my disappointment, my resentment, my anxiety, my boredom, my terror, my helplessness, my confusion, my ambivalence. All of the rejected images flood into my consciousness. I see myself hating the very people I also love, filled with dark desires—incest, rape, sadism, infanticide (especially at three A.M. when the baby cries). The dark, wiggly, and wicked side of me slithers to the surface. I am no longer nice or pleasant. My "won't power" replaces my will-power. The power of positive thinking gives way to the honesty of allowing negative feelings. To re-own my shadow, I must enter the dark night of the soul and learn the wisdom of endarkenment.

The practice of metanoia requires the rarest type of courage—the courage to be wrong, to repent, and to begin again. Magical thinking always tempts us to believe that we can purchase enlightenment without coming to know our darkness, that we can be saved by some vicarious savior, that we can be reborn without having to die. But in the moral world inhabited by persons who have chosen to know themselves, the path to healing involves the painful knowledge of how we dis-ease ourselves. The way we may find peace is by turning off the machine that manufactures enemies.

There are cases in which whole tribes or nations acknowledge their guilt, break their own myth, and waver on the edge of corporate metanoia. After World War II, Germany and Japan went through an upheaval in consciousness and a measure of repentance. For a brief time, after the blood bath of Vietnam, America questioned its self-righteousness. But true corporate repentance is difficult. Tribes and nations cannot exist long without a scapegoat and a ritual enemy upon whom to project their guilt. As yet, we have developed no "moral equivalent to war," no recognition that our common enemies are poverty, ignorance, disease, and the making of war.

Thus metanoia and the development of a genuine prophetic consciousness begins with the solitary individual. The discipline is always lonely. The moment I step outside my adult identity, it becomes obvious that my tribe is not significantly different than other tribes in its habitual projection of blame for conflict onto an enemy. It is disturbing for an individual to reject the tribe's claim to self-righteousness because it excludes him or her from the civil religion, the social immortality system, and the ritual of scapegoating, in which guilt is alleviated by being assigned to an outcast or enemy that the tribe may destroy in the name of God.* The dissenter who makes a separate peace will be called a traitor or a coward. It requires a great deal of personal power to abide unpopular knowledge. If loyalty to the mores of the group are the essence of morality, then clearly any compassionate individual must discover a basis for identity beyond morality.

But the loneliness of the outlaw creates the beginning of a new communion. Courage en-courages others. Once I have dared to repent, I find that I am not alone. There is a communion of men and women like myself who know themselves to have mixed motives, to be motivated at times by greed, to have a tendency to blame, to be animated by an antagonistic mind. The authentic outlaw is not the splendid beast of Nietzsche, not the *ubermensch*, the superman, the warrior, the master of the earth who is superior to the masses and might become the ruler of a purified society in the future. Far from it. The real outlaw is one who knows that all men, women, and communities are foolish and fallible, and that the pretense to self-righteousness is a prelude to violence. Since the human condition is to be a fragment and a fool (pretending not to be a fragment), our true safety lies in learning to forgive one another.

Forgiveness is the most radical way of moving beyond the law of history. It is by the act of forgiveness that we really step outside of the law of self-justification and power politics that governs the intercourse between nations, the battle between the sexes, and the civil warfare within our personalities. The history of the ego and the tribe is the story of the clash between the righteous and the enemy. The Hatfields and the McCoys, the Arabs and the Jews, the ego and the id are locked into a cycle of reaction and revenge. The law is an eye for an eye, a tooth for a tooth, blood for blood. The same old story. Warfare is the most boring of all human enterprises. Only the weapons are new. The warrior's mind is old, static, reactionary, driven by the old law—the obsessive compulsive cycle of self-righteousness and revenge. The only way to

*For a complete analysis of this process, see Ernest Becker's *Escape from Evil*.

break the law and introduce the spirit into human affairs is to practice the discipline of metanoia and forgiveness. We can never begin anything new without forgiveness.

Repentance and forgiveness change the fundamental structure of consciousness from antagonism to compassion. When I know my shadow, I know that "they" are like me. We share a common human nature. The 50 percent of the human race I cast into the category of aliens are fellow humans who, like myself, are faulted, filled with contradictory impulses of love and hate, generosity, and a blind will to survive. As I look at them, I realize we may have conflicts of interest, we may both want to occupy the same territory, but we are equally human. Neither of us is the righteous arm of the one true God, the defender of the Truth. When the face of the enemy is humanized, the issues separating us may be mediated. Conversation or dialogue rather than annihilation becomes the new model for conflict resolution. Metanoia brings the enemy within the circle of co-promising, conversation, and compassion, and restores half of my lost eros.

### OUTLAW SEXUALITY: AN END TO THE BATTLE BETWEEN THE SEXES

Metanoia also signals an end to the battle between the sexes. If identity is no longer centered around the need to combat an external aggressor, then the male no longer need think of himself primarily as a warrior. If battle, competition, conquest, and control cease to be the organizing metaphors, then the relationship between the sexes changes radically. There may be an end to the missionary position, to sadomasochism, to the superior-inferior game, to one-upsmanship, and any game in which there must be a loser.

Just as the outlaw consciousness demythologizes the enemy by re-owning its propaganda, it also demythologizes the rhetoric about the sexes. I must approach the opposite sex with a new innocence, an awareness of my ignorance, an act of genderal repentance. Male and female have created each other in the image of their fears and needs; we have imprisoned each other in roles for so long that we know the other only as stereotype. The result of this mutual conspiracy is that we don't know how many of our sexual differences are biological and how many are the result of behavioral conditioning. In sexual repentance, we see clearly the distorted faces we have painted upon one another. We cannot yet imagine our original sexual nature, our native carnality.

Outlaw sexuality is based on the same principle as the rest of outlaw consciousness—the quest for autonomy. When I lay down the burden of being superman, I am not initially certain about what I really want. What do I desire? What is the law of my own sexuality? For most people, the outlaw stage involves a period of experimentation beyond the boundaries of normal sexuality—breaking the taboo. For some, it involves homosexuality or adultery; for others, the reversal of the normal roles. Men must break the tenderness taboo and learn the virtues of softness—including the mode of making love with a soft-on. Women must learn to cease being victims and receptacles and learn the virtues and pleasures of firmness, focus, and aggression. In a sexually obsessive culture, our desires have become so highly sexualized that a period of voluntary celibacy is usually necessary for us to discover what passions we have that do not involve the sexual connection.

More than half in jest, I suggest that outlaw sexuality begins with a celebration of impotence and frigidity. We must embrace what we have feared.

To all lovers, the worst eventually happens. He says "yes" and she says "yes," but it says "no." He commands it to stand at attention, but it remains at ease. She pleads with the juices to flow, but they remain frozen. He is impotent. She is frigid. The key is bent. The lock is stuck. The gates of paradise are fast shut.

It's hell for both of them. They are cut off from the highest good, exiled from the kingdom of the coming. It is particularly grievous because the news of the day is filled with hints that everywhere sexually liberated couples are flocking to the utopian state of multiple orgasm.

He is unmanned. His ego is limp. He questions his masculinity, or suspects that she is just not hot enough to turn him on. He may try harder, only to find that it gets softer. He moves from fear to panic. He runs to easier women to reassure himself, or avoids women, or takes Vitamin E and begins jogging.

She questions her femininity. She can fake it, but that leaves her an unmoved spectator at a painful charade. She accuses him of being insensitive to her needs and suspects that he is too chauvinistic to understand her. She avoids men or looks for the prince whose magic wand will turn her into an erotic princess.

If they are bound together in wedlock, they endure their shame and lower their expectations. After all, sex doesn't matter that much, does it? Or they fight about whose fault it is. Or they read books that explain how joyful and natural it is and encourage them to get out of the missionary position. Or they go into therapy, and talk, and talk, and talk about what is not happening. And when all else fails, they go to the sex clinic where the white-coated Drs. Masters and Johnson cure them of their sexual dysfunction by teaching them to get pleasure by giving pleasure.

Stop!

What if we flipped things over, changed perspectives?

What if we played with a wild hypothesis that impotence and frigidity were not dysfunctions to be cured, but events to be celebrated?

What if impotence is not a power failure, but a coded message to be deciphered?

What if frigidity is not a shame to be endured, but an announcement about an emerging passion?

What if every authentic lover must pass through the valley of the shadow of impotence or spend a season in frigidity?

What if the genitals, like the heart, have a wisom that is deeper than the mind?

What if women who have never been frigid are impotent; and men who have never been impotent are frozen?

Words often give us the thread of Ariadne that leads out of the maze. Impotent: lacking in power, strength, or authority. The male crisis is a power failure, an energy crisis. A man may normally be cold and calculating, but no one will question his masculinity so long as he retains his defining characteristic—power. A man is a man so long as his gun is loaded and his tool is sharp. Frigid: very cold, markedly lacking warmth or ardor. The female crisis is a temperature inversion, an unexpected cold front in a normally warm area. A woman is warm-blooded. She may be dumb, dependent, and powerless, but her femininity is not questioned so long as she keeps her warmth. If she wants to be cool and sharp, she will be praised for thinking like a man and cursed for being castrating.

The current epidemic of frigidity and impotence reflects a change in the body politic, a revolution in self-understanding. Stereotypes are crumbling. Some very manly men are opting out of the power game and refusing to be warriors. Those who are secure enough to be soft have begun to see that there is a contradiction between following a path with heart and the accumulation of power—atomic or personal. Some very feminine women are learning the joy of assertion and discovering that power may be an aphrodisiac. The genitals are the bellwether of our changing images of man and woman. They are in open rebellion against the old tyranny. No more exploitation! The head commands the genitals to perform. They refuse. When you order an erection and it does not appear, you have an insurrection. When the privates refuse to march in public, the government is overthrown. Some generals and head men react by trying to impose law and order: Use will-power and firepower to force the rebels to obey. But the tyrannical effort to repress any member of the body politic eventually leads to a full-scale civil war. The only way to restore harmony within the body politic is to respect the demands of the rebels. Listen, negotiate, change. Justice means allowing every voice to be heard.

If a man could listen to all the voices within himself and respect the plurality of his emotions, he could speak clearly about his ambivalence. Then his penis would not have to bear the burden of his stuttering communication. What is the tongue-tied man trying to say by the gesture of impotence? The message is always mixed. It may be:

No.
Not now.
I don't feel desire.
I am not ready to be intimate with you.
I don't know you well enough yet.
I'm afraid you will swallow me up, take all my time, energy, freedom.
I'm afraid I am not a good enough lover to satisfy you.
I'm afraid of the consequences.
I'm afraid to lose control.
I'm angry.
I don't want to give you pleasure.
I want to punish you for betraying me, ignoring me, using me, not taking me seriously.
I don't trust you.
I choose to withhold myself from you.
I resent your demands.
I am tired of pretending I am always powerful and in control.
Sometimes I am small and frightened and I want to be held.
I don't want to *do* anything.
I want you to make love to me.
I am tired of making it.
I want to lie back and be soft and let it happen.
I don't want to make love until I feel trust, tenderness and desire.

And what fears, desires, and unspoken questions are coded within frigidity? When the unguents do not flow and a woman is not moved to passion, what is the message her body is uttering by its refusal? It may be any of the unstated fears or hopes that lie in back of male impotence. But the woman's voice has its own accent. Her gesture may also mean:

I am not moved.
I do not feel desire or love.
I do not want to be that vulnerable.
I am tired of being an object—a piece, a chick, a cunt, a wife, a thing.

If you do not want to engage my mind and my heart you cannot
    enter into my body.
I'm not ready yet; take more time; touch me.
I want to be by and for myself now; independent.
I am free to be closed or open.
I don't want to be passive; I want to make love to you but my
    aggression frightens you.
I am afraid that if I lose control I will overwhelm you, or myself.
I feel guilty.
I have been hurt too much in the past and I am still afraid.

The images we create recreate us. The old icons showed men and
women as different species. Iron-hard men and flesh-soft women.
Clint Eastwood and Catherine Deneuve. The Marlboro man and
the Breck girl. Ever-ready men and willing women. Now a new
image is emerging, a new ideal of the complete person. S/he has
the capacity and the need to combine the opposites previously
assigned to the separate sexes. The new person is aggressive and
tender, adventurous, and committed.

The passage from old ways to new ways is turbulent. Men often
feel unmanly when they first abandon making, doing, and controlling and begin to feel warm and welcoming. It seems so passive to
wait and wonder. Women are usually awkward when they first try
to move with angular force. Their slogans—"Womanpower"—
testify more to aspiration than achievement. Anger, long repressed, does not emerge nicely.

Beneath the confusion of sex roles and the new impotence and
frigidity, a new person is being born. It is time now for us to listen
to our deepest desires and to learn from each other. Time for a new
dialogue between power and love, the hard and soft ways of being
in the world.

By demythologizing our sexual stereotypes and proclaiming an
armistice (arm-in-arm rather than up in arms), we reclaim the
opposite sex as friends. Sexual or genderal metanoia allows us
to reclaim an additional 50 percent of the eros we disowned
when we agreed to become adults. Man and woman, dissolv-
ing their ancient enmity, may finally become teachers to each
other.

## ANDROGYNY: SELF-ROMANCE

The quest for Androgyny is the outlaw's equivalent of the adolescent longing for the one fulfilling romance. It is the introverted version of the old love story—man meets woman and they live happily ever after. Only now it is animus meets anima and the self lives happily, and self-sufficiently, ever after. The myth of the androgyne, like the romantic myth, is a necessary but not final stage in the transformation of eros.

The quest for androgyny follows naturally on the heels of demythologizing the enemy and ending the battle between the sexes. To reclaim the full range of the eros of the self, I must heal the schizophrenia that exists within myself between my "masculine" (approved and socially reinforced, since I am a male) and my "feminine" side (disowned, repressed, and therefore largely unconscious). Jung says the task of individuation involves the male in exploring his anima, his feminine side, which has previously been glimpsed only as it was reflected in his attitudes toward the women he loved and hated. The female must explore her animus, the masculine aspect of her psyche previously vicariously acted out for her by the men whom she loved and hated. Exploring the anima involves the man in examining how he relates to his soul. Exploring the animus involves the woman in examining how she relates to the external world. In the course of individuation, we lose the capacity to "fall in love" with another persona because we are in the process of falling in love with the self.

The fledgling shaman would often wear the clothes of the opposite sex in an effort to gain the knowledge of the other half of the psyche. Greek mythology portrayed Tiresias as the wisest of men because he had spent several years as a woman. In tantric symbolism, the reintegration and transformation of the person involves an erotic conversion. The female and the male deities turn to face each other. The embracing couples in the erotic statues on Indian temples are symbolic of the intercourse that takes place within the self. Individuation involves an intrapsychic love affair between reason and emotion, aggression and surrender, wonder and action

The erotic mind must be able to work and to play, to follow a disciplined linear path of logic, and to flow lazily through a tumbling stream of free associations.

Perhaps the simplest way to explore androgyny is to inhabit the characters of the opposite sex who appear in your dreams. It is easy to overlook the revelation that is contained in our "sexual" dreams, because we take sex so literally. Even the simplest dream about sex is about much more than sex. The sexual relationships in a dream are also symbolic of the relation of the masculine and the feminine within the self. By playing at psychodrama, our dreams will tell us much about parts of the self that are still alien to each other.

For instance:

I dream I am having intercourse with a young dark woman. She is dirty, but her smell excites me. No sooner do we finish than she runs away, laughing, to play with her friends.

On the surface, the dream is about simple sexual gratification. But my personality has been in-formed by the WASP ethic, which equates the good with being white, clean, pure, adult, serious. A voice calls to me in sleep, an invocation from a neglected part of myself that says: I am young, dark, and full of delight. I follow my instincts, accept pleasure easily, am uncomplicated and innocent. The woman in my dreams is my dark anima, the conscience of my carnal self recalling me to the wisdom of my body. She is the Song of Solomon singing in my ear: "I am black, but comely." No Calvinist she.

I dream that I come upon four men who are undressing a young woman. She cooperates with them, helps take off her clothes. I fear that they are going to rape her and throw her over a cliff. But she seems naively ignorant of the atmosphere of violence. I consider reporting the incident to the police, but feel double-bound. After all, she is consenting. What right do I have to interrupt?

When I identify with the males in the dream, I am a rapacious man who links sex and violence. I degrade the woman by ignoring her individuality. I have the courage to rape only in the company of the gang. In other words, I am the typical adult macho male. But in the dream I am also the moral observer who is shocked by the actions of my fellow men—my rapacious self—but I don't know what to do about my moral dilemma. And the authorities, the police, are of no help.

When I identify with the woman, the plot thickens. From some level beneath my image of myself as an aggressive and potent male, a message comes to me that says: I am a willing victim. I hide within my naivete. I play the masochist. I go along with the desires of the male gang even though I may be raped and injured, even killed, because I am unconscious of my own feelings and I ignore my intuitive sense of danger. I do violence to my anima.

When I remember the men and women of my dreams during my waking hours, I pause to reflect how often I aggressively march through the day, bending all obstacles to my single will, and how little I savor the feast of pleasure that is momentarily presented to my senses. Gradually, my persona and my self enter into a conversation and finally into a satisfying intercourse. I continue to work, but now more slowly. I pause frequently to enjoy the ray of sun that is now warming my skin, the rhythm of my breath, the kaleidoscope of images that floats up from my unconscious in the form of daydreams. When I move along the edge of awareness gracefully and am able to be active and receptive in alternating moments, I love the interplay within myself. At such times, solitude is rich and it is a great pleasure for me to be with my self. I want no one, male or female, to interrupt my intercourse with my self. My androgynous consciousness is playing with all the edges of awareness, dipping into a storehouse of memories, tickling new images into being, slipping into the stream of sensations, marching to the brass band of a new synthesis of ideas, plunging into the thick world of feelings.

In recent years, there has been much confusion about androgyny. Under the impact of rising feminism and plummeting masculinity, some have used the notion of androgyny to promote the unisex person. Radical feminists have made common cause with Skinnerians and have rejected the old idea that anatomy is destiny, proclaiming that all the differences between the male and female psyches are a product of social conditioning. Maternal instinct can be created or eradicated by behavioral modification. There are no innate masculine or feminine qualities. We are not both masculine and feminine, but neither. Thus, for those who believe in the social engineering approach to the psyche, androgyny has come to mean the new ideal of the unisex person, a person whose body might be male or female but whose psyche has no distinguishing marks. In the most radical forms of feminism and behavioral modification, the old Gnostic dualism creeps in in a new form. Nature makes the body, but society—the new god—makes the psyche. The dignity of the person is not related to anything so crude as anatomy or any of the biological functions, such as child-bearing. This form of argument usually goes along with the devaluation of the womb and the penis, the elimination of the vaginal orgasm, the elevation of the clitoris, and the celebration of the vibrator. With liberating masturbation, sex became a do-it-yourself project.

Unfortunately, the unisex solution distorts the mystery of sexuality in the effort to free us from the crippling effects of genderal stereotyping. It took a combination of God and mammon to create us male and female. Many of society's assignments are artificial and destructive, but there are radical differences between the sexes. Research into the differences between male and female brains and biochemistry is not conclusive, but it is generally agreed that the female brain is less lateralized than the male and that body chemistry, not conditioning, accounts for many differences. Donald Symons sums up the results of the research on hormones and patterns of sexuality:

> Data on late-treated AGS women [women who were masculinized *in utero* by progestins] suggest that some aspects of human sexuality, such as object choice, result largely from post natal experiences; but these data also suggest that the male's tendencies to be sexually aroused by visual stimuli, the specifically genital focus of male sexual arousal and relief, and the autonomous, fantasizing, initiatory, appetitive, driving aspects of male sexuality result largely from interactions of the affects of prenatal androgens on the developing brain; the activating effects of

postpubertal androgens on a brain already biased in a male direction; and peripheral stimulation from the genitals.[4]

We are neither completely determined nor completely free from the givens of our anatomy and gender. To be fully free and fully erotic, the self must abandon the artificial limits imposed by the social definitions of gender, but cherish the essential differences. Needless to say, there is no simple or scientific way to determine definitively which are artificial and which essential. As I witness the gulf between my male persona and my experience of myself as a sexual being, I find that I must decide for myself what it means to be a man, and I must still confront the mystery of the woman. The unisex alternative denies the radical difference between the sexes in a politically motivated effort to secure dignity and social and political equality. Male and female are of equal worth but of different natures.

Androgyny has also been taken to mean bisexuality. The most radical proponents of the sexual revolution announced that if we were freed from the cultural repression and the strait jacket of sexual roles, we would all be bisexual. In our unadapted state, the argument goes, we swing both ways. Whether this is true we have no way of knowing, since human beings are always socialized by a group that imposes some artificial genderal definitions. But even if bisexuality could be demonstrated to be a more unadapted choice than heterosexuality, it would still be no resting place on the pilgrimage of consciousness. Bisexuality still literalizes the myth of eros. It sublimates at the genital level a quest for fulfillment that must permeate every aspect of a person's life.

It is easy to see why the reunion symbolized by the quest for androgyny is a necessary but not final stage in the life of passion if we remember that the adult personality was created by a process of division. When we reach the outlaw stage, we must reunite what society has pulled asunder. Since it has introduced a false either/or (be either masculine or feminine) the outlaw must affirm the principle of both/and. I contain both of the supposedly contradictory virtues. I embrace the dichotomies.

St. Paul says that in Christ there is neither male nor female. I think this cryptic statement is a clue that indicates that there is a point in the trajectory of the self at which we go beyond the question of gender. When I ask the outlaw question, "Who am I?" and vow to have the courage to explore any feelings, fantasies, ideas, and thoughts (but not all actions), I pass beyond androgyny to a more radical form of self-love. It is not that I cease to be a man or a woman. Only that I become absorbed with a more embracing question than that of my gender. Until the end of my days I will be biologically a male. As an outlaw, or a lover, I may still experience the desire for genital sexual expression only with a woman. Or perhaps I might be moved by the desire for a homosexual expression. Or bisexual. It is difficult to speculate what kinds of sexual object choices we would make if we were free from the dis-ease of genderal schizophrenia and the obsessive concern with the sexual connection. As we will see, looking back from the perspective of the lover, the question of hetero, homo, trans, or bi is not of great importance.

For the moment, we need only note that the quest for androgyny has brought us to a point in our journey where the outlaw has begun to heal within his or her self the erotic wounds incurred in the process of becoming an adult. We now begin a more far-reaching exploration of the post-normal self.

## SELF-LOVE, SELF KNOWLEDGE: THE MENAGE À MOI

The taboo against self-knowledge and self-love guards the boundary between the adult and the outlaw. Self-knowledge is an offense against the authorities, self-love a crime. The conspiracy of membership in the tribe can be maintained only so long as the majority consent to be in-formed by the established myth, mystery, and authority. Conscience makes conformists, citizens, and cowards of us all.

The taboo is maintained in part by a verbal smokescreen, a barrage of misdefinition that identifies self-love with self-ishness, egotism, self-indulgence and, lately, narcissism. Within the Judeo-Christian tradition, the taboo against self-knowledge began with the identification of Adam's and Eve's *sin* as eating of the fruit of the tree of the knowledge of good and evil. God demanded obedience, not awareness. It is permissible to focus attention upon one's self only so long as one finds faults, examines one's conscience to disclose the sin that must be confessed. Christianity created a style of conscience in which the believer is expected to be alert for the failures of the self to live up to an impossible standard: "Be ye perfect even as your father in heaven is perfect." Self-knowledge is a form of self-judgment, an inquisition designed to provide the sinner with evidence of the depravity that must be confessed to be forgiven. Should a man or woman look within and find a clean conscience, it is a sure sign of pride. The standard Christian conscience does not permit the believer to look upon the self and find beauty, goodness, natural kindness, strength. Self-knowledge is tainted with self-hatred. The rules of the game of the Christian conscience are such that, when I look within, I must take the blame for all evil, all hardness of the heart that I find, but give God the credit for any evidence of love. The self, apart from God, is capable only of lust—eros. And should we find a loving self, it is only because God's love—agape—has replaced the natural principle of selfishness that rules the human heart.

It is not surprising that the practice of meditation and self-love has remained under a cloud in the West, and that we have, consequently, created a culture of extroverts. Secular culture, with the aid of psychoanalysis, has continued the old Christian habit of observing the self only to criticize it. In the theater of self, we keep hoping for applause, but get only suggestions for improving our performance, living up to our ideals, growing. Meditation, like masturbation, has until recently been considered a form of self-abuse. We have little permission to pay attention to the workings of our minds or to touch our bodies, to enjoy either the bliss of contemplation or sensation. Our mores prohibit us from doing for ourselves what we are commanded to do for others. A sensitive person may show love to a neighbor by listening, touching, and taking care, but should ignore the self.

The most recent form in which the condemnation against self

knowledge and self-love has arisen is in the new crusade against narcissism. Tom Wolfe has indicted the "me" generation and Christopher Lasch the culture of narcissism. Both have suggested that Esalen, the human potential movement, and gurus from the East are seducing the youth of America into the sin of navel-gazing. They charge that the new explorers of consciousness get lost in private experience and cannot love outwardly or care for the body politic.

Without doubt, there is an abundance of narcissism in modern society; but Wolfe and Lasch misidentify its most dangerous source. Our narcissism comes less from the small number of persons who have turned inward than from the unconscious majority who refuse to examine our values—our conspicuous consumption, our squandering of the world's resources, our unquestioned myth of moral superiority, our arrogant use of power, our opulent style of life that is maintained in a world where millions starve.

The difference between narcissism and self-love is a matter of depth. Narcissus falls in love not with the self, but with an image or reflection of the self—with the persona, the mask. The narcissist sees himself through the eyes of another, changes his lifestyle to conform to what is admired by others, tailors his behavior and expression of feelings to what will please others. Narcissism is eye trouble, voluntary blindness, an agreement to keep up appearances (hence the importance of "style") and not to look beneath the surface.

In the quest for self-knowledge, all images, comfortable illusions, self-indulgent ideologies must be questioned. All inherited certainties must be doubted. The self must be probed, stretched to the breaking point. The discipline is so torturous, so fraught with anxiety, that normal people question its value. Why endure greater loneliness, greater anxiety, greater ambivalence? Freud remarked that the best analysis can do is allow us to trade neurotic suffering for real suffering. Everyone who has begun the outlaw path knows the temptation to turn back and try to live in unconscious simplicity. Oh, how comforting it would be, Walt Whitman mused, to turn and live like animals who do not lie awake and worry about their souls. But there is no turning back. I cannot unsee what I have seen, cannot put uncertainties to rest merely because they are troubling, cannot cease asking questions that disturb my peace of mind. The mountain climber attempts Everest "because it is there." I explore my depths because I am here, cast up on the shore of life without an authorized map that tells me who I am, where I have come from or where I am going. My questions are my quest.

Is it worth it? When I strip off the myths and roles, do I discover some core, essence, soul that abides?

To love the self is not to come upon an unchangeable image or essence, but to welcome all the diversity of experience into consciousness. To love myself is to proclaim that I will live in a democratic rather than a dictatorial relationship to the plurality within. I will allow all my subpersonalities, contradictory impulses, alien wills, strange desires, forbidden needs to live together within the commonwealth of my consciousness. Once my self-image has been shattered, I will always be more than I can know. I will never wholly understand myself. The complexities that have been interwoven to form me are equal to the complexity of being itself. I can no more comprehend the width, height, depth of myself than I can embrace the totality of the world. Thus, knowing I will never be the all-knower, I learn to accept what I cannot comprehend. Loving myself, I respect the mystery that I am. I open myself to *be* more than I can ever *know.* It is in coming to respect the unfathomable depths of myself that I discover that love ranks higher than knowledge or action. Self-love is to the explorer of consciousness what curiosity is to the pure scientist. I must agree to respect what is the case before my quest for knowledge may begin.

THE DISCIPLINE OF SELF-LOVE

The practice of self-love involves a discipline of paying attention to the intricate interweavings of one's physical, mental, and emotional states. The earliest practice of yoga was based upon the observation that different rhythms of breath, the depth of inspiration and expiration, accompanied different states of mind. A speedy and disturbed mind will always be reflected in fast, irregular breath. Anxiety is shallow breathing of a narrowed mind. Calm the breath and you will calm the mind so that it can reflect the patterns and vibrations of things more accurately. Breathe into the rhythms of your life or your lover. Coordinate your breath with others and you will find out what they have in mind. Take three deep breaths between the impulse and the action and you will find the interim filled with myriad sensations and images. The key to tantric sexuality is breathing together with your partner (a conscious con/spiracy), arriving together at the plateau of excitement, rather than allowing the excitement to be discharged in orgasm. The point of love making (love allowing), like life, is the pleasure of the journey rather than the climax. The practice of self-observation is designed to slow us down so that we can allow breath, allow feeling, allow love, allow ourselves to be in/spired by spirit.

For over four thousand years, the East has refined disciplines such as yoga, meditation, tai chi, kung fu, and acupuncture that bring mind, body, and spirit, into harmony. Recently, with the aid of biofeedback machines (our permission givers!), we in the West are beginning to learn a minute amount of the ancient art and skill of self-knowledge and self-regulation. We are discovering what Tibetan physicians knew centuries ago; that active visualization has the power to heal us of many of our diseases, and that the proper foods are often our best medicine. Over the next decade, the emerging field of holistic medicine is likely to bring together many of the spiritual disciplines necessary for the intelligent practice of self-love. To love the carnal self means to accept responsibility for the body-mind. I cannot abuse my body with alcohol, stress, and self-indulgence and still claim to love my self. The outlaw must learn those modes of self-care that promote optimum health. The quest for a passionate life is inseparable from an intelligent and imaginative discipline of self-care. Eros must be well-fed, exercised, and allowed to grow. Since my body is my way of minding the world, and my senses are my only way to stay in touch, I must tend well the instruments of my knowing and loving.

## THE CARNAL SELF: HUMILITY AND SENSUALITY

The charge is often made that self-love leads to arrogance, pride, hubris. Focus attention upon the self and you become puffed up, take on airs. This is an old red herring that is frequently dragged across the outlaw's trail.

Nothing could be further from the truth. Self-knowledge never strays far from the awareness of death. Culture would like to trick me into believing I will be immortal so long as I follow the official civic religion. By being incorporated in the fatherland, motherland, the grand scheme of God in history, I might gain a kind of immortality.

The outlaw puts all that aside. No more loyalty to five-year plans or future utopias. I am my body. My primal certainty is rooted in the knowledge that, before all else, I am a carnal being. What is most real to me is what I taste, touch, smell, hear, see. No abstraction is as important to me as the flesh—my own and that of the people I love. I do not, for instance, believe that any value such as the "preservation of the free world" could justify a nuclear war in which my people and my place would be sacrificed.

To be carnal means to live with an acute awareness that time is of the essence. Like the grass of the field, I'm here today and tomorrow the wind will blow over this place and I will be gone. Even as I abide briefly, my flesh is subject to disease, accidents and the certain infirmities of aging. I may, suddenly, be struck down. There is no certainty that the tomorrow I plan for will find me alive to enjoy the fruits of my labors.

To be carnal, to be flesh, is to know myself in an earthy way. Imagination takes me on flights into merely possible worlds that might exist in the future, but sensation roots me in the here and now. Watching the pine tree gesticulate in the wind, I give up all thoughts of tomorrow. Caressing my lover, I give myself to the pleasures of the moment. Every act of yielding to sensation is a little death. I yield control, allow the scent of the jasmine to take over the corridors of my nose and tickle the circuits of my limbic brain. If I wish to go through this day with my senses aflame, I cannot program what I will enjoy. In the next moment I may be invaded by the aroma of roasting coffee beans, or a whiff of garbage. Sights and sounds come out to meet me. If I willfully stride through the day intent on some goal, I will be visited by very little strange beauty. Each time I yield to sensation, I surrender my will. I can only experience the pleasure of sex, or the beauty of a single jade wave backlit by the setting sun, when I accept, savor, and am thankful for a moment of fulfillment that is given me. Humility and sensuality go hand in hand.

THE BEYOND WITHIN: THE SELF AS NEXUS

Imperceptibly, the outlaw path merges into the lover's way. The quest for autonomy leads beyond itself. Deep solitude leads to an awareness of belonging. I struggle to climb to the apex of self-awareness, to know my original face, to test my limits, to inhabit all the contradictions of my experience, to understand the world as the first person singular. Then, suddenly, where there was only me, I run into you. At the heart of my privacy I discover how public I am. Self-love carried me into my neighbor's back yard.

## Passion as Compassion: The Ethic of Resonance

Sex is a parable that teaches that the self is an intersection. I am not an isolated atom, but a point of resonance, a vibratory event.

Suppose that I set out to "explore my sexuality" in a purely hedonistic and selfish way. I want *my* pleasure. Before long, I discover that the way I feel about my lover acts as a thermostat on my sexual sensations. If I am suspicious, or angry, or self-absorbed, I will come to her with a tight, defended body. I will be unable to allow the slow, soft pulsations, the ascending involuntary rhythms of deepening pleasure. Our movements will have the quality of a battle. I will try to make her respond so that I may prove myself superior to her. If I approach her merely as a body, a piece, an instrument designed to give me pleasure I, also, reduce my body to a machine that is divorced from feeling, a set of nerve endings that may be stimulated to produce pleasurable, or painful, sensations. When I divorce myself from the resonance of tender feeling that accompanies loving sexuality, I turn my body into an "it." I watch it perform, or not perform. I become a participant observer directing a sexual drama from afar. The more I try to limit touch to an exchange of sensation, the more I do violence to my full-bodied erotic potential. The proper name for this type of sexuality, which involves two personas, is mutual masturbation. No genuine passion develops because there is no com-passion between self and self, between self and world.

Carnal sexuality is mutual resonance, the tuning of one string to another. In the mathematics of the psyche, my pleasure is doubled by sharing your pleasure. The intensity of my sensation depends upon my openness to my feeling of you, your feeling of me, our feeling of we. This is the grammar of passion: two first persons singular become a first person plural. There is no way I can know my maximum sexual ecstasy apart from entering deeply into another self. My deepest form of knowledge of my self is mediated to me by another. In conversation or intercourse, my self is given to me through your gift of your self to me and my gift of my self to you. Apart from generosity and care, I know neither my self nor another.

Meditation upon the self leads inevitably to the conclusion that I can only love my self in the measure that I am willing to love my neighbor. The Heisenberg principle governs both personal and scientific perception: The observing eye always shapes and changes what it sees. It is an ironclad law of the psyche that I judge others as I judge myself. The "laziness" I cannot abide in A _____ is the same indolence that lurks just under the surface of my compulsive activism. The "promiscuity" I condemn in B _____ has the Dionysian leer and hoof of the satyr that keeps trying to run free in my dreams.

Watch the mind as it makes judgments based upon fear and desire—aversion and attraction—and you discover the world is a Rorschach test, a screen upon which you project your image of your self. What you see is what you are. And what you see is what you get. If you want to change what is "out there," you must first change the eyes with which you see. You want to love your neighbor? Then explore your multiple personalities until you know that nothing human is alien to you. Know your rage and you will understand the murderer, the child abuser. Know your death wish and you will not find Gary Gilmore alien. Know the victim and the master within yourself and you will have compassion for masochists and sadists. Allow your longing for the sacred to bubble up from beneath the facade of your secular personality and you will find that saints were not plastic statues, but are your companions and guides.

## My Unique Story and the Common Myth

My insistence upon my uniqueness leads to my commonness. In exploring my personal history, I begin to hear echoes from distant times and places. A host of heroes, shamans, and poets seem to have left their footprints on my path. Ulysses, Buddha, Socrates, Jesus, D. H. Lawrence, Kazantzakis, Wendell Berry, Susan Griffin, Norman O. Brown, Georgia O'Keefe, Hannah Arendt: all describe the human condition in ways that resonate with my autobiography. The tales of the "heroes with a thousand faces" are a part of the archetypal story that is woven into the substance of my self. What all individuals have in common is their uniqueness. Each of us has left the group mind and begun a solitary journey by entering alone into the forest at the point where it was darkest and there was no path. All who have survived and returned to tell the story talk about a similar process of ego-death and resurrection of the self. The demons faced may have worn different disguises at different periods in history—the minotaur, the devil, Frankenstein, the face of madness—but each time their power faded when they were faced, named, and claimed as projections of the self. With minor adjustments, the map I have constructed from my experience could fit the lives of uncounted modern men and women who are more interested in being human than in being modern. It is considerable comfort to know that I make my solitary journey in the company of so many.

*From Autonomy to Theonomy, From Freedom to Destiny*

My quest to discover the law of my own being—autonomy—leads me to the threshold of what Tillich called theonomy—the point at which freedom and destiny, the law of the self, and the law (or logos) of God coincide.

To know myself is to know my gifts. In exercising my freedom to its fullest, I find I am being moved by a destiny that is prior to my consciousness. As I peel away the layers of myth that have in-formed me, I begin to discover a certain core of givenness that seems primal. This core, which is discovered rather than invented, is difficult to describe. Call it my predisposition, my destiny, the essence that calls me into being, my soul, the bundle of desires that move me. No concept entirely captures the experience of following the scent of my being through the forest of distraction and false images of the self. You can think about it as the programming of my DNA that unwinds as I go through the trajectory of my life. Each year I am invited more fully into the way the genetic code (the latest biological incognito for "God") in-forms me. Or, in the old religious language, it may be named my vocation or calling. God, or the transmoral conscience, calls to me to become who I am meant to be—a lover. Humanists, who are embarrassed by overt religious language, might prefer to call it my potential.

Certainly, my destiny has something to do with my anatomy and disposition. As a male, testosterone charges my system with a certain style of desire. I respond to a woman with a different degree of erotic interest than I respond to a toadstool or a computer. I may choose to act upon the impulse of desire or not, but I cannot choose what I will desire. I cannot, for instance, choose to desire to grow a child within my womb, because I have no womb. My freedom is strangely interwoven with the acceptance and celebration of certain givens. As Merleau Ponty said (in condemning Sartre's idea that we are condemned to be totally free to create ourselves), "We are condemned to meaning." The world in which we find ourselves is already, in a large measure, in-formed.

Acorns regularly become oak trees, never lions.

But there is more than anatomy or DNA encoding to human destiny. We are, after all, not acorns. Our power of choice is so radical that we may even choose to distort our essential compassion and consciousness so severely that we become inhuman. Although we do not know how to make the notion of a human destiny intellectually clear, we are in virtual agreement that certain men and women violate the conditions that mark one as human. We identify the monsters—from Ivan the Terrible to Adolph Eichmann—as having chosen to refuse the destiny of becoming human.

The meaning that in-forms my life cannot be discovered by any general formula. Although I might fail so terribly to fulfill *my* individual destiny that it would be generally recognized that I had failed to fulfill a *human* destiny, there is no way that a universal formula can provide me with a map that will show me how to find meaning in my life. In other words, my destiny, the meaning of my life, my calling, is discovered only within the intimacy of my experience. My destiny is revealed only to me. We are each called by name. A small voice, easily ignored, whispers: "This is your work. This is your place. These are your neighbors. This is your mate. This is the burden you are to bear. This is the healing you are to undertake. This is the gift you are to exercise. These are the wounds you must suffer. This is the arena within which you must act the drama of your life."

Listening for my calling, following the scent of my destiny, is a constant and difficult discipline. I often miss the clues. Performing for others or judging what I should be doing by my culture's standards of success, I forget to pay attention to my dreams, my inner voices. There is one failsafe rule: Paradoxically, it is only as I have the courage to be an individual that I discover the destiny that links me to Being-becoming-itself. Only when I dare to be unique can I become grounded in common humanity. I might be able to en/courage you to listen to your calling, but only your ears can hear the vocation that whispers your name.

The voice revealing an individual's destiny is usually a matter of a slight inflection. Easy to miss. If I tell you stories of moments in which I knew the direction of my destiny, they will seem quite unimpressive to you. Just ordinary little flashes. For instance: Once in a dry time, Howard Thurman asked me: "What do you want, Sam? What are your dreams?" (He had previously warned me about the proper order of erotic priorities. "The first question an individual must ask is 'What is my journey?' Only then is it safe to ask the second question: 'Who will go with me?' If you get the questions out of order, you will get in trouble.") I didn't know how to answer him. I was a successful young professor with ideas and tenure, but no dreams. "I don't have any dreams right now," I answered. "Well," he replied, "you had better start looking for one." That night, I retreated to a quiet place with a libation of bourbon and sat. The emptiness was frightening. After a parched hour of waiting, a single image broke the surface of my consciousness. I kept seeing an Airstream trailer. I waited for something more organic. Nothing. For days I allowed the image of the Airstream to flicker on the edge of my awareness. Finally its meaning began to unfold. I heard the gypsy calling to me to abandon tenure and get back on the road. Within a year, I had resigned my position and started to freelance.

At the level of our most intimate experience of ourselves, all moments in time are not equal, all events are not democratically significant. Certain moments leap out and grab us. The revelation of the individual's destiny comes in just such ordinary moments that are saturated with extraordinary significance. Openings. Suddenly, I see a woman walk into a room and *I know* I desire her more deeply than others and that we are to be together. I don't know how I know, but I know. And we marry. It is only by responding to this particular woman in the pregnant moment that the universal human destiny to mate and cast my seed into history finds expression. Suddenly, one ordinary autumn day, an ordinary aspen leaf burnished with breathtaking luminescence in the sunlight falls within my ken. My stomach unknots, and something within me knows that death does not have final dominion. Contrary to Sartre's denial in *Nausea,* there are "special moments," privileged situations, timely (kairotic) moments, magical events that provide the individual with the clues to the meaning of life. It is in responding to these revelatory moments that the individual finds his or her tailormade destiny. In this way, the outlaw's pursuit of an individual calling leads through the threshold into the lover's world, where any flower in a crannied wall, any grain of sand may reveal eternity.

# 9.
# Outlaw Perversions:
# The Promethean Dis-ease

In our greatness lie the seeds of our self-destruction. The tragic flaw that undermines the hero is an oversized virtue. The individuated self stands alone, splendid, vulnerable, and intense—an iconoclast and breaker of boundaries. But the strength of the outlaw easily creates that form of spiritual blindness the Greeks called *hubris*—overweening pride.

Perverse individualism seduces us into the illusion of self-sufficiency and the belief that there are no limits to our ability to change the self and the world. An old hymn warns the outlaw who stands in the heroic Promethean posture: "When we are strong, Lord, leave us not alone, our refuge be." It is precisely at the peak of our potency as individuated selves that we must give up power as an organizing metaphor for life or risk that form of impotence that comes from pretending we are omnipotent. Man cannot live by adrenalin alone. By breakthroughs. By iconoclasm. The heroic posture, too long maintained, exhausts the system.

DIS-EASES OF THE BODY POLITIC: NATIONALISM AND TECHNOLATRY

The perversion of the outlaw impulse can be seen writ large in the dis-ease that now threatens western culture. The modern world suffers from a tug of war between perverse adults and perverse outlaws, or between nationalism and technolatry—the uncritical worship of technology. Nationalism is the pathology of the mass, the perversion of those who remain stuck at the adult level of consciousness and refuse to transcend their parochial morality and political interests. In the spread of technology and multinational

corporations, we see the outlaw impulse gone wild. The promethean spirit of the heroes who stole the fire and wrested knowledge and control from nature now threatens to burn the world up.
The light-bearers and fire-givers may incinerate us. An acupunc-
turist diagnosing the modern body politic would conclude that we
suffer from an excess of fire. Nuclear power or the greenhouse
effect may overheat us. Regaining our health depends on finding
a way to slow things down. Keep cool. Don't overheat the atmosphere. Speed, Type A behavior, leads to burn-out. Intensity must
always be balanced by contentment. Perhaps we can learn from
the fact that animals kept in a cooler-than-average environment
and fed less than is required for a full belly, live one-third longer
than their overfed, overheated counterparts.

The development of technology and the quest for self-knowledge are central chapters in the history of human heroism. The
impulse to know and to change what has been given to us by
society and nature is the heart of the outlaw impulse. The earliest
humans were, in a large measure, victims of nature. Because they
had no tools powerful enough to change things, they had to accept
the caprice of nature. Unfortunately the "laws" of Mother Nature
included hurricanes, drought, plague, disease, and early death.
And the worshipers of the Goddess accepted their lot with childlike passivity and sacrificed the lives of animals, slaves, sometimes
their beloved first-born children to ensure that the tenuous order
of the cosmos would prevail against chaos. With the development
of tools, we rebelled against nature and seized the power to exert
more control over our destiny. We studied to learn nature's laws,
forced her secrets out of her, and invented machines to do our will.
Knowledge led to power; power to the ability to challenge the
given conditions. The machines set us free from locality and from
captivity to fate.

The central error that turned the outlaw impulse into the
promethean perversion was the identification of knowledge and
power (a mistake at least as old as Adam, although it is usually
attributed to Francis Bacon). No doubt our advancing knowledge
has given us incredible power over nature. But healing knowledge

is always balanced by an awareness of ignorance, just as humane power is tempered by a sense of our essential impotence. We need only meditate on the inevitability of death to remind ourselves that our power is real but finite. In the same way, *our ignorance necessarily increases at the same rate as our knowledge.* Human consciousness is like a flashlight. It can illuminate anything upon which it is focused. But in order to know one object, it must ignore others. At best, we see 180 degrees out of a possible range of 360 degrees. The ignored darkness is always an accompaniment of the known light. At the present moment, we are so enamored of the type of knowledge technological reasoning has made available that we forget the types of potential knowledge we sacrifice. We have, for instance, lost the knowledge of kinship, of place, of the sacred, of our erotic connection with nature. Few moderns know how to grow their own food or survive in the wilderness. We can hardly imagine the skill an ancient Polynesian sailor used in sailing across thousands of miles of ocean without instruments, the acuity of the senses that allowed an Indian tracker to follow a mountain lion over hard-packed ground, or the control of breath and mind that permitted yogis to suspend animation and be buried alive for days. Ivan Illych has made a career out of showing how dumb our know-how has made us, how schools have destroyed our ability to learn; how medicine has destroyed our capacity for self-healing. The promethean disease tempts us to believe in progress and the perfectibility of the self because it rests upon the illusion that power can be expanded without limit and knowledge increased without adding to the sum of ignorance.

I have written elsewhere* about the process that leads a technological culture to its own nemesis. Suffice it to say that the promethean illusion that man is the omnipotent maker of his own destiny might be illustrated by an analysis of most any point of modern culture.

For instance:

Philosophically, it is reflected in Sartre's form of existentialism,

---

*Sam Keen, *Apology for Wonder* (N.Y.: Harper & Row, 1969).

which assumes that human beings are only what they make of themselves. His famous formula—existence precedes essence—expresses the belief that we are self-created.

Biologists and genetic engineers express the promethean illusion in the dream of recombining the elements of the DNA to produce a perfect human species. As Hannah Arendt says, "This future man, whom the scientists tell us they will produce in no more than a hundred years, seems to be possessed by a rebellion against human existence as it has been given, a free gift from nowhere (secularly speaking), which he wishes to exchange, as it were, for something he has made himself."[1]

Economists smuggle the assumption of omnipotence into the principle that only economic considerations limit our resources. Paul Ehrlich unmasks the illusion.

> In an extreme form the dissociation of economics from environmental reality can be seen in the notion that the market mechanism completely eliminates the need for concern about diminishing resources in the long run. . . . These serious, respected economists [Anders, Gramm, and Maurice] have written: "In a fundamental sense natural resources are not fixed but are functions of capital accumulation and with it of science and technology. . . . Man largely creates his own environment and his own resources. . . . Only if we eliminate the market incentives for motivation and investment or reduce the scope of market forces resources, must we face a real long term "resource crisis." The only non-renewable and non-substitutable resource is the set of institutions known as a market order, which eliminates crises with respect to physical resources.[2]

This omnipotent assumption rests upon a myopic, urban, elite, corporate individualism that divorces the human species from other sentient beings, does not recognize the rights or sacredness of harp seals, whales, or forests, and does not understand the connection between the humus and remaining human. It further severs the privileged technological peoples of the world, who consume most of the resources, from the have-nots of the Third World. In the effort to go beyond the limits that were once imposed by a medieval theological concept of nature, the new technologists have gone beyond compassion, beyond sanity, beyond the consciousness of the common bond that unites all living things in an interdependent web.

(I paused here for lunch. It being late October, I shook the tree and harvested the Carpathian walnuts. Lime-green pods and a beige lace filigree cover the dusky nut. After shelling them, my hands are stained with autumn. They match the aspen leaves that have fallen and cover the path up to my writing studio. The afternoon is filled with a blush of gratitude for sweetmeats miraculously given.)

Consider the perverse fortune of power in the twentieth century. Never have we had more fire-power; but Dr. Strangelove is leading us toward the apocalypse. We seem to be caught in the grip of Frankenstein. Our technological-economic-military machine is running amok. Never have we enjoyed more power to control our lives or felt more impotent. And all the while we tell ourselves that our problems will be solved by more of what we already have in excess—power. Hair of the dog that bit us. More powerful machines, weapons, drugs, energy sources. More omniscient information-processing systems. More knowledge. More experts. But the more we have the ability to shape our destiny, the less we have a sense that we have a destiny, or even a future. The message is clear: an obsession with power strangles desire. The quest for omnipotence leads to impotence. Inflation and depression hold hands under the table.

### DIS-EASED INDIVIDUALISM

If we switch our sights from the body politic to the single self, the outlaw perversion appears in a variety of forms of individualism.

Old-style capitalism idealized the rugged individual. The Robber Barons, Andrew Carnegie, Henry Ford, and other captains of industry provided models of self-made men. The Horatio Alger myth was the American pragmatist version of existentialism. "Real" men stand alone, are self-sufficient, and depend upon no one. They set goals for themselves and have enough drive to win. And winning, beating the competition, as Vince Lombardi said, "isn't everything; it's the only thing." The individual who gets to the top is the one who is tough and daring enough to impose his *will* upon others.

The myth of individualism is also celebrated nightly in the theater of our psyche in the great American morality play—the western. Cowboys and gunfighters incarnate the virtues of manhood. The macho male is rough, tough, hard to bluff, and takes no guff from the female of the species. He stands tall and alone. Doesn't cry. Avoids the tender trap of dependency. He can take it and he can dish it out.

In the "age of Aquarius," individualism has put on spiritual garb, adopted a soft tone of voice, and talks about "growth," "realizing the full human potential," and "total responsibility." Fritz Perls's Gestalt Prayer, which seems to have replaced the Lord's Prayer in the new age spirituality, reflects the new form of self-encapsulation:

I do my thing. You do your thing.
I am not in this world to meet your expectations.
You are not in this world to meet mine.
If we happen to meet it is beautiful.
If not, it can't be helped.

It should come as little surprise that in *In and Out the Garbage Pail,* Perls complained that in his seventies he is still struggling with the problem of masturbation. The stance "I do my thing, you do your thing" isolates the individual, overlooks the reality of mingling, ignores the link between passion and compassion, and hence reduces intercourse to mutual masturbation.

The new gospel of total responsibility as put forth by Perls, est, Wellspring, and the host of those offering instant prosperity and enlightenment is in reality a denial of respons/ability. Its solipsistic view of the self as a solitary center of autonomy, a self-creating entity, allows the new age spiritual individualists to ignore the wounds of class, the conspiracies of the power-elite, and the political reality of inequality. In the name of "personal responsibility," it destroys compassion and ignores the responsibility the privileged have for the poor and the disenfranchised. The old-style rugged individuals of early capitalism used social Darwinism and Calvinism to justify their political irresponsibility. Natural selection or predestination determined that there be sufficient poor to form a labor pool to contribute to the fortunes of the self-made entrepeneur and advance the cause of progress. The new age gurus appeal to the old Hindu idea of karma to show that they are responsible for being well-born and prosperous, and that the children of Vietnam were totally responsible for having chosen (in a previous incarnation) to be born where they would be napalmed. Such notions of "total responsibility" are functionally equivalent to the admission of complete impotence. The dogma that the individual has chosen everything that happens in his or her life requires us to suppose that much of this "choice" was made unconsciously or in a previous life. Hence there is nothing I can do now except change my *ideas* and feelings. Quite consistently, the isolated individual of the new age is largely committed to working on him or her self—even if the context for this is a group or commune. The Gurdjieff school, the new Tibetan Buddhist groups, and the Arica Institute are typical in their studied ignorance of politics. All provide a smorgasbord of spiritual disciplines —meditation, psychocalesthenics, mantras, mudras, rituals for cleaning karma and turning one's vibrations to the planets, and exercises in self-remembering. But they forget that real potency always involves the individual joining with other individuals to act in a way that changes the body politic. There is something painfully symbolic about the opulent spiritual feast offered in Boulder, Colorado, by the Naropa Institute, whose members have been virtually unrepresented in the group of protesters who, less than twenty miles away in Rocky Flats, have sat on railroad tracks in acts of civil disobedience in an effort to stop the production of plutonium weapons. The true outlaw quest may begin in individual consciousness, but it must lead into political action designed to change the hateful myth that in-forms society and systematically destroys our capacity to love.

Perhaps the most popular expression of the new age forms o

the promethean perversion is found in Castaneda's parables about Don Juan. A generation that felt itself politically impotent turned to Don Juan's magical, mystical quest for "personal power." But if we refuse to be enchanted by the beauty of Castaneda's style and examine the advice he gives, we find that his philosophy springs from the same root metaphor as the rugged individualist. Castaneda is the introvert's equivalent of the military conquistador. The spooks and obscure spirits his warrior confronts in his lonely vigils in the desert are the private equivalent of the Russian Bear of atheistic communism that shadows the dreams of the Pentagon. His man of knowledge is a warrior who must accumulate sufficient personal power by training his will and doing psychic battle with enemies who cast spells against him. Like Tom Sawyer, he walks in the graveyard at midnight and wrestles with the specter of ghosts, witches, and assorted occult spooks. But nowhere does Don Juan advise his apprentice to confront the real demons that rule at midday—the political tyrants, the arms race with its threat of nuclear holocaust, dehumanizing bureaucracies, the deteriorating environment, the escalating climate of violence. Nor does he suggest that "the path with heart" might involve the difficult discipline of learning to love another ordinary human being—a wife, a husband, a child, a neighbor, a friend.

Anyone practiced in listening with the third ear can hear, beneath the obsessive concern with the accumulation of power, the fear that is inevitably the unconscious motivating force of the promethean individual—the fear of impotence. It makes no difference whether the form of power sought is sexual, military, financial, political, muscular, personal, or spiritual. Men and women who become obsessed with power are driven by a repressed feeling of their own powerlessness and worthlessness. Power is sought to prove to some absent and critical eye that we are worthy of the love and acceptance we did not receive. Armaments are a substitute for the arms that were meant to enfold us. Spiritual power is sought when grace is missing. Sexual power is sought in the absence of passion. Military power is sought when men have lost the conviction of their potency to move others except by the use of violence. Economic power is sought when we fall into the illusion that commodities can compensate us for the absence of the household and the community—especially the absence of the father. Robert Bly's penetrating statement tells us much about the underlying motivation of our quest for power: "The boy and his father . . . are the love-unit most damaged by the Industrial Revolution." The quest to become a superman, an *ubermensch,* rests upon the fear that I am less than human, an *untermensch.* We get tough because we live in a world where we don't get touched.

### PROMETHEAN SEX

The promethean perversion reaches farcical proportions when it comes to dealing with sex. The makers, shakers, doers, and heaven-storming technocrats have recently replaced Miss Lonelyhearts as givers of advice to the lovelorn. The largest number of modern sex manuals seem to have been written by genital engineers who consider the problem of sexual satisfaction a technical matter to be solved by effective techniques. Consider the following sample taken from an unpublished *Manual on Psychosexual Integration.*

> *Bio-electrical nature of Orgasm.* Establishing responsive movements with complete genital contact activates sexual circuitry of a bio-electrical nature. The oscillation of the downward and upward strokes creates an energy field; it initiates an orgasmic buildup within each individual, and ignites an energy field between partners. As the movement is held constant, the field increases in volume and density until it reaches a point of capacity that is the combined potential of the two people, and evokes the involuntary responses of the rise to climax—triggering automatically a simultaneous merging in orgasm.

Lurking in the background of this fully dehumanized approach to the maximization of pleasure (which is usually accompanied by charts showing the plumbing of the genitals, the circuitry of the erogenous zones, graphs charting the rates, plateaux, and peaks of arousal, as well as instructions for using vibrators and other aids) is the mechanical mind of the technocrat. It is not difficult to imagine that we are only months away from a sexual utopia in which computer-dating services will arrange the coupling of individuals whose sexual profiles, genital proportions, and fetish preferences are compatible.

The new behavioral engineers, whether dealing with sexual or institutional problems, see human interaction on a stimulus-response model. Sex is reduced to a matter of applying the appropriate amount of stimulation to nerve endings to produce the intended result. Since it is so simple, we are all assured there need be no sexual maladjustment.

There is a hidden tyranny involved in the promethean effort to program, direct, and control the body or the body politic from above. Sexual engineers and behavior modifiers ultimately increase the alienation their techniques are designed to cure because they trivialize human beings by reducing them to mechanisms. The engineer, like the Grand Inquisitor, always stands in a superior position to the stuff upon which he is working, just as the pornographer always pictures the sadist as superior to his masochistic victim. When we seek to have *power over*, rather than a responsive relationship *with*, our bodies, our lovers, our children, our employees, our environment, we stand as masters to slaves, sadists to masochists. A technological model that reduces the complexity of communion-consciousness-cooperation to stimulus response makes of the other (even if this other is *my* body) a thing to be manipulated and controlled.

Whenever the promethean spirit is dominant, sex is turned into a contest and a proving ground. Man traditionally assumes the role of the sadistic controller of woman and nature. Woman is the enemy who may steal the fire-power of the hero. The will-full male sees woman as a part of the dark, forbidden, unconscious element that he must conquer. She is a threat to his autonomy, because she stirs him to desire which, when fulfilled, renders him soft and spent. The promethean hero worships only the erect phallus. He knows only the thrusting, the engine ramming the piston into the cylinder. Fearing the softness of his body, he knows only the armored body. Hence he blames the woman for what he experiences as the loss of his potency.

It is no accident that the men who have carried the outlaw impulse to a point of insane intensity have been fearful of women and related to them sexually either not at all or in a degrading manner. Nietzsche is typical in his advice: "When you go to a woman do not forget the whip." Or, "Woman! One-half of mankind is weak, typically sick, changeable, inconstant—woman needs strength in order to cleave to it; she needs a religion of weakness that glorifies being weak, loving, and being humble as divine: or better, she makes the strong weak." Thus Nietzsche asserts that the higher man must make war on the masses and on "everything that makes soft and effeminate."[3] Whenever mastery, will, and power are experienced as the center of the self's identity, women will be reduced to decorations or "cunts" to be used. They will be considered safe only when they can be controlled or demeaned. The Spanish bullfight vividly ritualizes and acts out this super-masculine stance, which is so characteristic of western culture. The bull, the ancient symbol of the Mother Goddess, the unconscious, is taunted, wounded, weakened, and finally killed by the phallic matador. In a less promethean age, in Minoan culture, acrobatic young men and women vaulted between the horns (the contradictions) and over the back of the bull and played with the incarnation of the dark forces that inhabit the labyrinth beneath the conscious mind.

SELF-CONQUEST: THE PERPETUAL STRUGGLE

The promethean remains a warrior whose battleground is finally the self, whose enemy is the dark "feminine" forces within, whose impossible task is to remake the image of the self into a guiltless and perfect being. No one has seen this more clearly than Thomas Merton. I can do no better than quote at length from his analysis.

> Prometheus transcends ordinary men by the intensity and power of his egoism, by the glamour of his adventure and by the violence of his self-hate. He has dared to reach down into the depths of his own spirit and find the forbidden, existential fire. . . .
>
> In relation to the rest of men, he is indeed a giant. For he who has

the courage to scale a mountain, even though the scaling be utterly useless, has at least a certain advantage over those who remain in the plain. He has the courage to admit that he is afraid, and he has the courage to do the thing they are all afraid of.

If Prometheus seems greater than the "right-thinking" herd at the bottom of the mountain, it is because he is to some extent more honest than they in his illusion. They claim to love the gods and to respect them. He admits he is afraid of them. They claim they can do without fire—that is to say, they are content not to exist, or to exist in a numbness without pain. He, on the contrary, determines to attack the problem of his own existence head-on, and demand that the gods tell him why he is not a person. And he has a certain right to be jealous of an answer which he thinks he has stolen from the summit of an Olympus which he found, to his surprise, to be without the gods he feared to find there. And so, finally, he marches off to Caucasus of his own accord, and chains himself to the rock, and calls for his pain and his vulture. Nor is it the vulture that is inexorable, but Prometheus, who insists that the bird be there. And so he stands and suffers, with a sorrow that is at once monumental and absurd, punishing and pitying himself because there are no gods and because, he, who wants to be his own god, realizes that he can only be so by being punished. . . .

Prometheus is not the symbol of victory but of defeat. Promethean mysticism has precisely this negative quality about it: since it cannot conceive of a true victory, it makes a victory out of defeat and glories in its own despair. But this is only because Prometheus believes in death rather than life. He is convinced, in advance, that he must die. . . .

The Promethean instinct is as deep as man's weakness. That is to say, it is almost infinite. It is the despairing cry that arises out of the darkness of man's metaphysical solitude—the inarticulate expression of a terror man will not admit to himself: his terror at having to be himself, at having to be a person. For the fire Prometheus steals from the gods is his own uncommunicable reality, his own spirit. It is the affirmation and vindication of his own being. Yet this being is a gift of God, and it does not have to be stolen. It can only be had by a free gift—the very hope of gaining it by theft is pure illusion.

The great error of Promethean mysticism is that it takes no account of anyone but the Self. For Prometheus, there is no "other." His spirit, his strivings, have no relation to any other person. . . . What Prometheus wants is not the glory of God but his own perfection. He has forgotten the terrible paradox that the only way we become perfect is by leaving ourselves. . . .[4]

The individual, the outlaw, the promethean, accumulates and uses the power necessary to conquer the fortress of the self. But once conquered, this fortress must be surrendered if the pilgrimage of love is to be continued.

# 10.
## The Lover

THE PROFESSOR AND THE POLYMORPHOUS ROSE

As a thin, young professor with a beartrap mind, I knew quite a bit. Of course, there was much I did not know; but I had made a study of the structure of knowledge and the pigeonholes into which the mind fits experience, and I was certain of the categories into which I might place the fact, theory, or myth I brought back from my expeditions into the unknown. Thus I was confident and willing to experiment with LSD when it was offered me in 1967.

One Friday evening, about 9 P.M., after the children were in bed, I took the magic wafer and waited. Close self-observation told me at 9:30 that nothing had changed. At 9:40 I began to feel soft, relaxed, and a little fuzzy. By 9:50, time vanished and all the objects in the room seemed to be fluid and rubbery. Anything that seized my attention claimed me totally. Or maybe it would be more accurate to say that "I" seemed to have vanished or transformed sequentially into a rubber ball, an oak rocking chair, the song that Donovan was singing.

In the eternity that preceeded midnight, I passed through one particularly vivid incarnation. A rose in a crystal vase, sitting on the coffee table called to me as I was passing. I sat down. The petals bent slightly, invited me deeper into the vermilion depths. As I entered the rose, I noticed a rich scent floating like a current in the spring air. Breathing deeply of the perfume, I was led down, down into a rose-red city where I saw, heard, smelled, intricate geometrical bursts of light and design—and Donovan singing in a cafe. All the while the rose also had the texture and aroma of a woman's flesh. And I was moving deeper into it-her; we were moving together to the scent of the music, to the rhythms of the colors, to the breath we shared.

From a great distance, a strange but somehow familiar voice called me. "Sam," it whispered, "do you want to go into the bedroom and make love?" I was confused. Where was the voice coming from? Why was it calling me to leave the rose world? With all the power I could muster I pulled myself back up into the room. It was then I noticed that I was sitting on the couch, looking at a rose in a vase on a coffee table. My wife was curled in back of me on the couch, spooned around my seated form. "You were moving back and forth and breathing fast," she said. "Do you want to go into the bedroom and make love?"

I looked at her, with complete puzzlement. "Why? Why," I asked, "would I want to do that?" Her body felt warm and friendly. I was aroused, but somehow at the moment, or non-moment, it seemed as if going away with her to the bed would be flagrant adultery, abandonment of the rose.

"Aren't we already doing it?" I asked.

"What do you mean?" she asked.

"I don't know how to explain," I replied. The pigeonholes were missing. I couldn't make any separations between knowing and loving, cognition and erotic union. And I couldn't even find the right words to tell her that I didn't know how to explain.

"It felt like we were already inside each other. You, me, the rose, Donovan, were inside each other. We were already making love, or, rather, we were all inside the same thing that was making love through us."

"Oh," she said. "I don't quite understand what you mean."

What did I mean? I started to puzzle. With the rose I had felt the same kind of sensations, the same intimacy, the same feelings of excitement and gratitude that I was accustomed to feel only when my wife and I were making love. I had lost myself, as in orgasm. The distinct functions and boundaries of my senses blurred. "How could that be?" I questioned. It was only a flower. The machinery of my mind went into high gear. I left the rose, my wife, the music miles behind me as I sped forward looking for explanations. Soon it occurred to me: It must be the drug. The drug has altered my mind. It made me crazy. Yes, that was the explanation. I blinked my eyes, looked carefully around the room, marshalled my will power, and tried to force myself into ordinary consciousness. I wanted things back in their familiar places. But the boundaries were still fuzzy. Every time I glanced at the rose it threatened to pull me back into its vaginal depths, to obliterate my clarity, to erase my self-consciousness. The more I fought its siren scents, the more frightened and paranoid I became.

For an eternity I wandered in darkness, my heart pounding with fear, I was exiled from my own mind. My passport stolen. "Just relax," my wife said. "The effects of the drug will wear off in a few hours." Like a zombie hoping that a draught of human blood would restore my humanity, I grabbed her wrist and looked at her watch. I was still in eternal damnation, but there was a glimmer of hope. I remembered about time.

"You mean, I won't always be like this?" I asked.

"Of course not, in a few hours you will be back to normal," she said. But there was a trace of uncertainty and fear in her voice.

"How long is a few hours?" I asked.

Like a mother teaching a child to tell time she held out her wrist watch. "When the large hand goes around three more times. Why don't you try to sleep now."

Thus reassured that time would bring me home to my own mind, I fell into bed and fitful dreams.

In the morning, I awoke. A shadow of terror hung over my mind. I trotted out a couple of syllogisms, followed a line of thinking from problem to solution, checked out my mental functioning. I was relieved to find that I was burnt-out but normal enough.

I walked into the living room and looked carefully at the rose in the vase. It was only an ordinary flower. Without understanding why, I cried. It was as if I had lost a lover.

LOVE AS HOLY BROKENNESS

We come to love wounded. The outlaw struggle between the ego and self leaves us scared, dis-integrated, de-structured, eccentric. Our old center gone. We begin the last and endless pilgrimage toward becoming a lover in the middle of a junkyard of broken myths, shattered relationships, smashed illusions, tarnished heroes, and obsolete gods. Our old identity is strewn in pieces around us. Our old badges of membership, our systems for assuring ourselves of meaning and immortality, are worn beyond repair.

But if we allow our eyes to become accustomed to the darkness of history we may glimpse a new light. Trust may grow to replace the tenacious beliefs and illusions of certainty to which we were accustomed to cling as adults. The enjoyment of endarkenment replaces striving after enlightenment. (Love is blind. It loves the dark.) Just where we encountered the insurmountable problem, we discover the mystery that heals us. We find wholeness in realizing our part/ialness. We are saved as we recognize that we remain sinners. We arrive home when we rejoice in being on the road. We are healed when we discover that the hole in our hearts is a fertile void. Our anxiety, loneliness, restlessness, incompleteness, doubt, longing is the emptiness of God, the presence within us of the nostalgia for Being-becoming-itself.

*The lover's glimpse of the splinter of light within the tragedy of the human condition is a momentary vision that the center is everywhere.* Everyplace and everytime is holy. The spirit of God, the in-forming energy of Life, the intention of Being is ubiquitous. As the Psalmist (139) says:

> Whither shall I go from thy spirit? Or whither shall I flee from thy presence? If I ascend up into heaven, thou art there: if I make my bed in hell, behold, thou art there. If I take the wings of the morning and dwell in the uttermost parts of the sea; even there shall thy hand lead me, and thy right hand shall hold me. If I say, surely the darkness shall cover me: even the night shall be light about me. Yea, the darkness hideth not from thee, but the night shineth as the day: the darkness and the light are both alike to thee.

There is no escape. Every being is within Being. We are insiders, not aliens; members of the family, not orphans.

*The lover's glimpse results in a new identity and a new citizenship—a change from mythical to mystical consciousness. The lover pledges allegiance to no tribal flag, but is a communicant in the cosmopolitan commonwealth, a co-creator in the family of God.*

To love is to be about the task of healing. The lover's vocation is to lure others (and that part of the self that nurses old injuries and fears, takes pride in autonomy, and harbors the illusion of self-sufficiency) into re-cognition of their true being and their true allegiance. It is to practice the art of forgiveness and to expand the circle of care. Love's way is always vulnerable because it abandons the rules of power-politics and the paranoid game upon which the social consensus is based.

In the passionate life, one is always in the process of forgetting one's self and becoming self-transcending spirit. The lover hovers on the edge of disappearing in empathy. In compassion we live on the boundary, a no-man's land. At any moment we may forget the self and slip into a wood thrush's song, the cry of an injured old man, or a lover's arms. In love, the moth becomes the flame. In compassion, we burn and bond with the other.

To love is to return to a home we never left, to remember who we are.

THE UNITIVE GLIMPSE

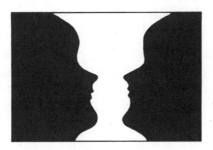

It happens suddenly. Everything turns inside-out. The gestalt changes. What a moment before appeared to be a picture of one goblet changes before your eyes to two faces looking at one another. Figure and ground reverse. Appearance and reality switch places. The dreamer awakens.

The transition from the outlaw's to the lover's perspective happens a thousand times in an individual's lifetime, but always instantly. In the twinkling of an eye one goes through the gate of the big paradox.

The big paradox is that every individual atom and self is singular and unique and at the same time an integral part of Gregory Bateson's "pattern that connects," the tightly woven fabric of being. The quantum change in the psyche's identity takes place as one realizes that the self, like light, is simultaneously a particle and a wave. The outlaw sees the self as an autonomous center in a Newtonian world; the lover experiences the self as a vibratory event within a quantum world—a spirit. In the unitive glimpse, we see the self-spirit as belonging both within the collection of individuals that make up the multiverse and within the network of life that makes up the universe.

Albert Einstein defines the viewpoint and the task of becoming a lover:

> A human being is a part of the whole, called by us the "universe," a part limited in time and space. He experiences himself, his thoughts and feelings, as something separated from the rest—a kind of optical delusion of his consciousness. This delusion is a kind of prison for us, restricting us to our personal desires and to affection for a few persons nearest to us. Our task must be to free ourselves from this prison by widening our circle of compassion to embrace all living creatures and the whole of nature in its beauty.[1]

I speak of a glimpse rather than a vision, because the initiation into the lover's perspective need not be a momentous affair. It is not usually a vision that gives us an overview or a Hegelian God's-eye view of the meaning of everything. It may begin simply with the shock of wonder.

Suddenly. The encrustations of sophistication fall away and we find ourselves standing in front of the bare fact of being.

One day, perhaps, you are watching an ordinary ladybug climb up an old beige curtain with sun-faded forget-me-nots still blooming in the background pattern. Suddenly, the bug crosses the invisible line between being an assumed part of the known world, with a name and a classification, and becomes a marvel. You find yourself wondering why there are ladybugs. And what would it be like to be a ladybug? And does it look at me and wonder?

Willi Unsoeld, who was on the American team that first climbed Mt. Everest, told me that when he was returning from the peak, he paused on a high col to admire the view. Turning around, he saw a small blue flower in the snow. "I don't know how to describe what happened," he said. "Everything opened up and flowed together and made some strange kind of sense. And I was at complete peace. I have no idea how long I stood there. It could have been minutes or hours. Time melted. But when I came down my life was different."

Accidentally, you conceive; think about an abortion; decide for vague reasons that it might be a good time to have a baby. It grows in your womb. Then comes the labor, the stretching, the pain of birth. And LIFE enters the world, squalling from the depths of your body. You can't quite believe it, but from then on you know that you are within the creative intelligence of Being.

In the middle of a long illness, you throw all the stones you have at the lurking shadow. But death still lingers near. And your remaining life is rare and precious, a moment-by-moment gift.

You are faced with the spectacle of a bombed village. Old and young bodies torn by shrapnel, roads clogged with refugees. You want to vomit. A primal cry of protest arises from the deepest part of your sacred sense of aliveness. "No. Goddamn it, *no*. Life *ought* not to be like this. We were made for something better, gentler."

It can happen anywhere, anytime. The shock of wonder is an earthquake that changes our perception of ourselves and the world and rearranges the foundations of our identity. A tidal wave of astonishment washes away the polite virtues of the adult, the self-sufficiency of the outlaw. Explanations, myths, ideologies crumble like so many sand castles. When the shock recedes, we are left with a memory of having been in the presence of the holy, the awesome and fascinating mystery (*mysterium: tremendum et fascinans*— as Rudolph Otto called it).

The glimpse shatters our categories and opens us to becoming a lover. It does not present us with a formula, a system, or a theology, a five-year plan for achieving utopia. As a result of our shift in perception and identity, we have not more answers but more questions. Or rather, we have a new quest—the search to find a way to live more fully in the presence of the grandeur of Being to which we belong.

Mystics, philosophers, and theologians have used a wide variety of languages to convey the experience of the unity of being. It is the vision of God, enlightenment, nirvana. In Tantrism, the opening of the third eye in the middle of the forehead is the symbol for seeing things whole. Greek philosophers spoke of the unity of the human logos and the Divine Logos. Eastern mystics emphasized the unity of substance between atman and Brahman, Christian mystics speak about the unity of the will of God and the will of the believer.

In every age, there have been skeptics and critical minds who found the anthropomorphic elements in God language abhorrent and have substituted more abstract, philosophical notions—the Prime Mover, the Absolute Spirit, Nature, the Life Force, Cosmic Consciousness, Energy. But all of the capitalized nouns that appear in nontheistic visions are pseudonyms of God. They are all designed to make the existential affirmation that there is a bond between the self and the cosmos, that every being is within Being, that human consciousness is interior to the consciousness that informs all things. God in His-Her-Its aliases is a cry the self makes: "I am not alone."

In spite of the testimony of visionaries of all times, there exists today a widespread skepticism about the legitimacy of the mystical experience of unity. Freud voiced one type of objection: "The oceanic experience is a memory of a wish to return to the womb. It is projection, a wish fulfillment of infantile minds who cannot accept the truth that we are orphans in a haphazard world." Marx voiced another objection: "Religion is the opiate of the people, it is ideology, a soporific that dulls our awareness of social inequalities and injustice." (One is tempted to reply: If religion is the opiate of the masses, then explanations are the librium of the elite.)

Certainly, history has shown us enough bloodstained crusades, inquisitions, five-year plans, and "just" wars perpetrated by true believers to make us suspect anyone who speaks authoritatively in the name of God, or Being, or History. The line separating the unitive vision and fanaticism is faint. Those who glimpse the Absolute have a tendency to become absolutists, speak *ex cathedra,* try to impose their vision on others. Mysticism (political or ecclesiastical) easily degenerates into spiritual tyranny. The children of light delight in defining and then destroying the children of darkness.

But the dangers of mysticism should not deter us from the vision quest. Fool's gold deceives us only because there is real gold. Counterfeit money testifies to sound currency. One of the most difficult tasks we will face in the twenty-first century is to coin a new nonrepressive, nonauthoritarian, nondogmatic way of thinking and talking about the "highest" forms of human consciousness. In a world dangerously fragmented by competing ideologies (economic and political gods), we urgently need more universally accessible ways to speak about the vision of the single cosmos. We need to demythologize our old religious and philosophical language and translate it into modern idiom. In an effort to make this translation, let us pick up our story of the ascent of consciousness where we left off.

As we have seen, the newly discovered autonomous self of the outlaw is beyond the social definitions of good and evil, beyond the masks of personality. But the outlaw is still alone within a context of an alien multiverse. There may be unity within the psyche, but there is chaos without. When the "psychological" crisis is resolved, the metaphysical or religious crisis begins. New questions emerge. Is the single self a bastion of meaning and purpose in an otherwise senseless world? Is there no bond that unites self and cosmos? Even a whole self cannot live in a completely fragmented world. Without some glimpse of cosmic unity, we are condemned to be aliens—alone and afraid in a world we never made. Both the Gnostics and the existentialists tried the experiment of pitting the lone self against a hostile universe. Neither found a way to create sufficient unity within the self to withstand the vision of a completely disunified world. Alienation can be healed only if we discover a cosmic bond that allows the self to recover "basic trust." Cosmic isolation is a burden that cannot be borne even by a mature self. The answer each person gives to the primal question—Am I alone?—is the religious solution. For, as Whitehead said: "Religion is what a person does with his solitariness."

Nor is the driving need for a unified vision a metaphysical crutch for those not strong enough to live without illusions. It is, rather, a demand of reason. William James has shown that what he calls "the sentiment of rationality" involves a balance between two cravings: the passion for distinguishing, for breaking things into their components, and a passion for simplifying and discovering the unifying principle that binds things together. Human rationality always moves between the many and the one, pluralism and monism. Complete pluralism leaves us in a sand heap multiverse. Complete monism condemns us to a monotonous prison in which individuals are reduced to illustrations of universal principles. An adequate science must investigate both individual species of facts and the pattern that connects. Without falling in love with the numerous pieces of data, there is no spice in life. Without some theory and glimpse of the whole within which the parts inhere, there is no security or existential unity for the individual. Or, as slang wisdom has it: A reasonable person must be able to let it all hang out as well as get it all together.

The shock of wonder is necessarily rare and intermittent. In the mystic's glimpse, as in the ecstasy of orgasm, the boundaries of individuality are melted. For a moment I see that I am a cell within the cosmic body, perhaps a nerve ending, or a neuron within the heart of Being. But like any part of an organic whole, I must rapidly fall back into my limited view and function, or else I cannot serve my purpose within the economy of the whole. The heart exists in some predetermined harmony with brain and liver. The knowledge of the overall operation of the body is somehow programmed into each cell. But the individual cell must function primarily within the definition of the organ within which it resides. Normal functioning requires that each fragment be both connected to and ignorant of the whole. Each person is a cosmic workhorse whose blinders slip for an extraordinary instant to allow a glimpse of the universal purpose. If, as Hegel says, "the truth is the whole," then to be a fragment is to exist in qualified ignorance. The flash of enlightenment in which we see the entirety with which we are bonded is as necessary to be fully human as it is impossible to sustain. It is moments of extraordinary illumination that allow us to live trustingly within Howard Thurman's "luminous darkness" of the ordinary.

It follows from the nature of the dialectic that is built into consciousness as it moves back and forth between:

| distinguishing | and | comprehending |
|---|---|---|
| the many | and | the one |
| the data | and | the unifying principle |
| individual beings | and | Being |
| particulars | and | the universal |

that the outlaw's and the lover's perspectives will remain in continual oscillation. For a moment, we may "see," "feel," "know," or have a premonition that all is one, that tragedy is not final, that the self is not alone. A moment later, however, our attention shifts, and we return to the chaos of everyday, to the struggle for existence and the will to power. The trust that allows us to surrender, to be a part of a larger whole, to accept our lives as a gift oscillates with the courage to exist as autonomous individuals. In speaking about the post-adult life, we may distinguish logically between the outlaw and the lover stages. But, *to be most accurate, we should speak of the second half of life as an escalating spiral in which the self-spirit of the outlaw-lover increasingly replaces the adult personality.* The deeper we penetrate into the mystery of our individuality, the further we travel into the unifying beyond of the cosmos.

Human beings are always parting and uniting; abstracting and healing. If we say that the mind separates, we must also say that the heart re-minds us that we belong. We are fully human only so long as we remain a-part and come together. It is this movement that has suggested to outlaw-mystics of all ages that the metaphor of love, and particularly loving sexuality between man and woman, provides us our best clue for understanding who we are.

Every religion has recognized that the lightning cannot be captured. The spiritual disciplines that spring up around the perimeters of the mystical experience are ways of remaining near enough to the ambience of the sacred so that normal life may reflect something of the radiance of the vision of God. Chanting, prayer, ritual, meditation, hymns, dancing, and all of the vocabulary of religion are ways of reminding us of the cosmic unity that we necessarily forget in order to be individuals. They provide ways to manage and celebrate the tension between the one and the many which is LIFE and life.

One example will suffice. Breath, will, and fire are common metaphors in religion. As the well loved hymn says:

> Breathe on me, Breath of God
> Until my heart is pure
> Until with thee I will one will
> To do and to endure.
>
> Breathe on me, Breath of God
> Till I am wholly Thine
> Until this earthly part of me
> Glows with Thy fire divine.

In the moment of the mystic glimpse, human breath is experienced not as a mere biological phenomenon, a process of taking in oxygen and dispelling carbon dioxide, but as a movement within the Divine spirit. Kabir says: "Student, tell me, what is God. He is the breath inside the breath." To be is to be inspired, and to be willing to expire. To the mystic, the human will is no longer the autonomous center of choice, but is experienced as interior to the divine willing. Autonomy is replaced by theonomy, as the lover finds that his or her deepest desires are identical with the divine purpose. And the unity of breath and Spirit, will and Will, is the experience of the passion that moves all life. Sexuality and religion are re-united in the mystic glimpse. To that story we now turn.

THE LOVER'S BODY: EMPATHY AND COSMIC EROTICISM

In the unitive glimpse, the entire cosmos is seen as a manifestation of the playfulness of divine energy. The world is Godplay or Leela. As a result, sexuality and eros are transformed and are henceforth experienced not as mere biological phenomena, but as forms of ontological attraction.

That the lover's body, and therefore the erotic and sexual style, are radically different than the outlaw's, follows inevitably from the axioms of the psyche that we have seen emerge in our study of the different stages of life. To restate: (1) the psyche reaches its fullest potential in a series of stages in which it develops toward a more universal understanding and compassion; (2) every stage has its characteristic philosophy of life and psychological orientation; (3) every philosophical and psychological stance shapes the body, its defense mechanisms and character armor; and (4) the nature of our motivation, our eros, changes each time we understand the world in a more inclusive way.

How is the lover's body changed? It is no longer a sealed, autonomous unit that may or may not be in communication with other selves. It becomes a nexus, a place of meeting, a crossroads, a center where all lines meet, a prism through which pure light passes and breaks into a rainbow of color, a regional being through which radiates the pulse, power, energy, intention of Being-becoming-itself.

In the strictest sense, it is not accurate to speak about the lover's body. No noun can capture the pulsing commonwealth of cells that make up any living thing. We exist as verbs, always in process. Each singular-plurality is a vibratory center in constant intercourse with other vibratory centers. There are no isolated events or entities in the universe.

Another way of thinking about this shift in identity is by using the notion of spirit, which has a long and honored history, but which has recently come under a cloud because of its vagueness.

Under the impact of both religious dualism* that juxtaposed spirit and flesh and honored only the former, and secular reductionism that carved humans into brain and body, the idea of spirit disintegrated and became an empty, pious phrase with no serious content. I propose to use the idea of spirit in characterizing the lover's identity in an exact way. *Spirit is the capacity to transcend the encapsulation of personality (the roles and myths that in-form the adult ego), as well as the autonomous individuated self of the outlaw. Spirit is the realization that we are embodied within a continuum, that we are alive only when a universal life force flows through us like breath through lungs, like wind through the evergreens.*

To think in contemporary categories about the transformations of the lover's body, we may best start with Norman O. Brown's monumental books, *Life Against Death* and *Love's Body*. By an intricate and elegant analysis, Brown shows that the psyche of western man has been constructed by desensitizing the total body and confining the experience of ecstatic pleasure and transcendence to the genitals. The obsession with genital sexuality designates one organ of the body as *the erotic center*. This centralizing of eros is an inevitable consequence of the adult identity that is based on loyalty to a single mythic center. Adults sacrifice their bodies to the body politic. Their reward for adhering to what they insist is "the reality principle" is the pleasure of role-governed genital sexuality and the prestige of status. We become obsessed with genital sexuality because it is the only erotic pleasure left for us to enjoy once we have committed our bodies, our time, our energies to a life of warfare and compulsive, alienated work. We punish ourselves by organizing our lives around abstractions, by sacrificing enjoyment of the here and now to pile up surplus possessions. We are always postponing gratification, promising ourselves we will enjoy life once the work is done. We are like the character in *Waiting for Godot*, who was asked: "Do you believe in the life to come?" and answered, "Mine always was."

Our eyes become so focused on goals that we forget to wonder in the presence of a rose. Our ears become so accustomed to

---

*See Sam Keen, *Apology for Wonder*, for a more complete analysis.

chatter, propaganda, and purposeful talk that we no longer listen to the changing winds. Our noses become so clogged by pollution, cigarettes, deodorants, our lungs so constricted by shallow, rapid breathing, that we lose the scent of life. The deep emotional centers of the limbic brain that are directly stimulated by smell lie dormant. Our bodies, in short, become erotic deserts, deprived of a multitude of sensory delights. And the genitals are assigned the role of oasis in a wasteland of pleasure. We expect the flowering of sex to make up to us for a desecrated life of the senses.

Brown suggests it is time to reorganize the psyche and to live by the pleasure principle, to resurrect the entire body, to become "polymorphously perverse." All the senses must be emancipated from our obsession with getting and owning. The tyranny of possession must be broken if we are to eroticize our bodies and minds. Brown has few suggestions about how we might accomplish this psychological revolution. His many critics, who have suggested that he is advocating androgyny, bisexuality, homosexuality, or promiscuity, seem to miss the point entirely. At the very least, Brown is trying to liberate eros from its genital moorings and envision a life in which a person would be connected to the entire environment with an intensity that was once reserved for the genital connection. The point is not that genital sexuality is abandoned, but that it ceases to be the dominant form of intercourse. To be animated by a vision of the unity of all things is to see that intercourse is the fundamental fact of the universe; it is not an act that must be accomplished.

The Christian notion of agape may help us edge closer to an understanding of cosmic eroticism. The Christian tradition recognizes many forms of love—*eros, philia, charitas, agape.* Eros is considered a lesser, merely human, form of love that is always determined by some ego hunger or need. It begins from deficiency. "I want, I need, I desire you because I am incomplete without you." Agape, on the other hand, is God's love that arises from plentitude and seeks nothing from its object. It is an overflow, a superfluous, giving form of love. Although the source of agape is divine, humans may be graced by it. We may rise above our needy-possessive-conquering orientation toward life and share the godlike perspective.

Agape may be understood as a metacultural ability to see with the heart, to penetrate to the depth of things. As cultural beings, we are always attentive to appearances. Fetishes govern our erotic lives. Propaganda and advertising create an *image* of the desirable object of love and promises. If you are beautiful (put disks in your lips if you are a Ubangi, wear designer jeans if you are American), you will be loved. Agape allows us to look beneath appearances, beneath any benefit we might gain by loving the other, to be *moved by* the *essential* being of the other. The accidents or predicates (old-young, ugly-beautiful, rich-poor, smart-dumb) are no aphrodisiac for the agapistic lover.

We need not accept all the overload of Christian theology to lay claim to agape. The capacity for radical empathy, which is the essence of agape, is universal. The human imagination can inhabit any conceivable being. We are all protean creatures; we change shape many times within a day. We normally flow in and out of our-selves. A mother watches a doctor as he prepares to give her child an injection. As the needle touches the child, she winces. At this moment, she has broken her identity with her own body and entered into the body of her child. This capacity for empathy was so developed in Ramakrishna, the nineteenth-century Indian mystic, that when he saw a servant boy being whipped welts immediately appeared on his own body. Experientially, my body is a plastic medium that may at one moment be contained within my skin and may at the next extend into a tree or another person. The more feelingful, open, and undefended our bodies become, the wider the range of our knowing. A godlike or agapistic consciousness would be polymorphous or protean enough to inhabit any entity. At the deepest level, knowledge is the awareness of our participation in the reality of the other. Ignorance is based on the illusion of our separation.

How far can we push human experience in this direction? How much can we develop the ability to leave the boundaries of our individual bodies (interests, viewpoints, ideologies, defense mechanisms) to intuitively-empathically-imaginatively-astrally inhabit other bodies? The only answer seems to lie in a paradox that mysticism and eroticism share:

It takes a strong identity to surrender.
The more we accept the limits of the body the more we may transcend "it."
The more secure I am the more I can risk.
The most ecstatic experience of the self comes when the boundaries of the self are transcended.
I am most I when I am aware of my participation in a world beyond me.

In mystical and erotic experience, self-transcendence, or the life of the spirit, is limited only by the unwillingness to die to the old self. Crucify the ego so the self may be resurrected—this is the core of every religion. In erotic experience, the same paradox holds. Orgasm is the little death. The ecstasies we love and fear take place as we cross the threshold between self and other. Carnal and mystical knowledge is limited by our natural reluctance to overcome our normal self-encapsulation and our fear of death. We become lovers (or philosophers, as Socrates noted) only by becoming well-practiced in the art of dying.

Whether we use the language of religion, eroticism, or psychology, the broad outlines of the theory of death and rebirth are easy enough to sketch. But the doing is difficult! "It is not easy to die and be reborn," as Fritz Perls and St. John both remind us. The vision of the dancing God within whom we all live and move and have our being is a prelude to the final journey in which the self, which has been so painfully re-membered, is forgotten and vanishes into the world.

THE LOVER'S SPIRIT: INCARNATION AND HOMECOMING

When the unitive glimpse occurs, the lover discovers that the kingdom of grace is everywhere. Until the last moment, the pilgrim ascending the mountain of consciousness struggles upward toward an imagined summit. Suddenly, there is no place to go. The peak experience destroys the mountain. When we get there, as Gertude Stein said, "There is no there there." The moment the self arrives at the vision of the unity of the cosmos, the eye (the I) that sees is dissolved into what is seen. At the top of the world, we discover it is an illusion to struggle to some point that is designated as the top of the world. There is no Holy Mountain upon which the gods live, no spine of the world *(axis mundi)* that supports the heavens and runs down into the bowels of the earth. There is no single center where God dwells. As Nicholas of Cusa said: "God is an intelligible sphere whose center is everywhere and whose circumference is nowhere." No temple, creed, ritual, or nation can contain the Holy. The One is in the many. Being sustains all beings. Thus any day may be a holy day, any place a sanctuary. Time is unconscious eternity. Enlightenment is awakening to the movement of consciousness in every episode of nature and history. At the end of the quest, we awaken from the myth of the quest: What we have been searching for has never been lost. We have always been at home smack in the middle of the eternity of life.

So what happens to the lover after the vision? Most begin by uttering a cosmic laugh (the opposite of the primal scream!) that destroys the demon of seriousness. The illusion dissolves with the realization that our carefully constructed unique selves were only anxious Maginot lines we built against imaginary enemies, our promethean struggle against the gods a shadow drama we played with ourselves. The mystical "Ah ha!" experience is getting the point of the big joke upon which the ego is built. What could be more foolish than:

a man riding on an ox, looking for an ox
searching for something that is not missing
ascending a nonexistent mountain
striving for contentment

dividing the world in searching for unity
killing for peace
running after happiness

working for grace
creating alienation so we can come together
questing for God when we are standing on sacred ground.

But when the laughter dies away—as it does inevitably, as soon as one casts an eye back into the bloodstained battle that is still being carried on in human history by those who haven't seen through the big illusion—the question still remains. What now? Where and how is the lover to live?

When we examine the stories, legends, and rumors that surround the mystics who are reputed to have glimpsed the divine unity, we find radically different accounts of their powers and manner of life.

Oftentimes saints, mystics, and holy persons are portrayed as near demigods with miraculous powers. In Tibet and India, all manner of extraordinary powers (siddhis) are attributed to those who have been enlightened. They can shrink their bodies to the size of an atom or expand them to encompass the universe; abolish time and see into the future and past; abolish space and teleport themselves in their astral bodies to distant places; become invisible; materialize or dematerialize objects; perform miraculous cures, and so on.

It is difficult to know what to make of reports of miracles. Perhaps Sai Baba could materialize gold toys from midair, or Jesus walk on the water, or Ramana Maharshi cure the sick. It is not my interest here to try to draw a hard line between fact and imagination (a game that scientists and poets play anew each generation). It would be an act of hubris to claim to know the limits of human consciousness. Perhaps the siddhis are real and the saints are evolutionary breakthroughs, the harbingers of what evolution intends for us all. One day we may all be masters of time and space, in telepathic communication with distant minds. We may perform feats of psychokinesis or accomplish healing by the laying on of hands. Considering the hundreds of millions of years the universe seems to have invested in the prologue before humans appeared, it seems safe to speculate that we are only at the beginning of the first chapter in the development of the powers of consciousness. It is too early to foretell what the human mind might be when it grows up. But all of this remains in the subjunctive, in the realm of maybe, perhaps, and someday.

There is a second, radically different tradition, within both Buddhism and Christianity, that portrays lovers as those who are able to live in the ordinary world with extraordinary grace.

In the Buddhist tradition, a Bodhisattva is an enlightened person who enters the outskirts of nirvana, and then turns around and goes back into the ordinary world to teach others the path. He takes a vow not to enter nirvana until all sentient beings have been saved. Although filled with compassion, he does not return out of "altruism," moral obligation, or sentimental concern for others. Rather, since all beings are united, he can't enter fully into nirvana so long as any one remains outside. His compassion springs from an awareness of a cosmic identity. Conscience and consciousness are the same. As Eugene Debs said, "While there is a lower class, I am in it; while there is a criminal element, I am of it; while there is a soul in prison, I am not free."

Once the illusion of the separate self vanishes, compassion for all living beings is inseparable from self-love. "I" am a part of the struggling mass of conscious and unconscious beings, of the creation that groans and travails (Romans 8:22) waiting to be delivered from bondage. The Bodhisattva recognizes the bond with all sentient beings in the same way the child accepts the bond with the mother. The radical trust in the intention of the cosmos is a repetition at the highest level of maturity of the childlike "basic trust" in the mother. We are all bonded, beings-with-one another. Empathy is the essence of human identity. Our beingness is our togetherness.

In both the tantric and the Christian myths, glory must be discovered in the lowest. Enlightenment or grace transforms the base functions of the body. The Protestant reformation began when the bowels of the chronically constipated Luther opened at the moment when he finally understood that "the just shall live by faith." The Absolute consciousness (which is inseparable from my consciousness of the Absolute) can be found in any manger or supermarket. Therefore, as Meister Eckhart said, if you are in rapture in the seventh heaven and hear of an old lady who is hungry, descend from your mystical experience and bring this creature of God a bowl of soup. Mysticism ends in politics. The prodigal consciousness climbs the heights and then returns to the heartland to dwell as a shepherd of being.

Zen Buddhism teaches that the miracle of the enlightened man is that he eats when he eats and sleeps when he sleeps and accepts the normal reality as the manifestation of Buddha consciousness. *Samsara* (the world of suffering and impermanency) is nirvana.

In a similar way, the Lutheran tradition within Christianity says that grace overtakes us as we remain sinners. The true miracle is not that we are transformed into morally perfect demigods with magical powers, but that we are enabled to be joyful within the contradictions and sufferings of history. Kierkegaard gives an unforgettable picture of the invisible saint whom he calls "the knight of faith." Although Kierkegaard admits he has found no certain example of the knight of faith, he is able to draw an imaginary portrait. The man looks perfectly ordinary, like a tax collector. His tread is vigorous and he is smartly dressed as he goes for his Sunday afternoon walks. He takes delight in everything, tends to his work, loves his wife, smokes his pipe. No outward activity marks him as unusual. Yet every instant he is surrendering his finite consciousness to his infinite identity.

> The man has made and every instant is making the movements of infinity. With infinite resignation he has drained the cup of life's profound sadness, he knows the bliss of the infinite, he senses the pain of renouncing everything, the dearest things he possesses in the world, and yet finiteness tastes to him just as good as to one who never knew anything higher.[2]

The most profound paradox of the struggle to explore the highest reaches of consciousness is that in the end we come home again to the ordinary. As T. S. Eliot wrote,

> We shall not cease from exploration
> And the end of all our exploring

Will be to arrive where we started
And know the place for the first time.

Everything is the same and everything is different. "God" is no more visible than before. The divine consciousness, the cosmic mind, is still invisible except in its manifestations—in mountains, trees, ladybugs, spaceships, and congressmen. But the enlightened person sees a single light-energy-consciousness radiating through all beings, and abides by St. Augustine's single moral principle— "Love and do what you want."

### The Sheaths of the Lover's Body

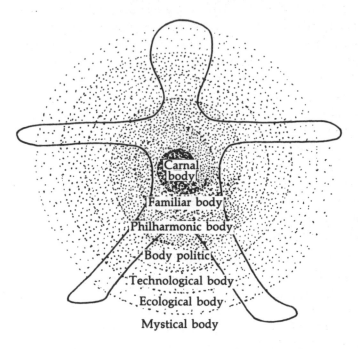

THE EMBODIMENTS OF LOVE: EROTIC POSTURES, OR SHEATHS OF THE LOVER'S BODY

From our being flows our doing. Ethics follows naturally from metaphysics. Who we are determines how we will act. The love glimpses the essential wholeness/holiness within which all being belong, but remains painfully aware of the actual dis-ease, suffering, and alienation that afflict us all.

Thus the task of the lover is to be an agent of healing, to embody health, to incarnate passion. Richard Baker Roshi suggests that we might substitute the word "healing" for the word "living." Whenever we are living fully, we are in the process of healing the artificial divisions, the needless diseases, the senseless tragedies.

Any account of the passionate life should include a description of the variety of the acts of love—a suggested repertoire for the complete healer. The following account of the concentric dimensions, realms, or sheaths that make up the lover's body may be considered the major erotic postures, the modes of intercourse that define our being and doing as lovers. They are the spiritual disciplines, the asanas, the acts of prayer, meditation, and ritual within which we incarnate our love and discover that the self exists fully as spirit—as a self-transcending being.

## The Carnal Body-Mind-Spirit

The carnal self is the first sheath of the lover's body.

We begin and return again and again to the individual carnal self. The outlaw-lover lives as a prodigal whose consciousness is always transcending the limits of being a citizen of Pittsburgh or Bethlehem, and yet is always returning to be embodied in a particular time and place. The self melts into the boundlessness of spirit and then returns home to the familiar perimeters of its own skin. If I answer the appeal to become a lover, it is no nebulous or general essence of mankind I am called to love, but my self, my children, my wife, my friends, my community, my land, my people, my tools, my world. The lover heals the world not by a vague and abstract love for everybody and everything, but by becoming passionate and vowing fidelity to concrete relationships, persons, institutions, and places. The only *Beyond* I can know is the one found *within* the intimate experience of the world as it is given to me. Only as I remain true to that being whose autobiography I alone can write and whose flesh I am, do I transcend my self, find my self encompassed in Being-becoming-itself. To be carnal means to re-cognize that *flesh is spirit*. My life, my time, my community is the locus of revelation. God is always incognito, hiding on a busy street, in falling rain, caressing us in every breath, in our DNA, encouraging us to become who we are.

## The Familiar Body: The Hearth of Kindness

The family is the second sheath of the lover's body. It is within the bonds of kinship that we may learn the practice of kindness and the potency of forgiveness.

We were, are, and always will be members of a family. We are embodied in a network that includes mother and father (present or missing) and the families to which they belong, stretching back in time beyond the memories of our grandparents and spreading out to include a web of uncles, aunts, and kissing cousins. For better, for worse, for richer, for poorer, carefully and carelessly, the warp of family will run through the tapestry of our days. The gifts and wounds we bear can be traced back to the ways in which we were cherished, encouraged, ignored, repressed, abused. Whether our families were good or bad, weak or strong, they imprinted us with our earliest self-images and expectations about the world.

Every family represents a challenge and a difficulty, a given that must be accepted and transcended if we are to grow into independent selfhood and beyond.

It was Freud who first discovered how much the adult psyche is still haunted by a shadow drama involving infantile feelings, memories, and habits. He taught us that to liberate eros we have to work through the unconscious family drama—relive the unbridled desire for forbidden persons, the pain of being misunderstood, frustrated, punished, ignored, the terror of abandonment and the fear of punishment. We live our chosen life only when we resurrect our unchosen past. To be healed we return to our brokenness. To know our power we remember our impotence. To love we experience the ambivalent hate-love we dared not feel when our earliest need for love was disappointed. To become free we must recall the captivity we knew within the bonds and the bondage of the family.

This archaeology of the self leads us to reexperience our anger and resentment against our parents and thus frees us from infantile dependence and obedience. In time, it brings us full circle to understand, forgive them, and feel the compassion that is the essence of the family bond. Until we have experienced both resentment and gratitude and have forgiven our parents and siblings, we remain stuck in the family and caught in the blame game.

At present, families are disintegrating at a rapid rate under the impact of economic pressures that force both father and mother into the workforce, easy divorce, constant mobility and rootlessness, and the new ethic of selfishness. The task of caring for and initiating children is increasingly turned over to professionals, as both mother and father choose to center their identity in the economic rather than the familiar.

More accurately, the crisis in the family goes along with a modern redefinition of "economic." *The word "economic" originally meant the art and science of managing a household.* Under the impact of the omnivorous market-mentality, it changed its meaning and became "the production, distribution, and consumption of commodities." The subversion and destruction of the family can be measured in the distance between these two definitions—between home economics and corporate economics. What is difficult for us to see, since *our myth is centered in the new definition of the economic order as the reality,* is that the destruction of the family is not an accidental but a necessary effect of our system. Our corporations need weak families. Industry needs work-defined men and women. The corporate world does not function "efficiently" with persons who find their center in familiarity. To get workers, warriors, and consumers, the industrial system must destroy and atomize the family, usurp the authority of the father, replace home economics with a consumer economy. We sacrifice the gods and goddesses of the hearth to the appetite for profit and convenience. We create isolated individuals and a philosophy of "self-realization" because our mythical system requires that our prime loyalty be given to the abstract world of professionalized labor rather than the intimate world of the family and community. Our daily bread is now the weekly paycheck, our father in heaven the boss in the executive suite who has the power of the purse.

No number of products, money, or abstract goods satisfies us. This is the fundamental mistake we make in substituting the economic for the familiar as the root of identity. Economic man is driven by insatiability because, as my friend Anne Valley Fox says, "You can never get enough of what you didn't want in the first place." Beyond the level of comfortable survival, goods become a substitute for the primal goodness we were denied—familiarity, intimacy, kindness. Freud reminded us that money does not satisfy us because it was not an infantile need. To the degree that we do not create families within which children are welcomed, cherished, touched, we will create a social order in which we produce more and more substitutes for absent kindness. And it will be ruled by distant authorities who keep the masses in control either by a glut of consumer goods or by repressive police-state tactics. In such a world, we will never have the feeling that we are known for who we are. We will always wear a mask, perform, hide.

Without recreation of the familiar—which means not only the nuclear and the extended family, but the integrity of place, environment, and community within which alone the family can thrive—there is no way we can advance the cause of peace. The possibility of extending kindness beyond the range of the biological family rests upon the experience of having been included within a loving kinship. It is only when we recognize that the stranger is one of our kinfolk that the normal rule of nations of paranoia and warfare may be changed.

It is well to remember that most utopian schemes and tyrannical states try to destroy the family by substituting an abstract allegiance to duty, country, and distant authority for the concrete fidelity to our flesh-and-blood intimates. Beware of programs that mechanize and streamline child care, replace parents with professionals, and demean the activity of creating a home and a home economics! From Plato to Marx to Mao, the family has always been the target of the "improvers" of mankind (always men).

For those interested in becoming lovers, the family is an essential school for compassion and the child is the professor who teaches us about unconditional love. No guru or program for reducing egotism is so effective as the discipline and sacrifice necessary to raise a family. Nor is any promise of immortality so believable, so palpable, as the sight of one's children growing into ripeness. By caring for a child, a man and a woman may recapitulate their own childhood, return to the terrible and wonderful corridors of early memory. Conscious parenthood is very nearly a substitute for psychoanalysis. Quite simply, a child invites us into a posture where we must humble ourselves to learn. Once again we crawl on the floor, see the world as a little person, remember what it was like to confront a dog who is taller than yourself. Listen to the way you address your child and you hear the echoes of your parents. Perhaps we never understand, appreciate, and forgive our parents thoroughly until we have ourselves become parents.

In large measure, the genital obsession that is rampant in western culture is a product of trying to sever sexuality from the context of familiarity. Language itself might have warned us that we invite trouble when we divorce recreational sex from creational sex. It is a piece of modern hubris to believe that sexual passion can be maintained when we conspire to forget the most powerful intentionality of the sexual act. Certainly, every sexual encounter need not intend a child in the conscious minds of the lovers. But, to be healing, it needs to create familiarity and kindness. Finally, the second innocence and care-fulness we learn when we tend the young is necessary to the maturation of a lover. When sexuality is completely divorced from the ambience of procreation and family, as it is among playboys and playgirls, it falls into sterility and loses its mood of kindliness.

Eros eventually dies when it is divorced from familiarity. In the western myth, the fabricating mind has taken over every activity, denying every possibility of grace. Everything must be made. We must *make* love. We must even *make* a name for ourselves. Yet we know that anonymity creates violence. Those who are not touched strike out to demand recognition from a reluctant audience, to make a name for themselves. John Hinckley, Jr., the man who attempted to assassinate President Reagan, did it to become known. In our mania for making, we have nearly forgotten that we each bear a *given* name. Unless we reject the gift of family, we do not, in the final sense, have to make a name for ourselves. The family gives us our first name, our first story, our first place to be. No matter how much we must struggle with the limits imposed upon us by families, there is no health possible apart from belonging within a circle of arms where we are known and accepted.

## The Philharmonic Body: Friendship

Friendship (*philia*) forms the third sheath of the lover's body, the birthplace of freedom. Within *philia,* the lover learns about self-transcendence, spirit, and freedom.

The bond of the family was imposed upon us. We were not free to choose our parents, our birth order, or our siblings. We start out in life with a biological destiny in which almost everything is necessary, little is free. Even when we rebel against the familiar bonds and try to sever them, we never wholly succeed. As Howard Thurman once said, "The bonds that hold us most tightly are those we have broken." Learning to love our family is an exercise, sometimes difficult, sometimes easy, in coming to accept one aspect of our destiny.

The bond of friendship, on the other hand, is joyfully and freely chosen. Although there are cultures in which friendships and marriages are arranged by parents, these are lasting only if they blossom into rich and free relationships. In friendship, we rise above biological destiny. Eros gains its wings, shows its true nature as the *power of transcendence* that sleeps within the human spirit. We struggle with our lovers and mates, but with our friends the way is easy. We fall into conversations that go far into the night. We reveal our deepest feelings. Our words flow together. One confidence breeds another. Precisely because friendships are formed when two people are drawn to each other by a mutual liking, and not by a mad, passionate, biologically driven need, they are usually more orderly and enduring than romance.

Within friendship we become transparent; and in self-revelation we come to know ourselves. We perform our social roles before an audience of our peers and authorities, but we tell the secrets that give the clues to our deepest feelings only to our soulmates. In friendship, the paradox of love shows another of its facets: I gain personal identity only in the presence of another with whom I share my self.

Friendship also teaches us the discipline of discrimination. I am not a friend to everybody. There is something exclusive about friendship. No less than marriage, friendship is based on a vow and a commitment that demands that I exclude many in order to include one. Mature friendships must be cared for and tended. My friend and I meet, spend time together, allow uncluttered hours to savor each other's company. We do not invite every passing stranger into our friendship. Our time with each other is limited. Over the course of a lifetime, we have a multitude of acquaintances but only a handful of true friends. To grow strong, eros must be planted and send its roots down deep into the soil of time. If we continually jerk the plant up, it remains feeble.

Friendship exists as a sanctuary that is situated between the private world of the family, the ambiguities of sexual love, and the public world of the corporation and politics. We dream of creating a society made up exclusively of friends. In hope, we dream that we may be Philadelphians to each other, dwellers within a city of brotherly love. But the ideal fails, and rightly so, because it is a false ideal. Friendship is a sanctuary precisely because within it we may be *more* than, and *different* from the destiny we must wrestle with in the family or the roles we must assume to enter the contractual order of civility. With my friend I am neither father, nor merchant, nor citizen. I am uniquely myself. The value of friendship lies in its exemption from the rules of usefulness, and from the compromises we voluntarily make as citizens. With my friend I may share my asocial, heretical, treasonous, antisocial, tabooed, or outrageous ideas, visions, and feelings.

Friendship also sets us free, for a moment, from the sweet burden of sexuality. Nowhere is it easier to confuse and identify the erotic with the sexual than in friendship, especially when it is between members of the opposite sex. We are drawn to each other. The pull is irresistible. We naturally have a fantasy and an urge to unite philia and libido. Wouldn't it be marvelous if our best friend could be our most passionate lover? But longtime experience testifies that it seldom works. The demands of genital sexuality and friendship overlap, but do not always mix well. Nowadays, in the dark ages of friendship, husbands and wives, or lovers, often claim they are each other's best friends. But I suspect this signals more a decline in the fortunes of friendship than an advance in the fortunes of marriage. The bonds of familiar and sexual love have their own special flavor—a warm, intimate, mixed fragrance of biology and choice. The deepest appeal of friendship is that it sets us free from the necessities imposed upon us by biology and politics. What is created within friendship is a relationship whose sole purpose is to be enjoyed. It is probably because it is rare and precious to know ourselves as useless and wonderful that we are willing to sacrifice genital pleasure to enjoy the dignities of friendship.

When men and women lose the habit of friendship, they become encapsulated within an incestuous family, or follow the illusion of romantic love, or sell themselves to the company store, or surrender their uniqueness for the security of a tyrannical political order that colonizes what was once their souls with an official ideology. Friendship is the surest antidote we have to self-betrayal and political tyranny. Friends bear witness that at the heart of each of us is something that can never be defined by an official ideology or doctrine, or contained within any institution. Our vastness and inexhaustibility can only be glimpsed when we are accepted by our friends without conditions, qualifications, ifs, ands, or buts, with warts, wrinkles, wounds, and, perhaps, halos.

Philia seems at first to be the most modest of the modes of love. It is as quiet as a shared cup of tea or glass of beer. Among men and women who dwell long together, it is so orderly as almost to escape notice. It is shared conversation. No howling on the full moon. No demonic explosions of contradictory passions. Friendships make gentlewomen and gentlemen open and unfearfu enough to give and receive as a matter of daily intercourse. It lacks romantic trappings; does not demand beautiful partners. Or youth. In fact, it is the solace of those who have nothing else. And when it is strong enough, we need little else—besides bread and shelter.

But look deeper and you will find in friendship the principle that allows us to abide the cruelties of fate and remain human. Isak Dinesen said, "All sorrows can be borne if you put them into a story." Storytelling is the heart of friendship. (The rise of the novel—the publication of the story—and later the cinema, correlates directly to a decline in friendship. We read or see others' stories in hope of finding our own, a hope that is vain so long as we do not have friends.) I am reminded of a woman from Israel I recently worked with who was having trouble breathing. As we talked, I saw the faded blue concentration camp numbers tattooed on her forearm. As she told me her story, she alternately coughed and cried. "When did you start having trouble breathing?" I asked. "When my friend died two years ago," she replied. "When she was alive, we could talk about anything. Although she had not been in the camps, she understood. But now there is no one to tell. And the nightmares haunt me. I can't sleep alone in the house. I know that if I want to live, I have to find another friend."

One of the foundation stones of an erotic philosophy is the philharmonic sense of the self that accompanies the experience of friendship. When I choose a friend, there is a convergence of my exercise of freedom; my surrender to the erotic impulse that attracts me to this particular person; the transcendence of my loneliness, self-encapsulation, paranoia, and narcissism; my meeting with a stranger who is in no way an enemy. We enjoy and celebrate a relationship that seems "like it was meant to be." As we create the words and lyrics of our relationship—en-chant each other—we seem to be moved by some preestablished harmony. Since I come to know myself within the mediating presence of my friend, I am a philharmonic being. I am embodied within the rhythms and harmonies of friendship.

## The Body Politic: The Compassionate Corporation

The body politic forms the fourth sheath of the lover's body. Here love as radical civility is potently expressed by acting in concert with others in a quest for justice.

### Idiotic Love and Political Compassion

One of the commonest perversions of love is the effort to limit it to the private sphere. The Greeks had a special name for those apolitical persons who thought eros was appropriately expressed only in privacy. They were called "idiots." In its original sense, "idiot" signified a purely private person. To Socrates, Plato, and Aristotle, human beings were social animals; hence those who took no part in the life of the body politic were less than human. Slaves, women whose horizons were limited to the household, lovers who became so fascinated with each other that they tended only to their private pleasures, religious visionaries who avoided the conflicts of political life—all were considered to be idiots. Any obsession that destroyed a person's public responsibility was considered demonic and not erotic.

In large measure, religious mysticism has historically shown a tendency to degenerate into idiocy. Many of the great visionaries who have seen through the illusions of the tribe and glimpsed the underlying, overarching unity of Being have fallen to the temptation to retreat from political involvement and remain in the bliss of mystical contemplation. From Plotinus to Ramanamaharshi, there is a line of mystical thinkers who see the soul's journey as "the flight of the alone to see the Alone," the return of atman to Brahman, the reunion of the naked soul with the Godhead. In this tradition of high mysticism, the true seeker is advised to turn his back on time in order to see eternity; to renounce the world, the flesh, and the devil and follow the spirit; to ignore politics or any effort to bring the kingdom of God on earth and take refuge in a direct, unmediated experience of the god beyond history.

In recent times, apolitical mysticism emerged in the psychedelic movement of the late 1960s and 1970s ("turn on, tune in, and drop out"), in the recent influx of gurus and religious communities devoted to the quest for enlightenment, and in orthodox psychoanalysis, which probed the psyche in the privacy of the consulting room.

All idiotic schemes for the salvation of the soul, whether by yoga, belief in Jesus, the guru, meditation, or the psychoanalytic process, are based on a mistaken isolation of inner and outer, the psyche from the community. All hold to the idiotic hope that the individual can be healed apart from the community.

Several lines of evidence converge to suggest why idiocy defeats the intention of love and becomes an erotic perversion.

First: All schemes for private salvation separate love and power and make a virtue out of a surrender to impotence. Those who forsake the world to cultivate the psyche abandon the exercise of power, accept the political status quo, and hence unconsciously conspire with the ideology of the ruling class. By refusing to enter the struggle to make the body politic more responsive to human need and more just, they turn their back on evil and leave the world as loveless as they found it. In India, for instance, centuries of transcendental mysticism and myriads of wandering holy men did little or nothing to change the systematic injustice of the caste system. Such voluntary impotence is often disguised as accepting the "will of God" who has ordained that the rain fall upon the just and the unjust. In effect, it equates love with sentiment and promises that when enough individuals' hearts have been changed, the community will practice justice. This radical separation of the sacred from the secular, private salvation from public policy, has rendered both fundamentalist Christian churches and orthodox psychologists mute about such major moral issues of our time as nuclear weapons, economic injustice, and ecological pollution. Love that does not act to change those conditions that allow humans to treat others in an unkindly way is a form of passivity and care/lessness. Underneath it lurks the impotence of the victim, not the potency of the lover. Those who care must use power.

Second: As Paul Tillich has shown, love, the exercise of power, and the quest for justice are inseparable. Love demands that we respect the integrity of the other, that we recognize each person's right to equality before the law. The practice of civility is the precondition that allows more intimate forms of love to blossom. Prophetic religion from Amos to George Fox to Martin Luther King, Jr., always enters into politics because it correctly sees that there is a necessary link between love and civil rights. Doing justice and loving mercy is the truest sign of walking humbly with God. True lovers always stand against the claims of Grand Inquisitors because they know that without freedom there is no dignity.

Third: Even if we reduce the matter to self-love, it is clear that if we do not love the body politic, we cannot love our own flesh. It is not accidental that idiotic mysticism and asceticism go hand in hand. Anyone who wants to cultivate a discarnate spiritual life must equally avoid the "temptations" of the flesh, the entanglements of the family and politics, and other carnal pleasures. What is being rejected in each of these instances is embodiment. This retreat from ordinary existence hides a hatred of the body and the Gnostic feeling that our incarnation in history is a fall into a prison of time and flesh from which the "spiritual" life should rescue us. This separation of the true self from the body and the body politic is a form of schizophrenic alienation and self-hate.

### The Agonizing Politics of Love

How is the lover, who has lost the illusions of the tribe and discovered a universal source of identity, to act within a community whose horizons and loyalties are parochial?

The lover's dilemma and agony follows inevitably from a radical difference between normal adults and outlaw-lovers—the question of *the scope of civility*. The politics of a lover is based upon the principle that the obligation of civility extends to all human beings. Probably to all sentient beings. The lover's social identity is rooted in the affirmation of a conscience that transcends all moral, national, and species boundaries, and a rejection of the consensual paranoia of the tribal conscience. In effect, the lover seeks to become a planetary citizen.

But here the dilemma deepens. For while the lover's identity is rooted in a transnational loyalty, there is no world community; therefore the lover, like the bodhisattva or the prodigal son, returns home to work among kinfolk, encouraging them to be more just, to open their hearts to aliens, to love their enemies.

The lover is always a prophet, standing with one foot in and one foot out of the local community. The majority will interpret the lover's criticism as an act of disloyalty, atheism, heresy against the official cult. Lovers bear the burden of being misunderstood because compassion obliges them to look upon the ideology, theology, and mythology of their own people as propaganda, which limits rather than expands consciousness.

Throughout history, cosmopolitan lovers have tried to alleviate their loneliness by affirming their membership in a coming kingdom of God, a now-and-future utopian community, a new age of the spirit, a united nations within which the demands of universal justice and civility could be honored. Every compassionate man and woman longs for a community in which one need not make the bitter choice between loyalty to one's kin and justice for all humankind.

But the hope for a body politic based upon compassion rather than power remains only a hope, or, as Kant said, "a regulatory idea." The image of a transnational community continues to inspire the prophetic efforts to make local communities more just, to weaken the claims of the state's sovereignty, and to topple the bloodiest idol of the twentieth century—nationalism. The nations of the world teeter on the edge of recognizing the necessity for radical civility and a cosmopolitan community, but they refuse to consider giving up their claim to sovereignty. Each nation demands obedience to the law of its citizens, but reserves to itself the right of the outlaw to go beyond good and evil. We have, to date, only a politic of power and the hope of a politic of love.

And so, the lover acts in agony, caught between a glimpse of an ideal, compassionate commonwealth and the hard actuality of power politics, "where ignorant armies clash by night." The glimpse does not lead to a blueprint for an ideal society, or a five-year plan, or a charter for utopia (all of which conceals the iron hand of a Grand Inquisitor, who offers people miracles, mystery, authority, and the illusion of security in exchange for freedom and justice). What it yields is something more modest, piecemeal, and vulnerable—a dedication to stand against individual instances of desecration and injustice. No one has given a more eloquent testimony to the lover's mode of action than existential writer Albert Camus:

> We are faced with evil. And, as for me, I feel rather as Augustine did before becoming a Christian when he said: "I tried to find the source of evil and I got nowhere." But it is also true that I, and a few others, know what must be done, if not to reduce evil, at least not to add to it. Perhaps we cannot prevent this world from being a world in which children are tortured. But we can reduce the number of tortured children.[3]

Those men and women who care inordinately—that is, beyond the requirements of duty—choose some place to take a stand against evil and injustice. It may be a narrow place—on a school board, where the fight must be carried on to educate rather than indoctrinate; in the executive committee of an investment firm that must decide whether to lend money to an electronics firm that manufactures guidance systems for missiles; in a rally to oppose the contamination of a river or the selling of public lands for private profit. But the choice to stand for compassion keeps alive the hope and the quest for erotic rather than neurotic corporations, healthy rather than dis-eased body politic.

### Political Vocation

The world is large and we are small, and those who try to love everything end up loving no thing well. Nowhere is it more true than in politics that we must find effective means and stringent limitations to express love.

So how do we love potently, justly, civilly?

The rules of private and public modes of loving are not that different.

1. To incarnate or incorporate love, we must commit ourselves to one body and forsake many. We must choose *an* arena, *an* institution, *an* issue and become informed and effective.

2. But how do we choose? Listen. We are called into love. Someone or something appeals to us. We are drawn. A voice calls us by name. Our vocation, like our destiny, is not something to be fabricated, but a response to make.

To find your political vocation, practice the art of compassionate listening. The daily newspaper brings a chorus of cries. Grieve with the family of Donald Teal, a carpenter, who died Wednesday at a local hospital after a lengthy illness at the age of thirty-nine. Rejoice with Mr. and Mrs. Bruce Hagman, whose son George, 7 lbs. 4 oz., was born yesterday. Share the worry of thirty-two men laid off yesterday when Specialty Electronics went bankrupt. Feel the anger rise in the blood as a fragile cease-fire between Israel and the PLO was broken for the fourth time. Allow the terror that comes with imagining the effect of detonating the nuclear missiles that the US and USSR have targeted at each other. Imagine the hopelessness of the new set of homeless refugees in Bangladesh. As you read each item, practice empathy until you find yourself moved.

3. Respond. Join. Act. Find like-minded people and pool your ideas, power, imaginations, energies to take some effective action. Create a responsive corporation. Make your company, church, school, government, bank, club, more compassionate.

## The Extended Technological Body

Technology forms the fifth sheath of the lover's body. Here love is caring for the means, media, and organs through which we interact with and upon other beings.

### The Neurotic Separation of Ends and Means, Values and Facts

It may seem passing strange to consider technology in a book about love. Machines are seldom mentioned in the same paragraph as eros. It is difficult to think about cold steel and warm flesh belonging together. By common agreement, we have segregated the objective, pragmatic modes of thinking required for science and technology from the subjective and intuitive ways of thought necessary to consider values, ends, and the destiny of the human spirit. As C. P. Snow has said, two cultures have grown up, one of hardheaded scientists and the other of soft-hearted artists and humanists. And the two seldom meet, even in the Faculty Club. Those scientifically minded persons, whom Robert M. Pirsig characterized as "classical" in his book *Zen and the Art of Motorcycle Maintenance,* delight in abstract forms and logical chains of thought but do not speak about vague subjects such as love. The romantics, on the other hand, wallow in oceanic feelings, but don't know how to tune a carburetor or tell a proton from a quark. Most parties to this schizophrenic covenant seem to agree that it makes sense to segregate matters of fact from matters of value, the realm of the I-it from the realm of the I-thou, and to have two separate professions and unions for the sciences and the arts. It doesn't.

If we look a little closer the division between:

| | | |
|---|---|---|
| science and technology | and | the arts, psychology, philosophy |
| the servile arts | and | the liberal arts |
| the realm of fact and means | and | the realm of values and ends |
| I-it relationships | and | I-thou relationships |
| the pursuit of knowledge | and | the practice of love |

we can see that it is only a slightly disguised modern version of that old schizophrenic dualism that has been dogging our steps since the beginning of western culture. It is the ancient disease that separates

| | | |
|---|---|---|
| Mother Nature | from | God the Father |
| the secular | from | the sacred |
| the flesh | from | the spirit |
| sex-eros | from | love-agape |

The division is not a division of labor, but a neurosis; a dis-ease in need of healing.

By every criterion we use to judge the presence of neurosis in a person, we may judge that the scientific-technological enterprise has become neurotic. How so? The heart of neurosis is the oscillation between omnipotent and impotent images, feelings and actions, and the neglect of a realistic sense of self. As psychoanalyst Karen Horney has shown in *Neurosis and Human Growth,* the neurotic has a godlike, idealized image of the self and a wormlike, degraded image of the self, but very little sense of real limits, abilities, or power. Wherever we encounter the assumption, "Everything is possible," whether in the moral realm (as among the creators of the concentration camps) or in the technological realm (those who believe there are no limits to human engineering), we may fill in the beginning of the sentence with words Dostoyevsky wrote a century ago: "God is dead, therefore everything is possible." The working assumption of the neurotic is precisely this functional atheism that proclaims the self omnipotent. And this leads inevitably to the nemesis—the collapse into the opposite feeling of failure, impotence and guilt.

The two opposite feelings about science and technology simultaneously present at the moment are the inevitable polarities of neurosis. When we allow ourselves to be seduced by omnipotent hope that some scientific discovery and technological fix will eventually allow us a global lifestyle of endless consumption, we will inevitably be haunted by the fear that the machines have gotten out of control and that the monolith of technology is on automatic pilot and can't be stopped. We will feel helpless to stop the scientists and technologists from doing anything that is possible—making new organisms that might escape and destroy life, or creating militarized space stations and laser weapons and driving us toward mass suicide. The promise of eternal energy is balanced by the suspicion that plutonium technology is the cyanide koolaid we are being asked to drink to preserve our way of life. Tools, machines, weapons—our only hope? Or the implements we are using to turn the earth into our own graveyard? This is the neurotic dilemma, the dead end we face as the result of the bankrupt ways in which we have thought about our relationship to our instruments.

To begin again, we must reject the old categories that lead us

inevitably into neurosis. We must rethink the relationship between our wheels and our feet, our hands and our tools, our minds
and our computers.

### I Am My Machines

The basic change we need to make is to stop thinking of machines as things, neutral means, mere instruments that are exterior
to our bodies and psyches and realize that, as Marshall McLuhan
has said, they are *extensions* of our bodies. The microscope and
telescope extend the range of the eyes and allow us to see the
infinitesimally small and the infinitely large. Telecommunications
extend the network of our nerves and sensors so that our body
may be present in places that were once out of reach. A bomb falls,
a famine happens in Uganda, and the effects are felt in New York.
We are accustomed to think about the difference between the
nuclear and the extended family. Now we need to become aware
of the differences between the nuclear body and the extended
body. Machines make up our *technodermis*—the new sensory in-
formation and feedback systems through which we relate to the
world. As such, they form a part of our spiritual body—our potentiality to transcend the limits of our skin and our locality and to
reach a more universal metanational form of consciousness.

A generation ago, such existentialist philosophers as Marcel,
Sartre, Jaspers, Merleau Ponty, and Heidegger made us aware that
we did violence to ourselves when we thought of our bodies as
something we *have*. When I say "my body is not important," I
suggest that there is some I who is separable from a thing I possess
that I call my body. They argued that in order to overcome our
alienation from ourselves, we have to learn to say and think "I am
my body." In a similar way, they extended this principle to include
all those dimensions of my existence from which I am inseparable.
Thus: I am my body. I am my family. I am my environment. I am
my community.

Now we must extend this principle a step further. *I am my machines.* They are no longer *its.* Those instruments that bring me
information about the world in-form my body-mind. The too

shapes the hand and the psyche that uses it. The machines we create return the favor. The means and media we employ in-form and misin-form us about what meaning is to be found. Consider, for example, the different types of in-formation we get from watching a picture of a starving Biafran mother and child on a television screen. In the comfortable twilight of a well-couched living room, eating as we watch, we do not have the sensory and emotional impact of actually being there touching the emaciated arms, brushing away the flies, feeling the final fatigue and hopelessness of a woman who must watch her child die. For better and for worse, we are married to the world through the media that brings us in-formation. And we need constantly to remind ourselves that *whatever in-forms us creates the mythical structure within which we live, move, and have our being.* Thus the machine is interior to our being. It enters our bloodstream. We breathe our imaginations into it. Into it we project our eros and thanatos, our life and death instincts, our images of hope to change the world to match our desires as well as the images of despair at our inability to control our destiny.

In the measure that machines, media, and data processors form our extended body, we must ask a new set of questions about technology that it will take many generations to begin to answer. What is the link between eros and techne? What does it mean to enter into a fully loving relationship with technology? In what ways may technology serve the cause of eros? It has been argued recently that we have created a new generation of machines that think, computers that respond to new situations and problems with creative intelligency, almost with feeling. The question whether machines think or not is academic. The more important question is, how do we exist in a relationship to our machines that maximizes our care-fulness? We have seen how the warrior uses the machine to serve the paranoid compulsion to manufacture and destroy the enemy. At this point in our inhuman history, a majority of scientific technological imagination is in the service of thanatos. Our most advanced technology is dedicated to murder sanctified by sovereign states and is created in the shadow of an evil imagination that will risk genocide, suicide, and cosmocide in the name of "national defense." If we are to survive, we need to ask how we may use the machine in the service of *metanoia* rather than *paranoia,* compassion rather than competition. How may we include the machine within the commonwealth of love? What are the principles of an erotic technology?

### Some Principles of an Erotic Technology

1. Technology has limits. Neurosis ends with the awareness that the self has limits. It is the human condition to be subject to dis-ease, tragedy, and death. As Camus said, it is only when we accept these absurdities that we can begin to write a manual of happiness. All utopian schemes—religious, political, or technological—that aim at reconstructing human life to make it perfect bring more evil into the world than they heal. Only when we give up the hope of engineering our way out of death and finitude can we begin to use our technology in a realistic manner. The men in the white coats are not going to save us. Nor can we abandon this planet after we have polluted it. This is our home.

2. An erotic technology must be sensitive, responsive to its impact on other domains—individual freedom, the economy, the family and household, the environment. To date, technology has developed under the sanction of the power and profit motives. And we have not counted its human or ecological costs until it was too late. We now need to consider which technologies will enhance the quality of planetary life and which will degrade it. Cost-accounting must reckon the loss that occurs when families are torn apart to accommodate production schedules and desert ecologies are destroyed by legions of off-road vehicles.

3. Technology cannot eliminate injustice. Herbert Marcuse suggested in *Eros and Civilization* that machines might set us free from the necessity of labor to live in a more leisurely and erotic manner. But his was still a vision of a society in which there would be no sacrifice or want because technology would provide a sufficiency for all. More recent thinking about global resources and the logic of energy usage shows that there are intrinsic limits to the devel-

opment of a triumphant technology. Even if we could develop a nonpolluting energy source to replace petroleum, we still could not sustain the levels of production and consumption that now characterize the affluent nations. There simply are not enough resources—minerals, clean air, and water—to support a global village of consumers. The hope that our technology can save us from having to share and conserve our limited resources is a self-serving illusion of the wealthy. If there is to be economic liberty and justice for all, it will be because we have decided that voluntary simplicity is preferable to a war between the first, second, and third worlds.

4. The principle of morality must be applied to the scientific-technological enterprise. Kant maintained that the essence of the moral imperative was always to act in such a way that "the maxim of your will could always hold at the same time as a principle establishing a universal law." What if everybody did it? Environmental impact statements must be extended to consider the rights of future generations. The principle of radical civility of the lover demands that we ask whether our actions will allow generations yet unborn, as well as those now living in the technological backwoods, the option of acting in the same way we act. For example: Our current level of industrial production and use of petroleum is clearly immoral because, if continued, it will deny future generations a similar privilege—both because it produces a greenhouse effect and because it depletes the resources at a rapid rate. The same holds true for our method of using water in highly technological agribusiness. Our children's children are included in the commonwealth of those who have a right to land, water, clean rivers, and unpolluted aquifers.

5. An erotic technology can only be embodied within a metanational body politic—a world commonwealth. Consciousness, compassion, and conscience require that we remain aware of the consequences of our actions. Every new technology affects everyone. The acid rain falls upon the just and the unjust. Communication satellites bring the visions of a Bloomingdale Christmas dancing into the heads of villagers in Chad. To date, the hidden costs

of technological developments that have made an elite class wealthy have been borne by us all. Polluted oceans and airstreams, rising levels of carcinogens in our food and tissue, these are the hidden taxation without representation we have paid. The economics and technology of the multinational corporations must give way to a genuinely representative world government.

6. An erotic technology must increase rather than decrease our sense of potency. Currently, we have created a paradoxical situation where our machines are so complex that they can only be serviced by experts. Thus we feel increasingly incompetent and vulnerable to any type of breakdown in the equipment upon which our lives depend. Our education must prepare us to have a hands-on relation to machines, to understand and be able to maintain more of what we use. We need to demystify and demythologize our relation to machines. And we can only do this by education that will make us all skilled. Our hands need to learn the skills of care.

7. As an instrument of the spirit, technology must *increase* rather than *decrease* our awareness, and aid us in transcending our captivity to merely localized consciousness and tribal values. Recently, many questions have been raised about the effect communications media, especially television, have upon consciousness. Some researchers have suggested that watching TV has the physiological effect of freezing the eye, placing us in semi-trance, and reducing our capacity for response and thought. Whether this proves correct remains to be seen. Certainly, the content of television programming, with its undue emphasis upon sports, situation comedies, and violence, does little to increase our awareness. The danger of television is that we will become passive recipients of the opinions and desires of others. Like dwellers in Plato's cave, we sit in a dark room watching shadows of shadows that we mistake for realities.

8. An erotic technology must increase rather than decrease the body's ability to respond. Clearly, technology serves neurotic ends when it causes more illness than it cures. The rapid rise of respiratory diseases suggests that the internal combustion engine and the

human lung are on a collision course. An excess of noise may destroy the ear's ability to hear. We need to develop sensitivity courses to make us aware of the impact our technology has upon our body. A trip through Secaucus, New Jersey, or Marcus Hook, Pennsylvania, provides sufficient evidence of our carelessness. The senses have a natural right to live in an environment that smells good. The eyes have the right to a sunset. The ear has the right to a mockingbird's song. The mind has the right to the unhurried rhythms that allow night dreams and daydreams to bubble into consciousness.

### The Ecological Body: Earthiness and Cohabitation

The ecosphere forms the sixth sheath of the lover's body. Here, love is expressed as cohabitation and care for nonhuman beings.

Carson McCullers tells a story that provides a parable to guide our thinking about the relation of humility and eros, land and passion. A young boy comes into an all-night diner to have a cup of coffee before starting his paper route. He falls into conversation with an old man, who pulls a picture of a woman from his wallet and tells the boy a story. "This woman is my wife," he says. "Many years ago, she ran away with another man. In those days I didn't know how to love. But now I am looking for her because I have discovered the science of love. Before you can love a person you have to start with simpler things and gradually build up your skill—start with a rock, a cloud, a tree."

The only hopeful way to approach the study of ecology is in the context of the problem of the recovery of passion. Our relationship to our bodies, to our land, to our sexuality is singular, cut from the same model. We cohabit either lovingly or carelessly. And our erotic impulses are fully satisfied only when we are within an environment in which we are continually stimulated to care and to enjoy. Eros is fully engaged only when we make the cosmic connection. Sexual love is both most passionate and most ordered when it assumes its rightful position within a nexus of erotic relationships that make up the natural world. Earthy love begins when we acknowledge our participation in an ecological bonding that joins all the species of life in a single commonwealth. Thus it is only when we deal with the dis-eased character of modern sexuality and the ecological crisis *as a single problem that is rooted in an erotic disorder* that we can begin to discover ways to heal ourselves of our alienation from our bodies and from nature.

Our eros defines our identity. The questions posed to us by the ecological crisis are: Who are we? With what do we identify? Where do we belong? Is our primary loyalty to the political or the natural order? Are we thoroughly domesticated animals or do we remain human only so long as we are in communion with something that is wild and earthy? These are, in reality, all the same question. The task of recovering our earthiness is the same as discovering the true meaning of cohabitation. We may approach this task best by searching for the principles of a new land ethic.

### The Desecration of Land and Body

The desecration of the land resonates in our bodies. Asbestos particles in our air, nitrates in our bacon, DDT in our calf's liver, monsodium glutamate in our nondairy coffee creamer. Caution: eating or breathing may be hazardous to your health. The sperm count of college-age American males has declined by 25 percent in the last ten years. That old carcinogenic devil is homogenized into all the sources of our nourishment. Better mix a little bourbon with your branch water to kill the bacteria.

I feel a little crazy because I don't know where to attack the problem. The system that is poisoning us pervades everything. The madness is within us all. I'm a part of the problem. I'm the very model of a modern man, a consumer. I like my coffee from Brazil and my pineapple from Maui, and perhaps some fresh asparagus just trucked in from South Carolina. I fly the friendly skies of United, have two cars, one dog, a stereo, and an appetite for the latest conveniences. My mind doesn't sink too deeply into the soil, and I feel rootless; afraid of dying, but equally afraid of slowing down. I wouldn't know how to survive if the gas stopped flowing or the carrots didn't come from the supermarket. I am not fat yet, but cholesterol is clogging my arteries. Privilege is my daily bread, and my minimum expectation is that I will have the maximum. I am a property owner, a taxpayer. I've worked hard and I want to be comfortable.

The future is rumbling and everything is changing, including what we think about change and growth and progress and the gross national product. We are on the edge of a new era, and we don't know how to be reborn. There aren't any little tricks. The entire understanding of what it means to be human must be enlarged. The new age must bring a new relationship between the human and the nonhuman, a new land ethic. How can we think about ourselves and our matrix?

### Approaches to a Land Ethic

Language governs perception. The metaphors we use limit what we can see and experience. The category into which we place a thing determines how we will deal with it. An entire logic and philosophy is smuggled into seemingly innocent words.

How are we to think about our relationship to the land, and the current ecological crisis? What category holds the most promise of healing the dis-ease?

Pragmatism?

Most commonly, we fall into the trap of thinking that we have a *problem* and therefore we must discover a *solution.* The modern technological mind automatically casts any dilemma into the problem-solution framework. The matter is pragmatic. If we lack water in Los Angeles, we will build aqueducts and bring it from Colorado. If our foods are dangerously polluted by carcinogenic chemicals, we will create new fertilizers. If we are depleting petroleum resources, we will discover how to make use of nuclear energy. The essence of this way of thinking is that knowledge and action—science and centralized control—govern the relationship between human beings and the land. Within this way of thinking, the problem of land ethics is: How can we make responsible *use* of the land. The question is utilitarian. We assume without question that we *own* land and have the right to *use* the land. Possession and utilization are the relevant categories.

The poverty of this way of thinking can be shown by some parallel questions: What is the responsible way to *use* a slave? How should I *manage* my children's future? How can I *control* my body? These questions suggest that much of our dilemma may arise from the unexamined assumption that land is an *it*, a possession, a *thing* that can be used, managed, and disposed of in any way that suits our needs. Our arrogance is hidden within the way we conceive the "problem." We do not even pause to question our chauvinistic assumption that the human species has the right to use and control all other life forms, or that we are wise enough to "plan" a system that is superior to the ecological balance. Without thinking, we spray the spruce bud worms to increase the yield of our timber, heedless of the destruction of bees, without which there can be no food, other insects, birds, and four-legged creatures.

Aesthetics?

Among landscape designers and some members of the Sierra Club, the question of a land ethic is often posed as: How can we shape an appropriate aesthetic to preserve the land so it may be enjoyed? The matter is one of beauty. We must learn to design our environment in a more pleasing and attractive way and preserve parks for campers and as sanctuaries for endangered species of animals. Land is landscape and a recreational resource.

The aesthetic mind is not so crass as the utilitarian. Beauty is a gentler mistress than pragmatism. But in the crisis we now face, the aesthetic approach to land is too precious to make much difference. We may easily enjoy enclaves of environmental art and sculptured parks, and neglect the more crucial question of toxins and chemical fertilizers and the destruction of the topsoil. When landscape architects such as Jacques Simon consider the land a "medium of aesthetic expression and an environmental building material," they miss the point. The earth is not material from which to fabricate a beautiful environment. It *is* our environment. To consider beauty the dominant category for a land ethic is as superficial as to relate to a lover on the basis of appearance. We must go beyond voyeurism.

Justice?

The ecological movement has raised the discussion to a new level by asking: Do trees have standing? Do redwoods and wolverines enjoy *legal* rights before the law? Do human beings have an *obligation* to all species of life? The shift from the language of ownership and use to *moral* language represents an enormous change in sensitivity. Land is not an it to be used, but a thou to be respected; it is not a thing but a presence. If squirrels and oak trees have rights, then a limit is placed on human action. If the cosmos is anything other than dead matter, we are obliged to discover what *respect* we owe to creeks, and warblers, and rolling hills. We must learn to apply the proper moral language to our actions and refuse to hide behind euphemisms. It is a small step to recognize that we must protect other species from human greed and to use the proper moral language to describe our violations: We murder the harp seals, practice genocide on the whales, rape the land, steal the territory of species who are powerless to defend themselves.

However, the ecological crisis we face is made more complex by introducing moral language. How must we live if other life forms have some purpose other than to serve human needs? How would we adjudicate the conflicting rights and needs? If trees have standing, how can we cut a forest to make a home? And who is to speak for the rights of blue jays? How do we render justice to all the species and still maintain human life?

A seldom noticed characteristic of legal language gives us a clue for deepening our approach to a land ethic. The liberal mind is always seeking to grant or recognize the rights of some previously disenfranchised minority. To recognize that trees and timber wolves have a claim to justice is an extension of granting rights to women, children, blacks, and homosexuals. Where the question of rights and justice is in the foreground, the question of love has not yet been raised with seriousness. The liberal fights for someone else's rights. By contrast, the radical or the lover understands that all society is bound together in such a way that if anyone's rights are denied, we are all imprisoned. It is not for the poor wolves that we demand rights—but for ourselves. The liberal mind defines and tries to solve problems from a position *exterior* to them: I'm OK (free, healthy, enlightened, educated, enfranchised), but my neighbor is not. The radical mind of the lover tries to heal dis-ease from a position *interior* to it: Neither you nor I can be free or healthy, until both of us dwell within a liberated community. To the liberal mind, land is a thing for which we are responsible; animals are lower species we should respect. To the radical mind, land, animals, and people are relatives with whom we cohabit, members of a communion of sentient beings bound together by the demands of kindness. Once we raise the question of a land ethic, not from the liberal perspective of protecting alien species but from the lover's perspective of protecting the delight we can experience only in plurality, we push the question deeper—from the moral to the religious and the erotic dimensions.

Religion—Eros?

The word "religion" comes from the Latin root meaning "to bind, or tie fast." The religious-erotic question is: What vows bind us to the land? A vow is merely the confession of an essentially inviolable bond. Whatever we are bound to as a condition of our existence is sacred. From a religious perspective, the land and its inhabitants are con-secrated—we share a sacred place. Our relationship, or bond, or the ecosystem is the precondition of our emergence and survival as individuals. Thus the connection between human and earth is not exterior or accidental, or a matter of ends and means. We are created for each other. Our bondage is mutual. Our dependence is absolute. We have power to destroy the land but not to live without it. The bond signifies that the relationship is a mystery and not a problem. We cannot abstract ourselves from nature to gain an objective distance from the envelope that enfolds our life. We cannot ask the question of the relation between person and land as if we were talking about two separate entities, one of which owns the other, any more than I can ask how I should relate to my body. The mystery of my carnality is that I am inseparable from my body. The mystery of my humanness is that I am inseparable from the humus.

Land and body are members of a commonwealth of interrelated cells and organisms. What poisons the liver destroys the heart.

What pollutes the air destroys the lungs. We are one organism: earthbodies; inspired humus; a commonwealth of consciousness.

Consider the ecosystem as a gestalt. What is figure today will be ground tomorrow. Today's individual is tomorrow's environment. A living organism passes into dust, and back again to a new form. The mercury in the fish will soon swim in your bloodstream, and your blood will eventually flow again into the ocean. We are destined to move through all the forms of creation. We who are today organisms will tomorrow take our turn at being the environment. The calcium in our bones will go from soil, to grass, to cow, to the bones of Alice McFay. The peregrine falcon, now nearly extinct, is resurrected in the serotonin that triggers my synapses into flights of images as wild as any storm that his wings battled. There is a fearful and wonderful justice at work in the body of this world. As we sow, so shall we reap. Each of us is a periodic table of elements organized by some cosmic dream that is dreaming us into an intricate democracy where heart and bone live in civil harmony. And our sins will be visited upon our flesh. As certainly as the chickens come home to roost, the DDT and the 2-4-D will find its way into the livers of the children of the third and fourth generation. The pollution we inflict upon one part of our cosmic body will return to trouble our gene pool and threaten our immortality.

The religio-erotic question is: How may we en-joy our body? How can we celebrate the coming together of the concentric realities (carnality, family, friends, corporations, technology, cosmos, mystical body) that constitute our shared body? There is no freedom if I do not respect my bonds, my bounds, my boundaries. I am not limited to the cells that are stuffed within this skin sack. I am the air I breathe. It is a question of identity. Psychology, ecology, and politics are inseparable. I am constituted by interchange. We are in this together. In fact, we *are* this togetherness. There is no *it* in the universe, only *we.* How do we reverence our bonds, perform our vows, celebrate our interchange, cohabit, make love together?

The issue of land is not practical. Nothing will be solved by a sprinkling of new programs. The question is metaphysical or religious, a matter of competing visions of reality. We are well into Armageddon; worlds are colliding; there is struggle between ideologies, philosophies, politics, economics, psychologies. How we relate to the land will be governed by which paradigm wins. The opposition is between:

| *The western individual, whose credo is:* | AND | *The lover, whose credo is:* |
|---|---|---|
| I believe in making, doing, fabricating, achieving, struggling, accumulating, competing. | | We believe in digging, planting, tending, harvesting, sharing, cohabiting. |
| The land is property that I own and have the rights to use for my profit. The value of land is determined by the market; it is a form of capital that may be accumulated, spent, and divided into neatly quantifiable parcels. Good fences make good neighbors. | | The land is our matrix, a living and shared body. We husband the soil and are nourished by it. Land and person are a seamless unity, a synergistic system, a couple of lovers. |
| A community is a collection of individuals who form a social contract to preserve law and order and ensure civil rights. | | A people is a communion, a family that roots in the humus. We are part of a commonwealth that includes land and animals and we all share the responsibility to preserve the health of our cosmopolis. |
| I believe in upward mobility, in movement through time, in advancement, in progress, in forging a new future, in the ability of man to solve problems and create a utopian society. | | We believe in taking root, in plunging deeper into a locality, in sharing space, in moving with the biorhythms, in the goodness of the eternally recurring seasons, in the sufficiency of this moment. |

### Learning to Cohabit

It is difficult to recover an easy relationship. The natural knowledge that is our birthright has become unnatural. It will require many artificial means to free the primitive. The path to second innocence leads through sophistication and wisdom before it circles round to simplicity. We do not know how to do what must be done, or rather, to un-do what must be un-done if we are to survive. I have spent too many of my formative years in a competitive, urban society that encouraged me to aspire to an alienated form of individuality to be an expert in the ways of loving the humus. But I have known some heroes and heroines of compassion whose lives suggest certain maxims for compassionate cohabitation. Here are some:

Begin with delight. Study the ways of a titmouse or an English sparrow until you see the intricate beauty of a single, strange life form.

Do nothing. Be silent and receptive until you begin to discover what is happening that does not depend upon your doing, making, or managing.

Practice the art of allowing, surrendering, being moved.

Know little, be a learner. Love comes before knowledge, and trust before authentic action. Dissolve the narrow focus; avoid positivism and scientific imbecility. Learn to be at home in the dark, to enjoy the obscurity of the human condition without having to feign omniscience. Avoid systems that give the whole picture; love the fragments.

Recover the animal within yourself. Descend into the limbic brain and discover the mammalian wisdom—the instinctual knowledge. For a time, silence the inner dialogue of the cortex. Practice smelling. Let your dog tutor your nose in the art of instinctual discrimination. Pay attention to kinesthetic intelligence, to the information that comes through movement. Learn to lope. Walk through a dark woods and trust your ambient vision; unfocus your eyes and take in the entire environment in a single gestalt, like a jackdaw waiting for a grasshopper. The American Indian practice of assuming an animal name testifies to the animalhood of all. Choose a totem animal. Symbolic bestiality is true intercourse between the species.

Invite inter-species communication. Study for a Ph.D. with a golden plover to find how the bird mind guides migration unerringly over ten thousand miles of ocean and mountains. Become a voyeur of the courtship dances of the woodcock to learn about the delicate rituals of intimacy. Contemplate the social habits of gorillas to appreciate how the powerful can tame their aggression and avoid war. Our species' chauvinism has thus far limited communication by our unwillingness to learn from "the inferior" forms of life. Begin with a working assumption of equality. Play with the radical idea of living in communion rather than the liberal idea of ghettoizing the poor dumb animals on a protected reservation.

Become a lunatic. Be sensitive to biorhythms, circadian cycles, and seasonal movements. How does the full moon affect the tides of your mind? The electromagnetic forces pipe a tune to which all cells dance. Anyone who insists on remaining an outlaw, a completely autonomous individual, chooses the illusion of separation and remains a wallflower in the cosmic hoedown. Find out how you are connected to the other dancers, the rhythms and melody that make the music. Take your own sweet time rather than accepting the tyranny of the 8:15 express. The rhythm method may allow you to conceive a new self.

Practice humble auto-eroticism: Do unto the humus as you would unto yourself. Love your body. Don't sow plutonium ("plutonium": from Pluto, the Greek god of the dead) or you will reap hell. Don't dump anything in a river you don't want your children downstream to drink tomorrow. Protect our common hope, our posterity, our communal immortality, our incarnate future.

Get dirty. From dust to dust; give back to the soil what you take from it. Compost. Be fertile-izers. A human being *is* a recycling system. Open your sphincters and let the energy flow through you.

Sink roots. Downward rather than upward mobility, incarnation rather than Gnosticism. Be in place. Be grounded in a locality. Learn to love some here and now rather than lusting after the exotic elsewhere. Co-habit.

Remain frail, vulnerable, open. Learn to respect delicate interconnections and thin membranes. Avoid macho. Disarm.

Cut nature at the joints. Respect the natural divisions: watersheds, creeks, timberlines. Create a politics of natural divisions. Why is there no advocate for the Ohio river? The Methow valley enfolds a natural constituency, a body politic gathered by the mountains.

Give voice to the inarticulate members of continuum. Every environmental designer and land-use commission has silent clients—bumblebees and, if you are very lucky, a cinnamon bear. Each human voice must advocate justice for all. Speech devoid of love is propaganda. Logos-eros-cosmos live or die together.

Be grounded in the organic rather than the fabricated. Right the balance between growing and making. Learn to tend as well as produce. Grow a carrot for food and to learn a metaphor. Cultivate your garden.

Use power to protect innocence. Make the body politic strong to protect against the enemies of the land—the profiteers, the conquistadors, the agribusiness oligopolies. Organize against carcinogens, toxins: Kepone, Aldrin, Agent Orange, DDT, 2-4-D.

Keep alive in yourself the painful awareness of desecration. Cherish outrage against the pollution. Even at the price of unrest, do not turn aside from the agonizing facts: The average depth of topsoil in the U.S. has fallen from three feet to six inches in two hundred years. Eleven million acres in Vietnam were defoliated by Agent Orange, a dioxin as deadly as atomic waste. The water table in the U.S. has dropped 16 percent. The quota for harp seals is 170,000 pelts, 20 percent of the less than one million that remain.

Adopt the principle of minimum interference. Never use a chemical toxin to kill an aphid when a ladybug will do the job for you. Take care that the remedy does not strengthen the dis-ease. (The overuse of "miracle drugs" has so strengthened the population of gonococcus that it now takes 4,800,000 units of penicillin to combat a case of gonorrhea that thirty years ago would have been treated with 400,000 units.)

The basic principle that may guide us to a new land ethic is the same that governs a compassionate relationship between people: Always act in such a way as to overcome existing alienation and deepen trust. In western culture, we have been on a prodigal journey. We left our homestead in the wilderness by inventing machines that gave us unprecedented control over nature. But the more control we exercised, the more we began to fear all that resisted the management of an urban mentality. The woods and wild places ceased to be sanctuaries and came to be unknown habitats of uncontrolled beasts. The more the majority lived within fabricated environments, the more the terror of nature has grown. The ecological movement, the rural renaissance, and the new romanticism are only a few of the signs that we are beginning to circle around toward a reunion with our original and abiding hearth. The twenty-first century may be characterized by both greater centralization and greater dispersion, by renewed cities and family farms. Along with our use of more appropriate technologies, we may come home again to trust that our natural matrix, our earthbody, is sustaining if we care for it. We may rediscover the wisdom of the primitive, so well spoken by Chief Standing Bear of Ogalala Sioux:

> We do not think of the great open plains, the beautiful rolling hills, and winding streams with tangled growth as "wild." Only to the white man was nature a wilderness, and only to him was the land infested with wild animals and savage people. To us it was tame. Earth was bountiful and we were surrounded with the blessings of the Great Mystery.[4]

## The Mystical Body: Fragments of an Erotic Metaphysic

The mystical body forms the seventh sheath of the lover's embodiment. Here, love assumes the form of radical trust and metaphysical play.

All that we are is a part of the mystery of Being-becoming-itself. Thus all knowledge (gnosis) rests within the cradle of ignorance (agnosticism). Intricate as our ecosphere is, there is yet a more encompassing reality, the ultimate setting for the cameo of human identity. The mystery out of which and into which all things flow may never be named, only hinted at with playful, poetic words and parables. Yet we must embrace the mystery or recoil from it, decide whether we will trust or mistrust it.

As we said at the beginning of our pilgrimage, we have no choice but to pick some fragment of experience and use it as a clue to help us interpret the unfathomable mystical body of Being-becoming-itself. There is no way to define the psyche without undertaking metaphysics. Our vision of the mystical body determines our mode of embodiment. Becoming a lover may be a high calling or the sentimental quest of a romantic illusion. If the context that supports human life is careless, it would be foolish to assume that nature has designed us to be caring animals. Whatever else we are, we are mirrors of the cosmos that surrounds us; microcosms of the macrocosm. If we see the world as a battleground, we become warriors. If it is a product of chance, we are accidents. If it is an evolving commonwealth, we are citizens of the kingdom of consciousness. If it is an erotic dance of particles that are drawn to combine to produce ever richer combinations of molecules and organisms, then love may be ingrained in our human essence.

Our final task in sketching the outlines of the lover's way is to play with the experience of love and see if we can make an erotic metaphysic from the fragments.

### The Epistemology of Love: Evidence and Intimacy

Before we can plunge into metaphysical play, we need to consider some of the unique problems connected with knowing about love. Before the search can even begin, we must examine the searcher. Who is looking for love? With what tools? Whose testimony do we accept? Does evidence for the presence of love have to be convincing to impartial observers? (Could Masters and Johnson study shared intimacy, the tenderness that is exchanged *only* where there are no observers?) In studying love, we obviously have a unique set of epistemological problems.

The evidence of love is peculiar in that it is unrepeatable, unquantifiable, and known only within a circle of intimacy that tolerates no observers. The signs are invisible to the scientific eye.

In a crowded room, lovers exchange a glance. He rolls his eyes and purses his lips for a moment. She repeats the gesture. They alone know each is remembering a moment two hours before the party when they were dressing and fell fully aroused onto the bed and came together. How could any objective observer know that at breakfast she meant (by bran muffins and steaming cups of tea) to celebrate a conversation they had the night before in which he listened to, and helped dissolve, her deepest fears of abandonment?

The evidence for love is known within a relationship between intimates; and it is the relationship that creates the intimacy that creates the evidence, that. . . . If this sounds circular, it is. I know myself as a unique and valued individual only within a relationship in which my uniqueness is recognized by another. There is no I without a thou. Individuality is created by relationship. Love is a relationship that creates its own terms. This means that the evidence that the universe harbors some kindly intent toward the individual can be collected and evaluated only within the courtroom of the individual's most intimate relationships. I can never prove to a neutral court of objective reason or to a scientific panel of inquiry that I am free, that I have a destiny, that the events of my life weave themselves together to form a pattern, a story that suffuses *my* life with a sense of kindly purpose. But I may experience it so. From within the privileged access of my spirit I may feel my life as a gift, my work as a vocation, my family and friends as the medium through which I am loved by God or Being.

### Metaphysical Love-Play

The lover's question is at the heart of religion and is the basis of a metaphysics of compassion: Is love a psychological phenomenon or an ontological current? Do the marks of love we observe in person-to-person relationships also apply to the relationship of the self and its world? Is the most profoundly satisfying human experience a lens through which we may legitimately view the cosmos? Does the microcosm mirror the macrocosm? Is there an analogy between human and nonhuman reality? How is life like a love affair?

Let's begin our metaphysical play by looking at the primal stuff

Once upon a time, philosophers and scientists thought reality was made up of unsplittable atoms that collided with each other like balls on a billiard table. Accident and the law of cause and effect created a complex world. Nowadays physicists, like wild-eyed mystics or old-fashioned idealists, are suggesting that consciousness may permeate everything.* As Alfred North Whitehead said (and Bell's theorem seems to demonstrate), the universe is a system of mutually prehending entities. There is nothing disconnected or frigid in the entire world; nothing that is unresponsive, immovable, untouched. It appears as if we are within some highly complex thoughtful organism that is evolving toward some inconceivable state of maximum consciousness. Since human perception of the whole is always filtered through the limited neural apparatus of the brain, our best visions are inevitably fractured or biased. Any evidence to support a metaphysic of compassion will necessarily be speculative—or playful—a matter of thinking in the subjunctive.

If everything is conscious, we are links in a network of knowledge. Reality is co-knowledge, or communion. And since knowledge always involves some degree of feeling, everything is linked in a compassionate system. The cosmos is a *menage ad infinitum.* Science is eavesdropping on an elaborate love affair, tracing the improbable liaison between quarks and black holes and studying the mores of particles. Until recently, scientists were content to view themselves as voyeurs; but Heisenberg showed that the prurient interest of investigators affected the erotic conduct of their subjects. Start observing a subatomic particle, and it performs for the camera. So now scientists must begin research with an acknowledgment that their desires limit the range of observations. This raises an interesting possibility. Perhaps only the most compassionate scientists may be able to discover the compassion of particles. Mystical physicists are discovering consciousness everywhere. A fully erotic generation of scientists might discover that the cosmos is moved by desire. If this seems farfetched, we have

*For a review of the new physics, see Fritjof Kapra's *The Tao of Physics* or Gary Zukar's *The Dancing Wu Li Masters.*

only to remember that when scientists were involved in a love affair with machines they produced a mechanistic worldview. Physics done from the heart might yield a vision of a heartful world.

Let's consider for a moment the wildest extension of our erotic metaphor. What if the mystical body of Being-becoming-itself, which is incarnate in the cosmos, is itself a climax of an act of love —an orgasm?

One day, when I was walking in San Francisco, I happened upon a building upon which someone had written: THE WORLD IS COMING. I imagined that some frustrated Jesus freak had been arrested just when he was about to write, TO AN END. (To the apocalyptic mind, history is *coitus interruptus,* an incomplete story waiting for a climax that never comes. Today the world ends; tomorrow the second coming. Promises, promises, promises. Fundamentalists and capitalists are always postponing satisfaction. Both believe the goal that makes life meaningful lies in the future. Someday, after a millennium of moral behavior and hard work, we will be ushered into a kingdom of leisure and joy. The eventual orgasm is the promised reward for diligence and the use of the right techniques. The kingdom is coming—tomorrow. In the meantime, we labor and fight.)

This morning it occurred to me that THE WORLD IS COMING might be a metaphysical maxim emblazoned for all to see by some unknown cosmopolitan lover instead of a warning by a frustrated prophet of the end. Perhaps some erotic visionary is making a daring suggestion: The world is an orgasm; the cosmos is a coming together of separate entities, a joyous union of particles.

The idea takes my breath away. It is wild enough to be interesting, and salacious enough to shock orthodox theologians, scientists, warriors, and serious thinkers. It is obviously worth pursuing, or perhaps I should say tickling out.

But what cold hard facts could possibly support such a view of the world?

Begin with a single atom. A neutral enough phenomenon, it would seem. Until we look closely. Under the microscope, th atom looks more like a love nest than a machine shop. The manly nucleus sits at the center of a kingdom, emitting a positive, musky charge. Electrons, like dancing girls, whirl and tease in orbit and keep their distance by a negative charge. Clearly, desire binds them together in a love dance. Scientists, not wishing to suggest that anything pornographic is going on among basic particles, have discreetly agreed to call the communion of particles by a single name—atom. In fact, there is no atom without an Eve, no plus without a minus, no yin without a yang. The least particle we know is already an organized bit of energy engaged in active intercourse with other particles.

Consider the molecule. Benzene is a convenient name for a love affair between hydrogen and carbon atoms.

$H_2O$ is a *menage à trois*.

$H_2SO_4$ is a multiple marriage with dangerous possibilities.

And who am I? An individual, of course. Nobody has fingerprints or a name that is the same as mine. I'm unique. Often I feel lonely. Then it occurs to me that I am a we. Within my permeable skin live a billion cells organized into elaborate communes called heart, liver, bone, and brain. When the moon is full and the sea swells, my sleep is restless because some surge that links the stars and the atoms washes through my body like the tide. And plants and cats and other living things tune to the vibrations I send and bloom and purr or shrink from my hostile intent. It's only when I forget how porous I am to the flowing world that I pretend to be a single self. When I am tuned to the rhythms of my inspiration and expiration I remember that I am a coming together of a community of atoms. I am a little world, a microcosm. Everything that is happening anywhere in the world is happening in me. The moon rises in my blood; lilacs bloom in my nostrils; suns are born and burst in the atoms that are my substance. I am one body with the world.

And what is the world? Explosions within explosions within explosions. A series of climaxes. It's already coming. Every beginning is an end. Every being is a becoming—a big bang. The cosmos is a divine orgasm. Hegel said it: the substance of things is the divine subject; stuff is mind; matter is consciousness; the world is the life of God; the cosmos is love disporting with itself. Each self is a communion of atoms and cells moving to unheard harmonies. What's happening is relationship. This instant is the product of the coming together of separate particles, which are the products of the coming together of separate particles, ad infinitum.

Here and now is where things end. Today is the climax. The world is coming. Creation or pro-creation; things are always coming together to give birth to new things. With each new thing there is a rebirth of hope. The moment is a manifestation of love, or relationship.

The news of the day is: the same old story—things are always new. What was and is and will be is be-coming. The world is a sexy place. God is love.

Let's put speculation about physics aside and stop playing with different worlds as if we might choose a raspberry cosmos instead of one covered with machine oil, and return to the ground—to raw human experience.

In the beginning is the gift. We are born into a world where there are already mothers and fathers, oak trees and blue jays. In philosophy, it is said that thought must begin with a datum (the Latin root is "gift"). To speak of beginning with hard data (just the *facts*, please) tempts us to forget that the world into which every human being emerges is already generously spread with nourishment to sustain life. The most misanthropic critics of mother nature can only bite the breast that feeds them. We are sustained. Our most righteous complaints against the universe are leveled by a species that lives by the grace of almost unlimited credit cards. When we see a crippled child, we curse the cosmos for being uncaring; but we are able to make our complaints only because we have seen so many healthy children. The presence of evil may break the heart, but it does not prove the cosmos is a loveless place. To the contrary, sacrilege helps us locate the sacred because, when confronted by torture or desecration, we *know* life *should not* be violated. It is because we have a presentiment that our destined fulfillment is in love that we react with horror to the most brutal instances of lovelessness.

The overwhelming order and sanity that preserves and nourishes a kaleidoscopic variety of life allows us the perspective from which we can object to disorder and lack of justice. Only a relatively orderly universe could produce and sustain a human consciousness that could play with the idea that the universe was a product of chance. If the cosmos has a sense of humor, mechanistic theories must be a shaggy dog story. There needs to be a God to appreciate the irony of our most noble minds bowing before the image of a machine they created for their own amusement. (Machines were originally invented as toys, not as a substitute for slaves.)

If we switch our attention from the absolute given of the cosmos as a whole to the more intimate world into which each of us was born, we find the entire landscape of birth and childhood strewn with intimations of love. We are conceived from mutual desire, encompassed within a matrix of absolute care, and born into a world where we are so important that we survive only if, for a time, we are the center of attention. A baby, like a lover, assumes without a shadow of a doubt that it is the focal point to which all blessings flow. The surrounding world is a combination of breast and circus designed for nourishment and entertainment. Everything is to be tasted and enjoyed. By powerful means—smiles and tears—the baby proves the primal proposition that the world is responsive to its needs and desires.

Moralists and developmental psychologists point out (with an almost audible sigh of relief) that the illusory state of infantile ego-centricity is soon outgrown. The little king or queen is dethroned. The pretender is taught the painful lesson that mother has other interests, and chairs and doggies and brothers don't always do what they're told. And as the age of reason dawns briefly, the child learns the hard lesson that the world is governed by universal laws that do not bend to accommodate merely individual needs. But before we rejoice at the end of innocence and the loss of the intimate and responsive world of childhood, we might note the strange fact that each of us was born and survived only because we had a necessary illusion of our own centrality. The first truth: It is my birthright to be loved. The mouth is programmed to expect the breast; the skin claims a natural right to be touched; the heart is quieted only by beating in unison with another; the hands reach out to a world presumed to be friendly. We each assume that this place was prepared for us, welcomes us, and rejoices in our becoming. We grow strong in exact proportion to our trust. In time, the context within which we live and move and have our being hardens, thickens, and becomes neutral or even hostile. As we mature, we are taught that the cosmos is ruled by law and chaos rather than love. In short, we fall into adulthood and put away our childish ego-centrism and become warriors animated by the perverse ego-centrism of paranoia.

It is hard to know what to make of this universal human story. Which world is the most real? The primal garden of love or the careless one to which we learn to adapt? What is wisdom? To put away childish things, or to become as a little child? Or both? I introduce the child's cosmos only as a fragment of evidence that eros is deeply programmed into the intentions of life and is not merely a psychological phenomenon. The jury within each person will have to determine how much to weight this piece of evidence. Much of how we think about, hope for, or despair of love seems to be determined by how we view childhood. If it is an illusory condition to be left behind as soon as possible, then we probably will have to settle for mature contracts and mutually satisfactory arrangements rather than love. Love seems to thrive only where something of the magical or graceful world of childhood is preserved. There is something terribly vulnerable, even foolish, about adults in love. They are always making mistakes, asking forgiveness, starting over, and they never seem to mind what other people think about them. They merely assume they have been graced by life and offer no proof except their continuing enthusiasm and their maddening hope. Adult lovers, like children, seem to have some primal trust that they are special.

On my best days, I think I know what it might be like to be a lover. You know the kind of days I mean. Traffic lights change as I approach; parking places appear in front of the store; I unexpectedly bump into an old friend I haven't seen for years; a neighbor returning from Hawaii drops in and leaves a ripe mango; my hidden and difficult thoughts rise up on wings; the entire current of life seems to be synchronized with the ebb and flow of my personal tides.

There are respectable philosophical names for such states of being: coincidence, good luck, synchronicity, serendipity. Tough-minded thinkers would insist that all seemingly magical events can be explained by such natural categories. It is somehow comforting to the skeptical mind to label a strange and meaningful coming together of unexpected elements with a word like "chance," and to explain it by the laws of probabilities. No doubt, in an infinite sea of possibilities in infinite time, the odds on the impossible are reasonable. But I have always suspected that the notions of chance, coincidence, or even synchronicity were threadbare philosophical garments constructed in a hurry to cover an embarrassing vulnerability in the armor of thinkers who are determined to be grown-up and reasonable at all costs. After all, "co-incidence" only means that two things happen at once—or come together. And coming together may be as easily a sign of a mystical harmony as a result of cosmic carelessness. If we remain at the level of experience, wild synchronicities seem the result of some special grace.

Several years ago, when I was living in the East, I flew to San Francisco, rented a car, and drove to Big Sur. My old friend Jane lived in Seaside and I wanted to see her, but I had not written because I did not know whether I would have time to visit. Passing through Monterey, I stopped to telephone. No answer. I walked out of the telephone booth and over to a garage one hundred feet away, and bumped into Jane as she was coming out the door. Coincidence? Chance? What does that mean? It *seemed as if* the meeting had been arranged. How? By whom? Why? I can't answer. I only insist upon staying close to the feelings of the experience, childish as that is. My hunch is that such experiences, although not daily, are common as thunderstorms or dandelions in most people's lives. Our embarrassment about unusual experiences and our mania to be mature and live in a scientifically respectable world makes us tend to repress such happenings and to write them off as chance. We do not easily report occult occurrences, because they shatter our secure categories of understanding and leave us feeling as if we were still in the magical world of childhood. Our adult egos know full well that if we begin to admit strange and miraculous events into consciousness, our laboriously constructed and passionately defended schemes of "reality" are in danger. A single, authentic synchronicity can shatter a rationalist's world and lead to personality disintegration. And then the radical questions begin: "Last night I dreamt I was a butterfly. Now am I a man dreaming I am a butterfly, or a butterfly dreaming I am a man?" asks philosopher Chuang Tze. Do we battle because the world is dangerous, or is the world dangerous because we battle? Is love an illusion or the fundamental reality that makes the world go round, the world go round . . . ?

This much I know for certain. The less I know for certain, the more mystical confirmation I get that I (and you and we) are in some cosmic dance in which each individual is central. The center is everywhere. This universe was created especially for each person. If that is too radical an idea, let me twist it around: To be a person is to live within a context in which one knows oneself to be intended, desired, created, nurtured, addressed. Or perhaps the world, like the *I Ching*, is an oracle that yields its meaning only when I take it personally. It seems as if the moment I decide to trust the world to provide the daily meaning and direction I need to live in harmony, ordinary events turn into omens that instruct me. It will not do to negate such experience by calling it magical, superstitious, or primitive. Sticks and stones may break my bones. . . .

As long as I am skirting the edges of foolishness and playing with the idea that we have an erotic relationship to the matri-

within which our individual lives are encompassed, I may as well confess that I suspect we are all recipients of cosmic love notes. Messages, omens, voices, cries, revelations, and appeals are homogenized into each day's events. If we only knew how to listen, to read the signs. . . . Many great lovers testify that life is vocation, it is constantly whispering sweet nothings in their inner ears. Paul Tillich says:

> All things and all men, so to speak, call on us with small or loud voices. They want us to listen, they want us to understand their intrinsic claims, their justice of being. . . . But we can give it to them only through the love that listens.[5]

Martin Buber says:

> Each of us is encased in an armour whose task is to ward off signs. Signs happen to us without respite, living means being addressed, we would need only to present ourselves and to perceive. But the risk is too dangerous for us, the soundless thunderings seem to threaten us with annihilation, and from generation to generation we perfect the defense apparatus. All our knowledge assures us, "Be calm, everything happens as it must happen, but nothing is directed at you, you are not meant; it is just "the world," you can experience it as you like. . . . What occurs to me addresses me.[6]

I could never prove to a spectator the extraordinary depth of meaning and reassurance that often reveals itself in an ordinary fact. Like the time the fuchsia that grows beside my dining room window was neglected by people staying in my house and I came home to find a dried stalk where red buds had once pirouetted in every breeze. Death seemed to sneer in triumph from the withered remains and threatened to engulf all passing beauty. Radical surgery was the one small hope. I cut the plant to the quick, watered the parched remains, and waited. Weeks later, the wizened stick turned green and, before the month was out, a pink blossom gave undeniable testimony to life's ingrained capacity for resurrection. The event was common enough. I have seen enough springs to know about the laws of growth. Yet that singular fuchsia's mes-

sage to me—"Life is alive and continuously regenerates itself"—
was as personal as Demeter 's words must once have been to some
Greek shepherd.

To carry the argument from the sublime to the ridiculous—we
also receive messages from overheard fragments of conversation,
or phrases of songs, or dreams. In a paragraph of grey conversation, a sentence will suddenly flash out in neon lights. For instance,
the other day I was walking in Muir Woods, looking at the redwoods and worrying about how to resolve an old and troublesome
contradiction. A group of tourists approached. As two men passed
me in deep conversation, I heard one say to the other, "Do nothing. Nine times out of ten that's the best thing to do." The omen
for the day. I find such experiences common, but slightly embarrassing to report. But my informal research has assured me that
most people received Delphic oracles from just such improbable
sources. A soda jerk, a disc jockey, a book title, a joke at lunch,
a face or gesture observed for a few seconds, no less than the
rebirth of a flower or the still small voice of conscience, may
become the medium for the revelation of the meaning of the day.
"Give us this day our daily omen, our synchronicity, our evidence
that the living context is responsive to our individual spirits."

Synchronicities, magical openings, omens, personalized revelations, oracles delivered by passing strangers or fuchsias—what do
these experiences prove? They certainly do not demonstrate beyond a reasonable doubt that the world is more like a love affair
than a battlefield. It is perfectly possible to dismiss such experiences as mini-schizophrenic episodes that illustrate the pathological tendency of ego inflation. Schizophrenics, mystics, and lovers
share a tendency to interpret events as if they were being personally addressed by what happens around them. Love and madness
are kin because both exist in a suprarational world where proof has
been abandoned. Loving or opening oneself to the perception that
one is being loved is always a risk. Love and proof are at opposite
ends of the scale. The point of love is not to verify, but to create.
The case for love rests with the future, not the past.

An erotic metaphysics, like a love affair, is a risk taken in the hope of creating. In playing the game "let's play as if the world were a love affair," we are agreeing to consider the possibility that we live in a world where play, freedom, novelty, and love are realities. The very act of agreeing to play the game is the first act in the game. Playing the game of "let's pretend" is a proof that the game is possible. Metaphysics is its own verification. That we are free to transcend the physical and play with different interpretations of the given is the evidence that we are necessarily free. And we may choose to play war games or love games.

What if I choose to live in the subjunctive mode and allow the world to play with me, caress me, address me as if I were its lover? This would require an awesome leap of faith. I would have to disarm myself and suspend critical judgment. Love does not grow in the atmosphere of criticism. Only by leaping into radical openness could I test the fantastic hypothesis that the world *is* like a love affair. To act *as if* turns fact into fiction and raises this interesting question: Who is the author of my life, what authority determines how I experience the world? To love is to seize the power of turning fact into fiction. If a human being is in essence a procreator, then we are not slaves to any past fact. Or better yet, the distinction between fact and fiction is itself a bad piece of fiction —pseudo-scientific prose from a nineteenth-century melodrama.

There is one final bit of evidence to support this free, fantastic, and erotic hypothesis. The more I act as if I were the nexus of some loving conspiracy, the more messages I receive, the more synchronicities happen, the more I come together with my cosmic environment and lose my sense of being an alienated atom in a billiard ball universe, the more porous I become to the waves-vibrations-intrusions-invitations of other people, animals, vegetables, and minerals that co-inhabit this planet. In short, the more I assume that I am intimately involved with an infinite commonwealth of compassionate consciousness, the more the old idea that I am a hermetically sealed individual with a mental computer following a preset genetic or social program falls away. The more I act as if the capacity for empathy was the human essence, the more my old American/white/Anglo-Saxon/Protestant/male/

modern/critical self begins to look like an illusion. When the recovery of compassion becomes the most human possibility, the quest for power begins to look like the source of our dis-ease. Topsy-turvy. The world just turned over. Fiction and fact from love's almanac. Notice how the head spins; the vertigo; the mixed fear and excitement in the pit of the stomach. It is always so when we walk on the razor edge of the awe-full possibilities of human freedom. We tremble to realize the vast power we have to create a world.

The terrible and promising conclusion we must draw is that we will create a world that gives us evidence to support the metaphors by which we live. Metaphysics, or basic analogies, govern our perception and our collection of evidence. A warrior's world will be filled with allies and enemies and evidence of conspiracy and malevolent intent. Power will be the only source of security, and a major amount of energy will be invested in "defense" systems. A lover will discover increasing evidence that he or she is welcomed, graced, nurtured, and taken personally. The world will be populated by potential friends and will give adequate evidence that we are all bound together in a compassionate commonwealth. To become a lover is to risk exploring the logic of compassion. In a dangerous world made even more dangerous by warriors who want to convince everyone to play the enemy game, the lover is a rare and vulnerable figure. Yes, a fool. When paranoia is the rule of the day, compassion seems like suicide or terrible foolishness. But to date the paranoid game has only increased the level of hostility and alienation to the point where the survival of the species is in question.

Einstein said that each of us must ask the ultimate question: "Is the universe friendly?" Is Being-becoming-itself a love story that is trying to get itself told?

At the moment, we face the possibility of the voluntary annihilation of life. History looks like a tragedy, or a tale told by an idiot in which evil finally triumphs. Certainly, we cannot claim that the universe is friendly enough to have eliminated suffering and evil. But it is care-ful enough to have raised a creature in which there is consciousness, conscience, and compassion. So we must reverse Einstein's question. Our survival now depends upon whether *we* are friendly. If there is to be a twenty-first century, it will be because we have finally learned to be kind to one another, to exist as a family.

In the presence of the threat that evil may overwhelm us at any moment and allow death to establish its final dominion, the only hopeful path left to us is to throw away our concern with bare survival, abandon the armored fortress of the warrior psyche, accept our vocation as healers, and set out on the journey that has no beginning or end. It may be that we will discover the promise that animates human beings only when we dare to become lovers.

Bon voyage.

# Appendix A:
# The Tantric Vision

Tantra, tantric yoga, or kundalini yoga is an ancient philosophy and practice linking sexuality and consciousness that has appeared in widely separated times and places.* It has cropped up in different forms in India, Tibet, and Mexico as well as in the writings of the alchemists, in mystical Christianity, and in theosophy. Its central idea, which seems to have occurred independently to a large number of early thinkers and spiritual adventurers, is that the body contains a number (usually seven) of physio-psychic centers that may become suffused by a current of "sexual" energy that leads to an expansion of consciousness or enlightenment. Although there is a lush variety of symbols in the various traditions, we can identify a common core of beliefs.

In Tantra, as in most forms of sophisticated mysticism, there is a fundamental belief that the human spirit and body are united with the cosmos. It can be stated in several ways: As below, so above; deeper in is further out; the microcosm reflects the macrocosm; every level of the hierarchy of being can be found within man; the human mind is a hologram of the universe.

In the concrete symbolism of religion, this belief is frequently presented in a pictorial way by showing how the human spine, with its seven ascending centers of energy (or chakras), is analogous to the seven-story cosmic mountain—Mt. Meru, Mt. Sinai, or Mt. Analogue. This mountain-spine forms a world pole *(axis mundi)* uniting the lower realms (Hades, the unconscious), middle earth (the everyday world of the ego), and the heavens (the ideal

---

*For more complete information, see Arthur Avalon, *The Serpent Power* (New York: Down Publications, 1974), or Mircea Eliade, *Yoga, Immortality and Freedom* (New York: Bollingen, 1958).

but unseen structures, powers, and presences that underlie and in-form all visible reality). Each of the seven centers of the body vibrates with its cosmic counterpart. We tune in to different levels of reality.

Physical/mental/spiritual illness results from any blockage that prevents us from communication or resonance. Health is being full-bodied, allowing the entire range of cosmic rhythms and intentions to inhabit and harmonize the various physio-psycho-spiritual systems within the body. The story of how we move from dis-ease to health is identical with the account of the ascent of consciousness and the metamorphosis of eros. We become whole by becoming citizens of each of the seven kingdoms of love.

The tantric consensus is that there is a single primal energy-spirit-consciousness that flows through all the cosmos and informs each person. The path of maturation, enlightenment, or transformation involves allowing this power (which is called kundalini or serpent power in the East) to rise up the spine and infuse each of the centers.

In tantric imagery, the food that nourishes the nervous system during the elevation of consciousness is the seminal fluid in men and the erotic fluids in women. The sexual fluid streams up the hollow channel in the middle of the spine (the susumna) and floods each of the chakras until it reaches the brain, at which point enlightenment occurs, with accompanying ecstasy. As the concentrated energy (called variously prana, chi, holy spirit, libido, or orgone) passes through the chakras, it purifies the body and mind and reunites sexuality and spirituality.

Among some scholars and esoteric aspirants, there is a tendency to take the symbolism so literally that it makes nonsense out of Tantra. Much of the interpretive literature discusses quite seriously whether there really is a channel in the spine through which sexual fluid might rise. Such literalism misses the point. The most valuable thing we may learn from tantric symbolism is a vision of how eros may be transformed, of how sexuality matures, of how desire expands, of how motivation changes, in the course of an authentic life journey.

## The Seven Energy Centers, or Chakras

Consider, for instance, the symbolic meaning hidden in the image of the sexual fluid as the fuel of consciousness. It is a fact of science as well as an abiding mystery that the intention and history of the entire evolutionary process is carried in the genes and chromosomes that flow together with the union of sperm and ovum. Whatever Nature or God is striving to create through this long drama of evolution is implicit in our drive to reproduce. The sexual organs do respond to the entire symphony of being. There is an intentionality, a telos, a purpose, a meaning, a direction encoded within our quest for pleasure. If we understand eros in its fullest sense, we may discover in sexual experience an impulse that may guide us in the unfoldment of consciousness. Perhaps our deepening desire is our surest path toward the sacred. Why should it be so startling to suggest that the cortex (a late-comer in the evolutionary story) might eventually fully understand the cosmic intention that is programmed into the sexual fluids? (Might the image of the kundalini serpent winding its way up the spine be an intuitive prefiguration of the helix of the DNA?)

We make best use of Tantra if we play with its symbolism. I suggest that the seven chakras are symbols of different stages of life and the philosophies and erotic practices that accompany them. The kundalini symbolism is an early developmental psychology. Each chakra represents an orientation to life that is appropriate to a certain stage of the pilgrimage of the psyche. These stages and their correlation to the progression of consciousness and the transformations of eros suggested in this work are as follows:

1. *Anal chakra.* Symbolizes bonding or possession, being held or grasping.

2. *Genital chakra.* Symbolizes the orientation to life as pleasure, play, and game.

Chakras 1 and 2 are parallel to the psychological development of the child, and the sexual awakening of adolescence. The rebel impulse is not encouraged within Eastern philosophy or culture.

3. *The solar plexus chakra.* Symbolizes the orientation to life as power.

Chakra 3 is parallel to the psychological development of the adult.

4. *The heart chakra.* Symbolizes falling in love with the ideal, romance, passion.

5. *The throat chakra.* Symbolizes purgatory, repentance, eating one's projections.

Chakras 4 and 5 parallel the psychological development of the outlaw, the first love affair with a transpersonal self, and the process of metanoia necessary to free the spirit from the myths, roles, and defense mechanisms that were a part of the adult life with its orientation to power and position.

6. *The third eye chakra.* Symbolizes the single vision.

7. *The crown chakra.* Symbolizes the homecoming, return of the Bodhisattva to the world, to live by the rule of compassion.

Chakras 6 and 7 parallel the psychological development of the lover, the unitive glimpse, and the return to the world to follow the vocation of the healer.

# Appendix B: Summary Chart

| | The Child's Being | The Rebel Temperament | The Adult Personality | The Outlaw Self | The Lover's Spirit |
|---|---|---|---|---|---|
| | Dependent<br>Unself-conscious | Counter-dependent<br>Self-conscious | Co-dependent<br>In-formed by the mythic consensus of the group | Independent<br>Self-witnessing | Inter-dependent<br>Self-transcending mystical consciousness |
| Primary Motivations and Modes of Loving | 1. Bonding *with* matrix.<br>2. Being encompassed by the patrix, carefully initiated into the taboos, oughts, and rites of family and tribe.<br>3. Playful sensuality and exploration. | 1. Rebelling *against* the authorities, breaking out of matrix and patrix, iconoclasm.<br>2. Conscious identification *with* a new peer group, new heroes, ideals, friends.<br>3. Romance, adoration of idealized beloved. | 1. Membership, belonging among, conforming, co-operating.<br>2. Playing a role, doing one's duty.<br>3. Taking vows, co-promising, pro-creating a home and family, caring for the young. | 1. Individuality and the Quest for autonomy.<br>2. Destroying the persona, myths, masks, roles, defenses, character, ego, constructed during the first part of life.<br>3. Self-love. Reconciling the opposites—male and female, good and evil; loving the carnal self. | 1. The unitive glimpse that the center is everywhere<br>2. Polymorphous eroticism.<br>3. The embodiment of love in the carnal body, the family, friendship, the body politic, the technological body, the ecological body, the mystical body. |
| Virtues That Characterize Health | Basic trust; dependency; openness, wonder; obedience—"yea saying"; enjoyment of intimacy; curiosity. | Ability to doubt and criticize; establishing limits and boundaries by "nay saying"; expression of outrage, anger and aggression; sustaining contest; ag- | Responsibility; loyalty to institutions; the discipline to postpone gratification, wait, sacrifice for the future; deciding; acting; moderation; consistency; predictability; | Metanoia, re-owning the shadow; repentance; demything the self; transmoral conscience; going beyond good and evil; spirit of adventure and experimentation; | Empathy; radical trust; forgiveness; second innocence; joyful acceptance of the actual; the ability to suffer voluntarily (an end to neurotic suffering); wise foolish- |

| | | | | |
|---|---|---|---|---|
| ...cess. | ...specting conscience and authority. | sionment and disintegration of the old; toleration of anxiety and guilt in breaking social taboos, roles; enjoyment of struggle to create; indifference to pressure of social opinion; the patience to be "artificial," to be awkward, to feel and act in new ways; exploring the excess that leads to wisdom. | | ...ing dis-armament and living in openness; the unification of consciousness, compassion, and conscience. |
| **Perversions** | The promise of childhood is perverted and we remain childish to the degree that bonding, initiation, or playfulness are deficient or excessive. This leads to different forms of arrested development: anhedonia, the bondage to pain, possessiveness, addiction, the obsessive quest for approval. | The promise of youth is perverted and we remain perpetual adolescents if we do not take the risk of rebellion or get stuck in an antagonistic posture. This leads to different forms of arrested development: resentment, hostility, the blame-game, passive dependency, sentimentality, niceness, incurable romanticism and idealism, the playboy and playgirl game. | Normality is a perversion of the human promise insofar as it is rooted in consensual paranoia, the making of enemies, propaganda, ideology, disowning and projecting the shadow. Normal defense mechanisms and repressions result in crippling eros, warfare between tribes, nations, the sexes, within the self, exhausting the energies of the body and body politic, chronic boredom, depression, and violence. | The outlaw impulse becomes perverse when the individual tries to maintain a posture of self-sufficiency, becomes inflated with Promethean defiance, obsessed with power and control. | The lover's spirit is the goal of the psyche, the standard by which health is ultimately judged. A lover is foolish but not perverse, vulnerable but not naive, dis-armed but not impotent, hopeful but not optimistic, mystical but not disembodied. |

# Notes

CHAPTER 1

1. Friedrich Nietzsche, *Beyond Good and Evil* (New York: Penguin Books, 1979), p. 73.
2. *San Francisco Bay Guardian,* June 10, 1981.
3. Robert Brain, *Friends and Lovers* (New York: Basic Books, 1976), p. 222.
4. Joseph Campbell, *The Masks of God—Creative Mythology* (New York: Viking, 1969), p. 59.
5. Gabriel Marcel, *Being and Having* (Westminster, England: Dacre Press), p. 167.

CHAPTER 2

1. Friedrich Nietzsche, *The Portable Nietzsche* (New York: Viking, 1954), p. 139.
2. Susan Griffin, *Pornography and Silence* (New York: Harper and Row, 1981), p. 253.
3. Joseph Chilton Pearce, *The Magical Child* (New York: E. P. Dutton, 1977), p. 53.

CHAPTER 3

1. Richard Restak, "The Origins of Pleasure" in *Saturday Review,* May 12, 1979; James Prescott, "Body Pleasure and the Origins of Violence" in *The Futurist,* April 1975.
2. James Prescott, quoted in ibid, p. 19.
3. Ibid.
4. Selma Fraiberg, *The Magic Years* (New York: Scribners, 1959), pp. 54–55.

CHAPTER 4

1. Selma Fraiberg, *The Magic Years* (New York: Scribners, 1959), p. 64.

CHAPTER 6

1. Erik Erikson, *Gandhi's Truth* (New York: Norton, 1961), p. 37.
2. Norman Cameron, *Personality Development and Psychopathology* (Boston: Houghton Mifflin, 1963), p. 113.
3. Mircea Eliade, *The Sacred and the Profane* (New York: Harper and Row, 1961), p. 33.
4. Donald Symons, *The Evolution of Human Sexuality* (New York: Oxford University Press, 1979), p. 57.
5. Ernest Becker, *Escape from Evil* (New York: Free Press, 1975), p. 4.

CHAPTER 7

1. Ernest Becker, *Escape from Evil* (New York: Free Press, 1975), p. 124.
2. Gilbert Derdt, *Guardians of the Flutes* (New York: McGraw Hill, 1981), p. 160.
3. Robert Stoller, "Sexual Excitement" in *Archives of General Psychiatry,* August 1976.
4. *The Sacramento Bee,* January 16, 1982.
5. Albert Ellis, *Sex and the Single Man* (Secaucus, New Jersey, 1963), p. 39.
6. Ibid., p. 56.

**7.** Helen Gurley Brown, *Sex and the Single Girl* (New York: B. Geis Associates, 1962), pp. 74 and 76.
**8.** Ibid.
**9.** Friedrich Nietzsche, *Beyond Good and Evil* (New York: Penguin Books, 1979), p. 73.

CHAPTER 8

**1.** Norman O. Brown, *Love's Body* (New York: Random House, 1966), p. 179.
**2.** Hannah Arendt, *The Human Condition* (Garden City, New York: Doubleday Anchor, 1958), p. 222.
**3.** Friedrich Nietzsche, *Beyond Good and Evil* (New York: Penguin Books, 1979), p. 51.
**4.** Donald Symons, *The Evolution of Human Sexuality* (New York: Oxford University Press, 1979), p. 175.

CHAPTER 9

**1.** Hannah Arendt, *The Human Condition* (Garden City, New York: Doubleday Anchor, 1958), p. 154.
**2.** Paul Ehrlich, "An Ecologist Stands up Among the Social Scientists" in *Co-Evolution Quarterly*, Fall 1981.
**3.** Friedrich Nietzsche, *The Will to Power* (New York: Vintage Books, 1968), pp. 458–460.
**4.** Thomas Merton, *The New Man* (New York: Bantam Books, 1981,) pp. 13–25.

CHAPTER 10

**1.** Albert Einstein, quoted in Michael Nagler, *America Without Violence* (Covelo, California: Island Press, 1982), p. 11.
**2.** Søren Kierkegaard, *Fear and Trembling* and *Sickness Unto Death* (Garden City, New York: Doubleday Anchor, 1954), p. 49.
**3.** Albert Camus, *Resistance, Rebellion and Death* (New York: Albert Knopf, 1961), p. 7.
**4.** Luther Standing Bear, *Land of the Spotted Eagle* (Lincoln: University of Nebraska Press, 1978), p. 133.
**5.** Paul Tillich, *Love, Power and Justice* (Oxford: Oxford University Press, 1954), p. 84.
**6.** Martin Buber, *Between Man and Man* (New York: Macmillan, 1965), p. 17.

# Index